Unless Recalled Earlier

DATE DUE

FEB 1 7 2002	

DEMCO, INC. 38-2931

Networks and Markets

Networks and Markets

James E. Rauch and Alessandra Casella
EDITORS

Russell Sage Foundation
New York

The Russell Sage Foundation

The Russell Sage Foundation, one of the oldest of America's general purpose foundations, was established in 1907 by Mrs. Margaret Olivia Sage for "the improvement of social and living conditions in the United States." The Foundation seeks to fulfill this mandate by fostering the development and dissemination of knowledge about the country's political, social, and economic problems. While the Foundation endeavors to assure the accuracy and objectivity of each book it publishes, the conclusions and interpretations in Russell Sage Foundation publications are those of the authors and not of the Foundation, its Trustees, or its staff. Publication by Russell Sage, therefore, does not imply Foundation endorsement.

Library of Congress Cataloging-in-Publication Data

Networks and markets / James E. Rauch and Alessandra Casell.
   p. cm.
   Includes bibliographical references and index.
   ISBN 0-87154-700-7
   1. Economics—Sociological aspects. 2. Sociology—Economic aspects.
   I. Rauch, James E. II. Casella, Alessandra.

   HM548 .N488 2001
   306.3—dc21   2001019328

The paper used in this publication meets the minimum requirements of American National Standard for Information Sciences—Permanence of Paper for Printed Library Materials. ANSI Z39.48-1992.

Text design by Suzanne Nichols

RUSSELL SAGE FOUNDATION
112 East 64th Street, New York, New York 10021
10 9 8 7 6 5 4 3 2 1

CONTENTS

Contributors

ALESSANDRA CASELLA is professor of economics at Columbia University and directeur d'études at l'École des Hautes Études en Sciences Sociales.

JAMES E. RAUCH is professor of economics at the University of California, San Diego, and research associate at the National Bureau of Economic Research.

RONALD S. BURT is the Hobart W. Williams Professor of Sociology and Strategy at the University of Chicago Graduate School of Business, the Shell Professor of Human Resources at the Institut Européen d'Administration d'Affaires (INSEAD) in Fontainebleau, France, and director of Raytheon's Leadership Institute.

GREGORY BESHAROV is assistant professor of economics at Duke University.

ROBERT C. FEENSTRA is a professor in the Department of Economics at the University of California, Davis, and a research associate of the National Bureau of Economic Research.

NEIL FLIGSTEIN is the Class of 1939 Chancellor's Professor in the Department of Sociology at the University of California, Berkeley.

AVNER GREIF is Bowman Family Professor of Humanities and Sciences at Stanford University.

GARY G. HAMILTON is professor of sociology and the Jackson School of International Studies at the University of Washington, Seattle.

DENG-SHING HUANG is a research fellow in the Institute of Economics at Academia Sinica in Taipei, Taiwan.

ALAN KIRMAN is professor of economics at GREQAM, University of Aix-Marseille, directeur d'études at l'École des Hautes Études en Sciences Sociales, and member of the Institut Universitaire de France.

JOHN F. PADGETT is research professor at the Santa Fe Institute and associate professor of political science at the University of Chicago.

REBECA RAIJMAN is assistant professor of sociology at Haifa University in Israel.

JOEL SOBEL is professor of economics at the University of California, San Diego.

MARTA TIENDA is Maurice P. During '22 Professor of Demographic Studies, professor of sociology and public affairs, and director, Office of Population Research at Princeton University.

ACKNOWLEDGMENTS

This book grew out of the workshop "Integrating Network and Market Models of the Economy" held at the Russell Sage Foundation September 19 to 20, 1997. We would like to thank Eric Wanner and Ronald Burt for their intellectual support and encouragement to expand the idea of the workshop into this book. Suzanne Nichols has been a very helpful and patient editor. We are also grateful for the financial support that the Russell Sage Foundation gave to the workshop and for the financial support that the National Science Foundation (SBR-9709237) gave to our work on the book.

Contributors' acknowledgments are included with their respective chapters and discussions. James Rauch served as editor for chapters 2 and 3 and the accompanying discussions, and Alessandra Casella served as editor for chapters 4, 5, and 6 and the accompanying discussions.

James E. Rauch
Alessandra Casella

Chapter 1

Networks and Markets: Concepts for Bridging Disciplines

James E. Rauch and Gary G. Hamilton

For most of their respective histories, economics and sociology have shared surprisingly little common ground. In recent years, however, practitioners of the two disciplines increasingly find themselves working side by side, exploring the same topics, being challenged by similar issues, and sometimes coming to the same conclusions. The two disciplines have different reasons for coming together. While economists are moving out from the traditional disciplinary center to explore topics such as family, ethnicity, and bureaucracy, sociologists have moved into the heart of economics to uncover the institutional and organizational features of phenomena formerly understood only through a neoclassical lens.

Among several areas of overlap, one particularly promising site of disciplinary exchange is forming around two key concepts: networks and markets. Following Joel Podolny and Karen Page (1998, 59), we can define an economic network as a group of agents who pursue repeated, enduring exchange relations with one another and, at the same time, lack a legitimate organizational authority to arbitrate and resolve the disputes that may arise during the exchange. The qualification regarding authority is necessary to distinguish a network from a hierarchy. By contrast, exchange in a market is episodic and anonymous and is mediated by competitively determined prices. Most simply, then, one could say that this book is about the intersection and interaction of personalized exchange with arm's-length exchange.

Matters are not so simple, however. To begin, many sociologists would consider the Podolny-Page definition of economic networks too restrictive because, for example, it excludes agents connected only indirectly and occasionally by referral.[1] We might then substitute for the repeated-exchange definition of networks a weaker definition such as "a group of agents who know each other's relevant characteristics or can learn them through referral." Going still further, Mark Granovetter's (1985) work, which has served as the guiding formulation for economic sociology, stresses that *all* economic action is embedded in networks. Likewise, economists are no longer willing to refrain from applying the concept of "market" to personalized exchange, if in fact they ever were.[2] Indeed, the term "market" has become so elastic and ambiguous as to prompt one sociologist (Lie 1997, 342) to write: "The market is a central category of economics. . . . It is then curious that the market receives virtually no extended discussion in most works of economic theory or history. . . . The market, it turns out, is the hollow core at the heart of economics." One could even say that "market" has become the conceptual banner that economists carry when they move beyond the traditional subject-area boundaries of economics, and "network" has become the equivalent banner that economic sociologists carry as they move into the base of economics.[3]

On the one hand, this use of the concepts of "network" and "market" maintains what we feel is a healthy lack of disciplinary convergence between economics and sociology. On the other hand, such an indiscriminate approach obscures what economists and sociologists can learn from each other. We argue that by recognizing personalized exchange among many agents as a network, economists can draw upon insights from economic sociology that they will find valuable, and that by recognizing arm's-length exchange mediated by prices as a market, sociologists can draw upon insights from economics that they will find valuable. The promise for such a mutual enrichment was the inspiration for the workshop that led to this book.

This book concentrates on the core concepts of networks and markets and is designed to allow economists to think more deeply about how networks might be useful in economic analysis and sociologists to think more deeply about how markets might be useful in sociological analysis. At the same time, the contributions to this volume may cause practitioners from both disciplines to define and clarify the concepts that they normally take for granted. Each chapter brings a disciplinary, but innovative, use of the two key concepts to bear on a quite specific empirical phenomenon: the formation of trusting relationships in large organizations (Burt); the sizes of business groups and the internalization of transactions within them (Feenstra, Hamilton, and Huang); the formation of stable buyer-seller relationships in wholesale markets (Kirman); the recruitment of business partners in banking (Padgett); and the exchange of information among small retail businesses (Rauch). With only one exception, the discussants are sociologists if the chapter author is an economist, and vice versa; they were asked to write about how they would approach these same empirical phenomena from the standpoints of their own disciplines. The empirical focus helps to bring out not only the implications of this volume for the practice of economists and sociologists but also its implications for policy, about which Alessandra Casella writes in her concluding remarks.

In the remainder of this introduction, we first survey some recent work by economists employing the concept of networks, then argue that economists could benefit from a deeper understanding and use of the sociological approach to networks, giving examples and illustrating our argument with chapters from this volume. Next, we do the same for sociologists and markets. In the last two sections of the introduction, we review the methodological tensions between economists and sociologists that are revealed by the discussions of the various chapters and conclude that these differences maintain a healthy division of labor between the two disciplines.

The Study of Networks by Economists

Sociologists have studied the impact of business and social networks on economic life for decades.[4] Their work has included fundamental theoretical analyses, statistical testing, and many specific case studies. In contrast, economists have come to the subject, in a self-conscious way, only in the 1990s. It is true that in prior years many applications of industrial organization and game theory could be interpreted as shedding some light on the functioning of networks, from the study of the conditions necessary to support cooperative equilibria to the functioning of teams. What was new in the 1990s, however, was the attempt to include business and social networks in models and empirical applications that go beyond the level of individual organizations or isolated games to the level of markets, industries, or even the entire economy, at which level networks interact with general equilibrium forces of price determination and resource constraints. In other words, some economists in the 1990s began to try to integrate network and market models of the economy and to apply the integrated models in empirical analysis.

There are many examples of economists using this new, integrated mode of analysis. Avner Greif (1993) and James Rauch and Alessandra Casella (1998) have examined how transnational networks of traders can overcome informal barriers to international trade, such as a weak international legal system and lack of information regarding trading opportunities. Steven Durlauf (1993) has demonstrated that network interactions between firms in technologically related industries can generate multiple equilibria for the aggregate growth of the economy. Rachel Kranton (1996) has shown how anonymous markets and networks can form alternative means of exchange and how the growth of one may undermine the functioning of the other. In the same vein, Raja Kali (1999) recently argued that the existence of a network has a negative effect on the functioning of the anonymous market in an unreliable legal environment because it absorbs honest individuals and thereby raises the density of dishonest individuals engaged in anonymous market exchange. Gérard Weisbuch, Alan Kirman, and Dorothea Herreiner (2000) have demonstrated that the underlying network relationships help to explain the pattern of transactions in the wholesale fish market in Marseille. Robert Feenstra, Tzu-Han Yang, and Gary Hamilton (1999) have found that differences in business group networks across South Korea, Taiwan, and Japan are reflected in differences in the quality and variety of the products they export.

In the next section of this introduction, we argue that economists' work could be greatly enhanced by incorporating into their models a richer approach to networks than they have used to date. Many elements of a richer approach are present in the sociological literature. We focus on three that are well illustrated by the sociologists' chapters in this volume. First, the formation of dynamic alliances and concentrations of power tend to occur at certain nodes in networks that Ronald Burt (1992) calls "structural holes." Second, not all network ties are equivalent; they can differ in strength and meaning (Granovetter 1973). Third, if individual agents are conceived as relationally or socially constructed, networks can be "constitutive" in the sense that they shape agents' identities and thus their preferences, as well as their action capacities or rules (White 1992; Padgett and Ansell 1993). We have ordered these three elements of a richer approach to networks by the ease with which we think economists could assimilate them.

How Economists Can Benefit from a Deeper Understanding and Greater Use of the Sociological Approach to Networks

For economists, networks can be a way to structure interactions between large numbers of agents that are not at arm's length—that is, not mediated by competitively determined prices. An explicit accounting of network ties is a clear advance over assuming that such interaction is mediated through summary statistics (usually the mean) for the relevant agents, a very popular approach in both theoretical work (for example, Lucas 1988) and empirical work (Borjas 1992; Rauch 1993b). Indeed, a network approach gives a much clearer idea of which agents are "relevant" and why.[5] Networks are both an alternative and a complement to game-theoretic approaches to non-arm's-length interaction. Network relationships do not need to be specified in game-theoretic terms, but when they are, the network structure can be used to channel and simplify the game-theoretic interactions. This flexibility allows a network approach both to encompass a broader range of relationship types and to reduce or avoid the complexity of n-person game theory in applications where the latter would make analysis intractable.

In view of the fact that flexibility is a major advantage of a network approach to non-arm's-length interaction, it is surprising that economists have typically assumed a very restrictive form of network, especially in models used empirically.[6] In this network form, agents are divided into disjoint "groups." These groups interact only through the market. Within each group, every agent is tied equally to every other.

The chapters in this volume by Robert Feenstra, Gary Hamilton, and Deng-Shing Huang; Alan Kirman; and James Rauch all follow this restricted approach, though they apply it in nuanced ways with an unusual level of institutional detail. Feenstra, Hamilton, and Huang apply it to the sizes and levels of product variety and the internalization of transactions of Korean versus Taiwanese business groups; Kirman applies it to the formation of buyer-seller pairs in the Marseille fish market; and Rauch applies it to the information flows within coethnic groups of small-business owners.

We can gain greater insight into both the nature of the restrictions imposed on network structures by economists to date and the potential gains from deeper use of the sociological approach by using a standard tool from network analysis, the sociomatrix. In the figure 1.1 sociomatrix, three groups of equal size are shown. All agents under study are arrayed, in the same order, both horizontally and vertically. A 1 in the ith row and jth column indicates that agents i and j are "tied"; a 0 indicates that they are not tied. Every agent is trivially tied to himself, so we leave all diagonal entries blank. We also assume that if agent i is tied to agent j, then agent j is automatically tied to agent i, so that the sociomatrix in figure 1.1 is symmetric.[7]

Figure 1.1 is a stylized representation of the theoretical model of Feenstra, Huang, and Hamilton (1997). Each block of 1s is a business group within which firms share profits and sell to each other at marginal cost. The large 0s indicate that no other ties exist. Business groups are assumed to consist of equal numbers of firms. Profits are not shared across groups or between groups and unaffiliated firms, and in transactions outside the group, market power is exploited to its fullest, with prices marked up above marginal cost.

We wish to focus on two particular limitations of the network structure shown in figure 1.1: the absence of ties across groups and the dichotomous nature of ties. As noted already, these restrictions characterize the bulk of the work by economists who are trying to integrate network and market models of the economy, and thus figure 1.1 can be adapted to describe the various papers without relaxing these restrictions. In the model and empirical application of Greif (1989, 1993) and in the model of Rauch and Casella (1998), there exists only one group within the set of international traders, rather

Figure 1.1 Sociomatrix Showing Disjoint "Groups"

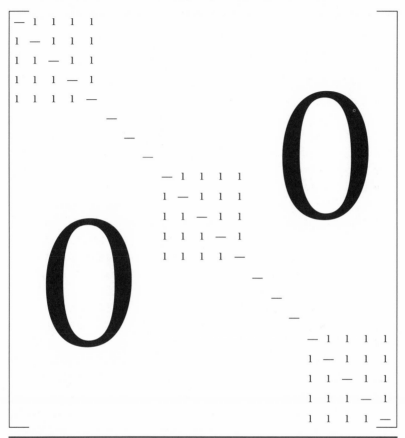

than several as in figure 1.1. The same is true for the set of all traders in the model of Kali (1999). Within the group, information is shared completely, while group members do not share information with traders outside the group (nor do unaffiliated traders share information with each other), so ties are dichotomous. In the model of Kranton (1996), every agent has one and only one partner with whom he can engage in reciprocal exchange outside the market if he chooses. In terms of figure 1.1, there are no unaffiliated agents in Kranton's model, and every group has two members. In the model of Weisbuch, Kirman, and Herreiner (2000), each buyer either forms a "group" with a given seller or remains unaffiliated, searching anew for a seller in every period. Network structure in their model cannot, however, be completely captured in figure 1.1 because there are many more buyers than sellers and the two types of agents cannot be described symmetrically.[8]

We consider first, and in most detail, how the restriction of the absence of ties across groups could be productively relaxed. Following Burt (1992), we can see the absent ties across the groups as "holes" in the network structure. Burt is mainly concerned with showing how agents whose ties span these structural holes, such as i and j in figure 1.2, benefit economically by acting as "brokers" between the groups.[9] Note that agents span these holes by virtue of luck of the draw in network ties rather than by virtue of any special "human capital" that allows them to interact with different groups. Indeed, an emphasis on network position over human capital as an explanation for individual economic outcomes is a hallmark of the sociological approach to labor "markets" (see, for example, Granovetter 1988). Interesting though this explanation is, what we wish to argue here is that ties that span structural holes ("bridge ties") can be a useful device for explaining not only individual economic outcomes but also economic phenomena at a higher level of aggregation—that is, the kind of phenomena that economists began to use networks to explain in the 1990s.

We make our case by example. Let us think of the three groups in figure 1.1 as three firms or joint ventures of firms that are making three different products. Let us also assume that for technological reasons only one product will become the "standard" in the long run. In this sense, the situation depicted in figure 1.1 is an "unstable equilibrium." An economist analyzing this situation would typically assume that one of the three groups will be the sole survivor when a "stable equilibrium" emerges. The economist would then try to predict the survivor on the basis of a combination of initial conditions, or "history," and expectations.[10] The economist might look at a number of initial conditions, such as whether one group has some kind of head start (for example, in marketing), but he or she would not normally

Figure 1.2 Relationship Between *i* and *j* Spans a "Structural Hole"

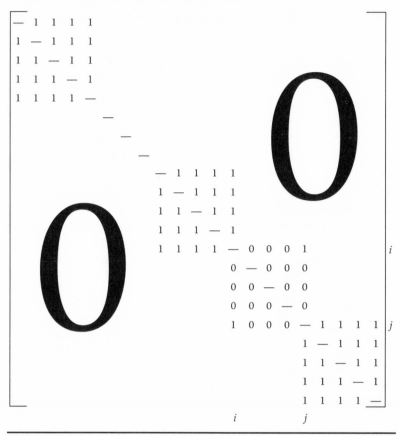

include the structure of network ties in the set of initial conditions to be examined. If a careful tally of network ties were to yield figure 1.2, however, one might predict that the two groups tied by the relationship spanning a structural hole would discover synergy between their products and form an alliance to make a new product that combines the best characteristics of the two old ones. The resources of the alliance and the superiority of the new product would lead to its becoming the standard. Figure 1.3 depicts the stable equilibrium

Figure 1.3 Agglomeration in a Stable Equilibrium

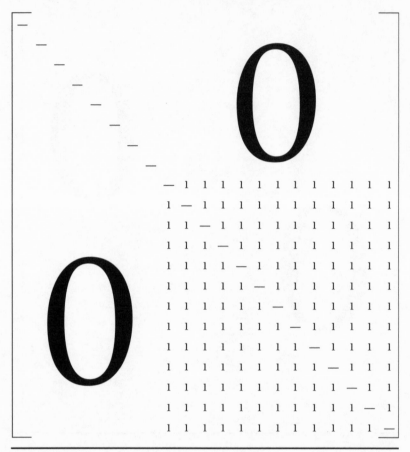

outcome. Note that the surviving group in figure 1.3 is larger than the sum of the two allied groups, representing agglomeration effects that attracted previously unaffiliated agents.

Our example is intended to make two points. First, the pattern of network ties can influence the outcomes of path-dependent processes of interest to economists, especially if the pattern contains ties that span holes in the network structure. Second, the pattern of network ties may suggest outcomes that economists would not otherwise have considered—in this case, the formation of an alliance between groups rather than the survival of one of the original three. Although our example is completely artificial, Mark Granovetter and Patrick McGuire (1998) have shown how the structure of preexisting ties among principal actors in the nascent electric power industry influenced the path-dependent choice of central over distributed power generation.

We now consider how the restriction that ties are dichotomous could be relaxed. Rather than assuming that agents are either tied or not (either 0 or 1 in the sociomatrix), ties could vary in "strength," as in the classic article by Granovetter (1973). Strength can be measured by frequency of interaction (Granovetter 1974/1995) or by emotional intensity (Marsden and Campbell 1984). Granovetter's (1973) division of ties into "weak" and "strong" could prove especially useful to economists. For example, he shows (1974/1995) that weak rather than strong ties are the most valuable type of contact in the context of job searches. In his survey of professional, technical, and managerial employees, the modal means of finding a job was to get information from someone with whom one had once worked and whom one now saw "occasionally" or even "rarely" (less than once a year). This counterintuitive finding can be explained by the tendency for strong-tie networks (for example, kinship groups) to contain redundant rather than new information, because everyone knows everyone else. Another example of the importance of weak ties is given by the current work of Wai-Keung Chung and Gary Hamilton (1999) on the means by which Chinese entrepreneurs in Hong Kong have expanded their businesses. They find that contacts made in voluntary associations, such as those based on native place (the location of one's lineage roots) in China's hinterland, have more importance in economic activity than impersonal market means or strong ties, such as extended family relationships. In job searches and among ethnic traders, economists attempting to apply dichotomous-tie network models could easily focus on strong ties to the exclusion of weak ties, thereby obtaining misleading results because the latter could be valuable bridge ties.

The chapter by Ronald Burt shows how skillful application of the concepts of structural holes and weak-versus-strong ties can help us understand agents' abilities to form trusting relationships with new acquaintances and thereby take advantage of potential business opportunities. In line with the preceding analysis, Burt first observes that a potentially valuable tie that spans a structural hole is more likely to start out weak than strong. (For example, the relationship is with someone in a complementary line of business whom one happens to meet, as opposed to a good friend who happens to be in a complementary line of business.) If the relationship in question is embedded in an agent's strong ties, his natural inclination to distrust the new acquaintance is amplified by their gossip because to be polite they go along with his inclination. If, on the other hand, the new acquaintance is relatively unknown to the agent's trusted colleagues, he must gather information independently and thus forms a more accurate judgment. Burt's hypothesis is supported by three different surveys of managers, all of which show that weak relations embedded in a manager's strong third-party ties are much more likely to be cited for distrust than weak relations not so embedded.

Burt's chapter highlights aspects of sociologists' approach to networks, especially the importance of structural holes, that we believe could be relatively easily assimilated by economists working in the neoclassical tradition. In contrast, the chapter by John Padgett highlights aspects of sociologists' approach that are less assimilable, in particular the "constitutive" view that social networks shape agents' identities and rules of action. In this view, agents activate and identify their economic interests through membership in a business or social network, and thus their interests are not independent of the "cognitive frame" that the network establishes.[11]

The constitutive view of networks conflicts with the bedrock neoclassical assumption that the preferences of individual agents are stable and exogenous.[12] Yet the idea that social interactions can alter individual preferences is making gradual inroads among economists, as work by Matthew Rabin (1993) and Uzi Segal and Joel Sobel (1999) demonstrates. These papers suggest the possibility that many elements of the constitutive view of networks could be made acceptable to economists by models that depict agents as engaged in "social learning."

In chapter 5, Padgett argues that, in fourteenth- and fifteenth-century Florence, political developments acted as a selection mechanism for deciding *which* social networks would constitute agents' identities: those of family, guild, social class, or court patronage. These identities in turn determined which relationships and strategies agents would use for recruitment into Florentine banking partnerships: father-son lineage in the family regime, master-apprentice in the guild regime, intermarriage and elite friendship in the social class regime, or court connections in the patronage regime. We might think of Padgett's analysis as telling us which relationships would have counted as "1"s in a sociomatrix relevant for this recruitment. Padgett goes on to argue that these different regimes determined different stylized paths of individual bank growth and division and of interbank financial relationships.

The Study of Markets by Sociologists

Sociologists have never been reluctant to study markets and economies more generally. Karl Marx and Max Weber, both recognized today as founders of contemporary sociology, devoted much of their scholarly lives to the examination of capitalist market economies.[13] Following this legacy, sociologists through most of the twentieth century developed a very broad but also very non-economic view of markets and economies. This view concentrated on the transformations of societies from traditional (feudal, mechanical, gemeinschaft) to modern (capitalistic, industrial, organic, gesellschaft).[14] Although the development of a capitalist market economy is at the heart of this view, very few sociologists tried to understand the transformation in economic terms. Until recently, few scholars matched the rigor of even Marx's and Weber's understandings of how markets work.

Since the mid-1980s, this situation has changed considerably. Sociologists began to use two new and closely related approaches to analyze the working of modern economies. The first approach stemmed from Mark Granovetter's (1985) influential article "Economic Action and Social Structure: The Problem of Embeddedness," in which he emphasizes the importance of social relationships in establishing economic organization. Expanding from this base to establish an economic sociology, other researchers (Swedberg 1991; Granovetter and Swedberg 1992; Friedland and Robertson 1990; Zukin and DiMaggio

1990) further argued that complex economic networks do not arise exclusively from technological or economic factors but also have social and institutional foundations that structure ownership, control, and exchange relationships in the economy.[15]

The second approach arose as a reaction to a number of publications in related fields, especially Chandler (1977, 1990), Piore and Sabel (1984), and Harvey (1990). Sociologists critiqued and then quickly reinterpreted the conclusions of these studies (for example, Fligstein 1985, 1990; Gereffi and Korzeniewicz 1994; Perrow 1981, 1990; Stinchcombe 1990; White 1981, 1992). These researchers also emphasize networks, as well as the spatial components of economic organization, but here networks do not necessarily imply socially defined relationships. Instead, networks connote a web of ties that arise out of the processes of work and economic calculation of long-term gain. Brian Uzzi (1996, 693) makes this point very clear when he concludes, based on an empirical study of the apparel industry in New York City, that network "embeddedness is a logic of exchange that shapes motives and expectations and promotes coordinated adaptation."

Although this rapidly growing literature addresses many issues at the heart of economics, work directly on markets is only a small part of it (Lie 1997). To be sure, market dynamics are implied in much of this literature, but core market processes—such as price, competition, and equilibrium—are rarely discussed. Aside from a few very notable exceptions (for example, White 1981, 1992; Podolny 1993), research on specific markets stresses network and interaction (Abolafia 1997; Abolafia and Biggart 1991; Baker 1984, 1990; Swedberg 1994; Mizruchi and Stearns 1994), as well as politics and regulation (Fligstein 1996; Fligstein and Mara-Drita 1996). Most sociologists would conclude, as do Neil Fligstein and Iona Mara-Drita (1996, 25), that "markets are social constructions that reflect the unique interactions of their firms and nations." As valuable as such insights may be, the sociological literature obscures the fundamental economic features of markets—the exchange of goods and services and the setting of prices in complex and increasingly global organizational settings characterized by cooperation and competition. What are the effects of institutions on market processes? An equally important question is: What constraints do these processes place on the social constructibility of markets? In the next section, we work in parallel with our procedure in the last section and begin with aspects of economists' work on market processes that we believe are more compatible with current approaches in economic sociology.

How Sociologists Can Benefit from a Deeper Understanding and Greater Use of Economists' Approach to Markets

For sociologists, markets represent a structure of organized interdependence between economic actors (Swedberg 1994; White 1988; Podolny 1993). Markets are constituted through the nature of the interdependence. Exogenous social networks may provide a foundation of trust on which to build economic exchanges (Granovetter 1985). Equally, interdependence may arise endogenously through repeated exchanges leading to reputations and reciprocity as organizing features of competitive markets (Uzzi 1996). Harrison White (1981, 1992) and Joel Podolny (1993) also find that repeated competition in price-based product markets leads to the formation of status-based hierarchies among producers, an outcome that has direct effects on product prices. Finding structure to be a significant aspect of market actions, most sociologists are content simply to conclude that market structure shapes market outcomes. The economists' chapters in this volume can add substance, but also complexity, to the sociologists' conclusions.

In chapter 6, Rauch addresses the market for retail products in ethnic neighborhoods. Whereas sociologists (for example, Bonacich 1973) have analyzed this situation in terms of middleman minorities, Rauch looks at the economic mechanisms that help or hinder the process of matching final consumers with supplies of the products they want to buy. In many neighborhoods, members of ethnic minorities have an advantage in linking producers of goods with final consumers owing to the trust that can be established between pairs of buyers and sellers. However, in Rauch's particular case—the African American neighborhoods of New York City—he finds that African American retailers do not establish extensive business networks similar to those of other ethnic groups, such as the Korean minority, and therefore have considerable difficulty establishing a market-sensitive trading system. It would appear that, as we saw in the discussion of the work of Granovetter (1974/1995) earlier, furnishing information is a particular strength of weak-tie networks. The low density of business associations in the African American community makes it difficult to create weak-tie networks.

Rauch takes his analysis one step further. Observation of how the market attempts to mimic networks can help us better understand how networks themselves operate.[16] The large-scale, commercial intermediaries studied by Rauch attempt to link their retailer clients to a very broad array of vendors despite the potential problem of dilution of expertise, suggesting that one advantage of weak-tie over strong-tie networks in this area is simply their ability to grow large. The fees charged by these market institutions can at least give us a lower-bound estimate of what weak-tie networks are worth to their members. At the same time, the fact that such institutions have not displaced networks provides insight into what is unique about the latter. Rauch suggests that what is special about ethnic weak-tie networks is their ability to provide a shared cultural framework for understanding.

Alan Kirman's survey of the Marseille fish market—a classic setting where all buyers and all sellers meet daily to clear the market of all goods—provides a cautionary study for both economists and sociologists. Kirman notes that loyalty is a strong feature of buyer behavior in the fish market: many buyers return to the same seller, day after day, rather than shop around for better prices. Kirman's finding is exactly what sociologists would predict: transactions are embedded in social relationships in which loyalty is generated by reinforcement learning—buyers stay with sellers with whom their past experience has been good. This learning undoubtedly involves some mutual adaptation on the part of the buyers and sellers. Loyalty becomes profitable to both buyers and sellers when, for example, sellers learn to give priority in service to loyal buyers (but to charge them higher prices than shoppers), and buyers learn that they are more likely to be served by loyal sellers (even though they pay higher prices).[17] The results would seem to confirm that embeddedness pays.

Kirman's study also confirms, however, economists' prediction that, in the aggregate and despite the absence of individual maximizing behaviors, the fish market acts like a perfectly competitive market: the market clears every day, prices of each variety of fish are stable over time, and the aggregate demand is downward-sloping. As Kirman notes in his chapter and Alessandra Casella also observes in her discussion of it, this finding "breaks the link" between individual- and aggregate-level behavior. The economic characteristics of the Marseille fish market cannot be adduced from individual behavior, but rather can be explained only by understanding how the fish market functions as an organized system. Prices are consequences of the dynamics of the system, not decisions made by individuals. The implication of this conclusion is a blow to rational-choice theories in that there is no demonstrable progression from microlevel processes to macrolevel outcomes. This conclusion also implies that embedded social networks can be delinked from macrolevel outcomes in that the same price structure may be consistent with different network arrangements.

Kirman's conclusions emphasize the importance of a Walrasian framework as a way to break out of the theoretical preoccupation with individual-level phenomena. In much of the theoretical work in which economic and sociological theories are set in opposition to each other—for instance, the Granovetter-Williamson debate—writers focus on the micro level and debate the nature of human nature. They ask whether individuals are rational maximizers or whether it makes sense to assume they are. The normal proclivity is to state the primitive case and then generalize the conclusion, inducing complex economic organization of firms, of sectors, and even of whole economies from relatively simple propositions. Sociologists, no less than economists, make this leap of faith.

Feenstra, Hamilton, and Huang's chapter, like the closely related paper of Hamilton and Feenstra (1998), also emphasizes the importance of the Walrasian framework. Feenstra and Hamilton argue that "bottom-up" descriptions of economic organization are misleading, if not incorrect, accounts of what happens at the level of entire economies. Bottom-up descriptions have a pernicious effect on economic analysis because they ignore the fact that, at any one point in time, an economy is a going concern, a complex, interdependent organization of industries and firms engaged in joint economic activity. Conceptualized in this way, economies consist of interconnected markets that are linked together by, among other things, price structures (the prices of inputs and outputs as well as the price of money for financing) and capital accounting systems (the systematization of financial information about firms).

In economics, the way to model cross-market economic systems is through the Walrasian framework known as a general equilibrium theory. The formal theory of general equilibrium proposed by Kenneth Arrow and Gerard Debreu (1954) is highly mathematical, very restrictive in terms of its assumptions, and of interest to few, if any, sociologists.[18] For instance, in the Arrow-Debreu version, the idealized Walrasian world contains two internally undifferentiated classes of agents, labelled producers and consumers, each of whom plans on the "right" prices but none of whom possesses the agency to alter price systems independent of their joint actions.

The Walrasian framework, however, can be opened up by incorporating a more organizational and institutional view of cross-market economic systems. Feenstra, Hamilton, and Huang's chapter represents an initial step toward reformulating a Walrasian framework. The economic focus of their chapter is a simulation model of how business groups are incorporated in an organized economy. The stylized model depicts an organized economy consisting of upstream sectors producing intermediate inputs and downstream sectors using those inputs to produce final consumer goods. In the model, manufacturing firms decide whether to buy intermediate products at marginal markups from a firm within a group or at full markups from independent firms. Solving the model based on the pricing decisions of firms in general equilibrium reveals multiple equilibria in the form of two distinct and economically stable (that is, stable in an ideal world only) solutions to business group integration in an organized economy: a high- and a low-concentration organized set of firms. Multiple equilibria suggest that, even in an ideal world of pure economics, there is no single efficient solution, and hence that, in the real world, theorists should expect to find multiple forms of capitalistic economic organizations, the origins of which economic theory cannot explain. Treating the multiple equilibria solutions as ideal types, Feenstra, Hamilton, and Huang demonstrate the plausibility of these solutions with industrial survey data from South Korea and Taiwan.

For sociologists, one of the significant aspects of this study is its focus on how price systems influence the economic performance of different kinds of socially embedded networks. Although economic networks may be socially embedded, they are not immune to fluctuations in price structures and capital accounting systems, as the recent Asian business crisis shows so clearly. Models drawn from general equilibrium theory can serve as simulation models—computerized ideal types—that indicate which types of networks may be maintainable under which market conditions. As in Weberian theory, one of the tasks for economic sociology is to specify how economically active networks deviate in the real world from the ideal types.

The Discussions

The discussions of the various chapters reveal many interesting methodological tensions between economists and sociologists. Indeed, the discussion of Padgett's chapter by Gregory Besharov and Avner Greif is a miniature treatise on differences in method between economists and sociologists, written from economists' point of view. In a book on networks and markets, it is especially worth noting methodological differences in the treatment of these two concepts.

Let us consider networks first. Economists typically prefer to treat networks as outcomes (endogenous), as in the chapters by Feenstra, Hamilton, and Huang and by Kirman, though they occasionally treat network membership as exogenous, especially when determined by ethnicity or similar demographic attributes (see, for example, Greif 1993; Rauch, this volume). Sociologists, on the other hand, prefer to treat networks as givens (exogenous). This methodological difference is brought out especially clearly by Joel Sobel's discussion of Burt's chapter. Sobel asks why agents do not choose more open networks if agents with such networks do better than agents with dense networks. Burt's answer would be that agents largely accept the networks that they are dealt as a by-product of their other activities. Sobel's question is akin to a sociologist suggesting that when conflicting preferences create a problem (for example, the "battle of the sexes" game), the solution is for the agents to harmonize their preferences.

Turning to markets, economists typically believe that market competition plays a strong role in shaping institutions, especially within the private sector, and that it operates in a manner analogous to Darwinian natural selection. This belief leads economists to describe the various existing institutions, and even their individual features, as efficient solutions to some problem. In other words, when economists try to explain the features of an institution, they ask: What problem do these features solve? The well-known book by Paul Milgrom and John Roberts (1992) is one of the leading examples of this approach. Contemporary sociologists deride this view as crude "functionalism." They believe that institutional structures are much more constrained by history and much more strongly influenced by political and cultural forces than do economists. This debate is joined from the sociologists' side by Neil Fligstein in his discussion of the chapter by Feenstra, Hamilton, and Huang, and from the economists' side by Besharov and Greif in their discussion of the chapter by Padgett.[19]

These differences between economists and sociologists as to whether networks should be treated as endogenous or exogenous and regarding the strength of market competition as a force for selection of institutional forms are not unrelated. An extreme economists' position would be that market competition causes "efficient" networks to form and eliminates "inefficient" ones. Although he does not take this position, Rauch does (implicitly) argue in his chapter that efficient networks (or commercial institutional substitutes) can be constructed if government provides incentives lacking in the market; Marta Tienda and Rebeca Raijman, in their discussion of Rauch's chapter, are much more skeptical.

Conclusions

Sociologists and economists studying networks and markets are now crossing the disciplinary divide and working with and scrutinizing each other's concepts. Economists have always known, of course, that personal relations are important in economic life, but they are now starting to use network conceptions of personal relations as a way to qualify their understanding of markets. Likewise, sociologists have always known that price and profit-led markets are important in capitalist societies, but now the new economic sociologists are trying to show not only the sociological underpinning of markets but the ways in which price and profit-led markets interact with social organization. These cross-disciplinary incursions are leading to frequent exchanges between the two disciplines and to a mutual recognition that each discipline has something to learn from the other. The chapters in this book reveal that despite their disciplinary differences, economists and sociologists share common ground on a surprisingly large number of issues.

Nevertheless, we do not believe that these more intensive exchanges will lead to a disciplinary convergence of economics and sociology. It seems more likely that such exchanges will provide a clearer recognition that a division of labor exists between economics and economic sociology of a kind similar to that envisioned by Joseph Schumpeter and Max Weber nearly a century ago (Swedberg 1998; Hamilton 1996).[20] The details of this division of labor are still forming, but the starting points are already fairly clear and roughly correspond to the market and network approaches described earlier.

The disciplinary core of economics has been, and will continue to be, markets. Markets and the possibility of markets, as captured in rational calculations of all types, permeate modern societies as never before, and so economists will never run out of subject matter to scrutinize. As new generations of economists enter the scene, however, the focus of economic work is likely to change, perhaps leaving the rigid assumptions of neoclassical economics for less constricting perspectives.

Economic sociology is a relatively new field whose agenda is still being formulated. The current direction of research is to examine the organization of economic life, the structure of markets, and the institutional environment in which economic activities occur. Networks are one of the primary ways by which institutional and market structures are conceptualized. As the division of labor between the two disciplines matures, economic sociologists are likely to become specialists in how economies are institutionally framed and internally structured, and economists will continue as specialists in how economies perform in both the ideal and real worlds.

We would like to thank Joel Sobel and two anonymous reviewers for helpful comments. Rauch gratefully acknowledges support from National Science Foundation grant SBR-9709237, and Hamilton gratefully acknowledges support from the Center for Advanced Study in Behavioral and Social Sciences.

Notes

1. The study of Australian Chinese by Constance Lever-Tracy, David Ip, and Noel Tracy (1996, 137–38) leads them to state: "The power and flexibility of the Chinese system of networking lies in the way it can indefinitely extend the range of these personal contacts," and they quote one Australian Chinese: "When you know one person you know others. My contacts have their contacts. You can't know everyone yourself."

2. Alfred Marshall (1920, 182) wrote: "Everyone buys, and nearly everyone sells . . . in a 'general' market. . . . But nearly everyone has also some 'particular' markets; that is, some people or groups of people with whom he is in somewhat close touch: mutual knowledge and trust lead him to approach them . . . in preference to strangers."

3. Economic sociology is a very recently proclaimed subfield of sociology. As an identifiable field of study, economic sociology dates back to the works of Max Weber and Joseph Schumpeter (Swedberg 1998). Throughout much of the twentieth century, however, interest in this area was sporadic, and it languished until the mid-1980s, when a group of sociologists began to concentrate on demonstrating the sociological underpinning of economically identified phenomena. With the organizing efforts of a core group of specialists and a highly successful drive for members, the American Sociological Association formally accepted economic sociology as a fully recognized subfield only in 1999. See Smelser and Swedberg (1994) and Granovetter and Swedberg (1992) for programmatic statements and substantive discussions of the field.

4. For some reviews of the literature, see Powell and Smith-Doerr (1994) and Nohria and Eccles (1992).

5. Timothy Conley and Christopher Udry (2000) provide an especially nice empirical illustration of this advantage.

6. Purely theoretical work has increasingly moved away from this restrictive form. Examples include Jackson and Wolinsky (1996) and Kranton and Minehart (in press).

7. Symmetry itself is a restriction, but not one we consider relaxing. A good example of a sociomatrix that need not be symmetric is a matrix in which the entries are 1s when agent i states that agent j is his friend.

8. The restriction in figure 1.1 that groups are of equal size is not essential to the work discussed in this paragraph. In chapter 3, Feenstra, Hamilton, and Huang note that business groups vary widely in size within both Korea and Taiwan. In chapter 6, Rauch points out that groups of small-business owners are formed on the basis of ethnicity and may differ in size in part because population sizes differ across ethnic identities. Another restriction in figure 1.1 is that the position of each agent within a group is symmetrical. When economists relax this restriction, they mainly do so by assigning a coordinating or leadership role to one agent in the group; this agent is sometimes called a "club entrepreneur." Land developers (for example, of industrial parks) are concrete examples of club entrepreneurs (see Henderson 1985 and Rauch 1993a).

9. Edward Glaeser, Bruce Sacerdote, and José Scheinkman (1996) allow for uniform overlap between groups as a way for groups to interact outside of the market. In their model, all agents are arrayed along a line and every agent interacts directly only with his left and right neighbors. (This network structure is also used, as a special case, by Blume 1993 and by Durlauf 1993.) A sociomatrix showing the network structure of this model would start by showing all agents affiliated with a group of size two, and then add a 1 immediately to the right of the second agent and immediately to the left of the first agent in every group. This uniform departure from the restriction of absence of ties across groups is quite different in spirit from the analysis of "structural holes" in that ties that span structural holes are valuable precisely because they are not found everywhere.

10. For a succinct illustration of how history and expectations can both play roles in determining the outcomes of path-dependent processes, see Krugman (1991).

11. Perhaps the most sophisticated version of the constitutive view of networks is found in the work of Harrison White (1988, 1992).

12. Gary Becker (1976, 5) states: "The combined assumptions of maximizing behavior, market equilibrium, and stable preferences, used relentlessly and unflinchingly, form the heart of the economic approach as I see it."

13. Both Marx and Weber considered themselves economists more than sociologists. Weber was a trained economist and held a chair in economics, not sociology. Marx lived before sociology became an academic discipline. Though self-trained, he was a rigorous economic observer.

14.   For a summary of this literature, see Hamilton (1994).

15.   From this beginning, a number of researchers began to show that some of the most successful industries and economies are organized specifically to take advantage of institutionalized networks of firms (Nohria and Eccles 1992; Smelser and Swedberg 1994, part 2). Some have even argued that specific industries (Powell and Prantley 1992; Uzzi 1996) and specific economies (Gerlach 1992; Fligstein 1996; Whitley 1992; Hollingsworth and Boyer 1997; Stark 1996; Stark and Bruszt 1997; Orrù, Biggart, and Hamilton 1997) are founded on institutionalized social networks.

16.   An important strand of recent research in economics is the evolution of market institutions (for example, North 1981; Milgrom, North, and Weingast 1990), which are often conceived as providing benefits that substitute for participation in social networks.

17.   Economists (for example, Dixit 1992) have recently devoted considerable attention to examining how the combination of the irreversibility of many investment decisions with uncertainty can generate another explanation for loyalty, which they prefer to call "hysteresis" or "lock-in." If accepting what appears to be a better deal requires making an investment for which an agent has little alternative use, he may prefer to stick with what he has and knows rather than risk forfeiting his investment if the deal goes sour. Investments that are relationship-specific are especially unlikely to have good alternative uses, so hysteresis naturally arises in the context of networks.

18.   It is missing even a theory of the firms.

19.   This debate parallels one within evolutionary biology itself (Gould and Lewontin 1979).

20.   Both Weber and Schumpeter believed, but in rather different ways, that an adequate study of economic life could be achieved only by dividing the analytic work between economic theory, economic history, and economic sociology. Each subject area has a different theoretical and substantive focus, but combined they give the full view of the place of the economy in human life.

References

Abolafia, Mitchel Y. 1997. *Making Markets: Opportunism and Restraint on Wall Street.* Cambridge, Mass.: Harvard University Press.

Abolafia, Mitchel Y., and Nicole Biggart. 1991. "Competition and Markets: An Institutional Perspective." In *Socio-Economics: Toward a New Synthesis,* edited by Amitai Etzioni and Paul Lawrence. Armonk, N.Y.: M. E. Sharpe.

Arrow, Kenneth J., and Gerard Debreu. 1954. "Existence of an Equilibrium for a Competitive Economy." *Econometrica* 22(3): 265–90.

Baker, Wayne. 1984. "The Social Structure of a National Securities Market." *American Journal of Sociology* 89: 775–811.

———. 1990. "Market Networks and Corporate Behavior." *American Journal of Sociology* 96: 589–625.

Becker, Gary. 1976. *The Economic Approach to Human Behavior.* Chicago: University of Chicago Press.

Blume, Lawrence E. 1993. "The Statistical Mechanics of Strategic Interaction." *Games and Economic Behavior* 5: 387–424.

Bonacich, Edna. 1973. "A Theory of Middleman Minorities." *American Sociological Review* 38(October): 583–94.

Borjas, George J. 1992. "Ethnic Capital and Intergenerational Mobility." *Quarterly Journal of Economics* 107(1): 123–50.

Burt, Ronald S. 1992. *Structural Holes: The Social Structure of Competition.* Cambridge, Mass.: Harvard University Press.

Chandler, Alfred D., Jr. 1977. *The Visible Hand: The Managerial Revolution in American Business.* Cambridge, Mass.: Harvard University Press.

———. 1990. *Scale and Scope: The Dynamics of Industrial Capitalism.* Cambridge, Mass.: Harvard University Press.

Chung, Wai-Keung, and Gary G. Hamilton. 1999. "Personal Ties: The Normative Foundations of Chinese Business." Unpublished paper. University of Washington, Seattle.

Conley, Timothy G., and Christopher R. Udry. 2000. "Learning About a New Technology: Pineapple in Ghana." Working paper. Chicago and New Haven, Conn.: Northwestern University and Yale University.

Dixit, Avinash. 1992. "Investment and Hysteresis." *Journal of Economic Perspectives* 6(Winter): 107–32.

Durlauf, Steven N. 1993. "Nonergodic Economic Growth." *Review of Economic Studies* 60(2): 349–66.

Feenstra, Robert C., Deng-Shing Huang, and Gary G. Hamilton. 1997. "Business Groups and Trade in East Asia: Part 1: Networked Equilibria." Working paper 5886. Cambridge, Mass.: National Bureau of Economic Research (January).

Feenstra, Robert C., Tzu-Han Yang, and Gary G. Hamilton. 1999. "Business Groups and Product Variety in Trade: Evidence from South Korea, Taiwan, and Japan." *Journal of International Economics* 48(1): 71–100.

Fligstein, Neil. 1985. "The Spread of the Multidivisional Form Among Large Firms, 1919–1979." *American Sociological Review* 50: 377–91.

———. 1990. *The Transformation of Corporate Control.* Cambridge, Mass.: Harvard University Press.

———. 1996. "Markets as Politics: A Political-Cultural Approach to Market Institutions." *American Sociological Review* 61(4): 656–73.

Fligstein, Neil, and Iona Mara-Drita. 1996. "How to Make a Market: Reflections on the Attempt to Create a Single Market in the European Union." *American Journal of Sociology* 102(1): 1–33.

Friedland, Roger, and A. F. Robertson. 1990. *Beyond the Marketplace: Rethinking Economy and Society*. New York: Aldine de Gruyter.

Gereffi, Gary, and Miguel Korzeniewicz. 1994. *Commodity Chains and Global Capitalism*. Westport, Conn.: Praeger.

Gerlach, Michael. 1992. *Alliance Capitalism: The Strategic Organization of Japanese Business*. Berkeley: University of California Press.

Glaeser, Edward L., Bruce Sacerdote, and José A. Scheinkman. 1996. "Crime and Social Interactions." *Quarterly Journal of Economics* 111(2): 507–48.

Gould, Stephen J., and Richard C. Lewontin. 1979. "The Spandrels of San Marco and the Panglossian Paradigm: A Critique of the Adaptationist Programme." *Proceedings of the Royal Society of London B* 205: 581–98.

Granovetter, Mark. 1973. "The Strength of Weak Ties." *American Journal of Sociology* 78: 1360–80.

———. 1985. "Economic Action and Social Structure: The Problem of Embeddedness." *American Journal of Sociology* 91: 481–510.

———. 1988. "The Sociological and Economic Approaches to Labor Market Analysis: A Social Structural View." In *Industries, Firms, and Jobs: Sociological and Economic Approaches,* edited by George Farkas and Paula England. New York: Plenum Press.

———. 1995. *Getting a Job: A Study of Contacts and Careers*. 2nd ed. Chicago: University of Chicago Press. (Originally published in 1974)

Granovetter, Mark, and Patrick McGuire. 1998. "The Making of an Industry: Electricity in the United States." In *The Laws of the Markets,* edited by Michel Callon. Oxford: Blackwell.

Granovetter, Mark, and Richard Swedberg, eds. 1992. *The Sociology of Economic Life*. Boulder, Colo.: Westview Press.

Greif, Avner. 1989. "Reputation and Coalitions in Medieval Trade: Evidence on the Maghribi Traders." *Journal of Economic History* 49(4): 857–82.

———. 1993. "Contract Enforceability and Economic Institutions in Early Trade: The Maghribi Traders' Coalition." *American Economic Review* 83(3): 525–48.

Hamilton, Gary G. 1994. "Civilizations and the Organization of Economies." In *The Handbook of Economic Sociology,* edited by Neil Smelser and Richard Swedberg. Princeton, N.J.: Princeton University Press.

———. 1996. "The Quest for a Unified Economics." *Industrial and Corporate Change* 5(3): 907–16.

Hamilton, Gary G., and Robert C. Feenstra. 1998. "The Organization of Economies." In *The New Institutionalism in Sociology,* edited by Marcy C. Brinton and Victor Nee. New York: Russell Sage Foundation.

Harvey, David. 1990. *The Condition of Postmodernity*. Oxford: Basil Blackwell.

Henderson, J. Vernon. 1985. *Economic Theory and the Cities*. Orlando, Fla.: Academic Press.

Hollingsworth, J. Rogers, and Robert Boyer. 1997. *Contemporary Capitalism: The Embeddedness of Institutions*. Cambridge: Cambridge University Press.

Jackson, Matthew, and Asher Wolinsky. 1996. "A Strategic Model of Social and Economic Networks." *Journal of Economic Theory* 71(1): 44–74.

Kali, Raja. 1999. "Endogenous Business Networks." *Journal of Law, Economics, and Organization* 15(3): 615–36.

Kranton, Rachel E. 1996. "Reciprocal Exchange: A Self-Sustaining System." *American Economic Review* 86(4): 830–51.

Kranton, Rachel E., and Deborah F. Minehart. In press. "A Theory of Buyer-Seller Networks." *American Economic Review*.

Krugman, Paul R. 1991. "History Versus Expectations." *Quarterly Journal of Economics* 106: 651–67.

Lever-Tracy, Constance, David Ip, and Noel Tracy. 1996. *The Chinese Diaspora and Mainland China*. New York: St. Martin's Press.

Lie, John. 1997. "Sociology of Markets." *Annual Review of Sociology* 23: 341–60.

Lucas, Robert E. 1988. "On the Mechanics of Economic Development." *Journal of Monetary Economics* 22: 3–42.

Marsden, Peter, and Karen Campbell. 1984. "Measuring Tie Strength." *Social Forces* 63: 482–501.

Marshall, Alfred. 1920. *Industry and Trade*. 3rd ed. London: Macmillan.

Milgrom, Paul, Douglass C. North, and Barry R. Weingast. 1990. "The Role of Institutions in the Revival of Trade: The Medieval Law Merchant, Private Judges, and the Champagne Fairs." *Economics and Politics* 1(March): 1–23.

Milgrom, Paul, and John Roberts. 1992. *Economics, Organization, and Management*. Englewood Cliffs, N.J.: Prentice-Hall.

Mizruchi, Mark S., and Linda Brewster Stearns. 1994. "Money, Banking, and Financial Markets." In *The Handbook of Economic Sociology*, edited by Neil Smelser and Richard Swedberg. Princeton, N.J.: Princeton University Press.

Nohria, Nitin, and Robert G. Eccles, eds. 1992. *Networks and Organizations: Structure, Form, and Action*. Boston: Harvard Business School Press.

North, Douglass C. 1981. *Structure and Change in Economic History*. New York: Norton.

Orrù, Marco, Nicole Biggart, and Gary G. Hamilton. 1997. *The Economic Organization of East Asian Capitalism*. Thousand Hills, Calif.: Sage Publications.

Padgett, John F., and Ansell, Christopher K. 1993. "Robust Action and the Rise of the Medici, 1400–1434." *American Journal of Sociology* 98(6): 1259–1319.

Perrow, Charles. 1981. "Markets, Hierarchies and Hegemony." In *Perspectives on Organizational Design and Behavior,* edited by A. Van de Ven and William Joyce. New York: Wiley.

———. 1990. "Economic Theories of Organization." In *Structures of Capital: The Social Organization of the Economy,* edited by Sharon Zukin and Paul DiMaggio. Cambridge: Cambridge University Press.

Piore, Michael J., and Charles F. Sabel. 1984. *The Second Industrial Divide: Possibilities for Prosperity.* New York: Basic Books.

Podolny, Joel M. 1993. "A Status-based Model of Market Competition." *American Journal of Sociology* 98: 829–72.

Podolny, Joel M., and Karen L. Page. 1998. "Network Forms of Organization." *Annual Review of Sociology* 24: 57–76.

Powell, Walter W., and Peter Prantley. 1992. "Competitive Cooperation in Biotechnology: Learning Through Networks?" In *Organizations and Networks,* edited by Nitin Nohria and Robert Eccles. Cambridge, Mass.: Harvard Business School Press.

Powell, Walter W., and Laurel Smith-Doerr. 1994. "Networks and Economic Life." In *The Handbook of Economic Sociology,* edited by Neil Smelser and Richard Swedberg. Princeton, N.J.: Princeton University Press.

Rabin, Matthew. 1993. "Incorporating Fairness into Game Theory." *American Economic Review* 83: 1281–1302.

Rauch, James E. 1993a. "Does History Matter Only When It Matters Little?: The Case of City-Industry Location." *Quarterly Journal of Economics* 108(3): 843–67.

———. 1993b. "Productivity Gains from Geographic Concentration of Human Capital: Evidence from the Cities." *Journal of Urban Economics* 34(November): 380–400.

Rauch, James E., and Alessandra Casella. 1998. "Overcoming Informational Barriers to International Resource Allocation: Prices and Group Ties." Working paper 6628. Cambridge, Mass.: National Bureau of Economic Research (June).

Smelser, Neil, and Richard Swedberg, eds. 1994. *The Handbook of Economic Sociology.* Princeton, N.J.: Princeton University Press.

Segal, Uzi, and Joel Sobel. 1999. "Tit for Tat: Foundations of Preferences for Reciprocity in Strategic Settings." Discussion paper 99–10. University of California, San Diego (June).

Stark, David. 1996. "Recombinant Property in East European Capitalism." *American Journal of Sociology* 101(4): 993–1027.

Stark, David, and Lásló Bruszt. 1997. *Postsocialist Pathways: Transforming Politics and Property in East Central Europe.* New York: Cambridge University Press.

Stinchcombe, Arthur. 1990. *Information and Organizations.* Berkeley: University of California Press.

Swedberg, Richard. 1991. "Major Traditions of Economic Sociology." *Annual Review of Sociology* 17: 251–76.

———. 1994. "Markets as Social Structures." In *The Handbook of Economic Sociology*, edited by Neil Smelser and Richard Swedberg. Princeton, N.J.: Princeton University Press.

———. 1998. *Max Weber and the Idea of Economic Sociology*. Princeton, N.J.: Princeton University Press.

Uzzi, Brian. 1996. "The Sources and Consequences of Embeddedness for the Economic Performance of Organizations: The Network Effect." *American Sociological Review* 61(4): 674–98.

Weisbuch, Gérard, Alan Kirman, and Dorothea Herreiner. 2000. "Market Organization and Trading Relationships." *Economic Journal* 110(463): 411–36.

White, Harrison C. 1981. "Where Do Markets Come From?" *American Journal of Sociology* 87: 517–47.

———. 1988. "Varieties of Markets." In *Social Structures: A Network Approach*, edited by Barry Wellman and S. D. Berkowitz. Cambridge: Cambridge University Press.

———. 1992. *Identity and Control: A Structural Theory of Social Action*. Princeton, N.J.: Princeton University Press.

Whitley, Richard D. 1992. *Business Systems in East Asia*. London: Sage Publications.

Zukin, Sharon, and Paul DiMaggio, eds. 1990. *Structures of Capital: The Social Organization of the Economy*. Cambridge: Cambridge University Press.

Chapter 2

Bandwidth and Echo:
Trust, Information, and
Gossip in Social Networks

Ronald S. Burt

There are two schools of thought on how network structures create the competitive advantage known as social capital. One school focuses on the advantages of closure. A network is closed to the extent that people in it are connected by strong relationships. Typical forms of closure are dense networks, in which everyone is connected to everyone else, and hierarchical networks, in which people are connected indirectly through mutual relations with a few leaders at the center of the network. Both forms provide numerous communication channels, which facilitate the enforcement of sanctions against misbehavior. Closure lowers the risk of trust, thus facilitating collaborative efforts that require trust. A second school of thought focuses on the advantages of brokerage. Markets and organizations are assumed to be networks of interdependent groups in which information flows at higher velocity within than between groups such that separate groups come to know about different things. Boundaries between groups define holes in social structure, or "structural holes," creating a competitive advantage in networks that span the holes. Brokerage across structural holes is an advantage for detecting and developing new ideas synthesized across disconnected pools of information.

The two schools of thought are reviewed in detail elsewhere. The available empirical evidence clearly supports brokerage over network closure as the source of social capital, though closure can be a significant factor in realizing the value buried in a structural hole (Burt 2000).

Trust remains an unresolved concern. The social capital of brokerage depends on trust—since the value created by brokers by definition involves new, and so incompletely understood, combinations of previously disconnected ideas—but trust is often argued to require network closure, precisely the condition that brokers rise above.

My purpose in this chapter is to show how the trust association with network closure is more complex, and decidedly less salutary, than argued in closure models of social capital. Building on earlier work (Burt and Knez 1995; Burt 1999a), my argument is framed with respect to two hypotheses describing how closure affects the flow of information in a network. What I discuss as a bandwidth hypothesis—presumed in closure models of social capital and in related work such as reputation models in economics—says that network closure enhances information flow. The echo hypothesis—based on the social psychology of selective disclosure in informal conversations—says that closed networks do not enhance information flow so much as they create an echo that reinforces predispositions. Because information obtained in casual conversations is more redundant than personal experience but not properly discounted, recipients come to an erroneous sense of certainty. Interpersonal evaluations are amplified to positive and negative extremes. Favorable opinion is amplified into trust. Doubt is amplified into distrust.

In the first section, I summarize as a baseline model the dyadic exchange theory of trust production that ignores social context. The bandwidth and echo hypotheses are introduced in the second section as contextual extensions of the baseline. In the third section, I use network data on three study populations to illustrate the contradiction between the hypotheses and the empirical support for the echo hypothesis over the bandwidth hypothesis.

Trust Without Context: A Baseline Hypothesis

Take as the unit of analysis the relationship between two people, ego and alter. The baseline for any network argument about trust is a description of how trust would emerge between ego and alter in the absence of a network around them. This is the setting for much of exchange theory and a convenient setting in which to define trust. Two prominent examples are George Homans's (1961) analysis of social behavior and Peter Blau's (1964) analysis of social exchange, but James Coleman (1990, chapter 5) captures trust more concretely for his systems of two-party exchange: Trust is a willingness to commit to a collaborative effort before you know how the other person will behave. Distrust is a reluctance to commit without guarantees about the other person's behavior. This is trust, pure and simple. You anticipate cooperation from the other person, but you commit to the exchange before you know how the other person will behave. A university faculty granting tenure to a professor trusts the professor to continue to be productive. A faculty committee allocating a fellowship to a graduate student trusts the student to work toward the degree. Anticipated cooperation is a narrow segment in the spectrum of concepts spanned by richer images such as Bernard Barber's (1983) distinctions between trust as moral order, competence, and obligation. However, much of the trust essential to market competition can be described as anticipated cooperation. The issue is not moral. The market requires flexible cooperation. This point is nicely illustrated in fieldwork by Stewart Macauley (1963) and Brian Uzzi (1996). Macauley (1963, 61) quotes one of his local Wisconsin purchasing agents: "If something comes up, you get the other man on the telephone and deal with the problem. You don't read legalistic contract clauses at each other if you ever want to do business again. One doesn't run to lawyers if he wants to stay in business because one must behave decently."

Viewed as anticipated cooperation, trust is twice created by repeated interaction, from the past and from the future. From the past, repeated experience with a person is improved knowledge of the person. Cooperation in today's game is a signal of future cooperation. Across repeated games with cooperative outcomes, you build confidence in the other person's tendency to cooperate. The cumulative process can be cast as a statistical decision problem in which you become more certain of the other person across repeated samples of the other person's behavior. The repetition of cooperative exchange promotes trust. More generally, the cumulative process involves escalation. From tentative initial exchanges, you move to familiarity, and from there to more significant exchanges. The gradual expansion of exchanges promotes the trust necessary for them. Whatever the cumulative process, past cooperation is a basis for future cooperation. (See, for example, Zucker 1986, on process-based trust; Staw and Ross 1987, on commitment escalation; Stinchcombe 1990, 164–65, on the information advantages of current suppliers for building trust; Kramer 1999, on history-based trust; Kollock 1994, for illustrative laboratory evidence; Gulati 1995; Gulati and Gargiulo 1999, for field evidence.) Moreover, the history is an investment that would be lost if either party behaved so as to erode the relationship—another factor making it easier for each party to trust the other to cooperate. Blau (1968, 454) summarizes the process:

> Social exchange relations evolve in a slow process, starting with minor transactions in which little trust is required because little risk is involved and in which both partners can prove their trustworthiness, enabling them to expand their relation and engage in major transactions. Thus, the process of social exchange leads to the trust required for it in a self-governing fashion.

Where sociologists explain trust emerging from past exchanges, economists look to the incentives of future exchanges (for example, Tullock 1985; Kreps 1990; Gibbons 1992, 88ff). The expectation that violations of trust will be punished in the future leads players to cooperate even if defection would be more profitable in a single play of the game. The information contained in past experience and the potential for future interactions are inextricably linked. A player's willingness to forgo short-term gains is based on the expectation that current behavior will be used to predict future behavior.

In sum, the baseline prediction is that *trust is a correlate of relationship strength*. A history of repeated cooperation strengthens the relationship between two people, increasing the probability that they trust one another. *Where people have little history together, or an erratic history of cooperation mixed with exploitation, or a consistent history of failure to cooperate, people will distrust one another, avoiding collaborative endeavors without guarantees on the other's behavior.* There is research to be done on the relative weight to be given to dimensions of relational strength, or their impact on trust relative to the level of risk in a proposed collaborative effort (for example, Kollock 1994; Snijders and Raub 1998; Buskens and Weesie 2000), but it is sufficient here to take as a baseline that trust is a correlate of relational strength.

Figure 2.1 is a quick illustration that is useful in distinguishing the bandwidth and echo hypotheses. The dots in figure 2.1 are people,

Figure 2.1 Whom Does Henry Trust?

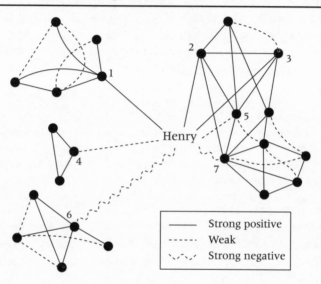

Henry Trust	Baseline hypothesis	(1, 2, 3)	>	(4, 5)	>	(6, 7)
	Bandwidth hypothesis	(2, 3 > 1)	>	(5 > 4)	>	(7 > 6)
	Echo hypothesis	(2, 3 > 1)	>	(5 >4)	>	(6 > 7)
Henry Distrust	Baseline hypothesis	(6, 7)	>	(4, 5)	>	(1, 2, 3)
	Bandwidth hypothesis	(6 > 7)	>	(4 > 5)	>	(1 > 2, 3)
	Echo hypothesis	(7 > 6)	>	(5 > 4)	>	(1 > 2, 3)

Source: Author.

and the lines indicate relations: a solid line for a strong positive relationship, a dashed line for a weak relationship, and a wavy dashed line for a strong negative relationship. In distinguishing strong and weak relationships, I have in mind the usual dimensions of emotional closeness and history between two people (compare Granovetter 1973, 1361). Henry in figure 2.1 has strong positive relations with three contacts (1, 2, 3), weak relations with two (4, 5), and strong negative relations with two (6, 7). According to the baseline hypothesis (bottom of figure 2.1), if Henry were asked to name the people he trusts, he would be expected to name contacts 1, 2, or 3. He would be less likely to name contacts 4 or 5, and unlikely to name contacts 6 or 7. If Henry were asked to name the people he distrusts (where distrust is not the complement to trust so much as an opposite extreme separated in the middle by contacts a person neither trusts nor distrusts), he would be expected to name contacts 6 or 7. He would be less likely to name contacts 4 or 5, and unlikely to name contacts 1, 2, or 3.

Trust in Social Context

Expanding the ego-alter unit of analysis to include friends, acquaintances, and enemies as third parties to the relationship between ego and alter adds several dimensions of meaning to exchange between ego and alter, but information flow is my concern here. In particular, I am concerned with the way third parties affect information flow in casual conversation by telling stories—not stories in the sense of deception, but stories that are personal accounts about people, in short, gossip. Ralph Rosnow and Gary Fine (1976, 87) offer a definition of what I have in mind when they define gossip as "nonessential (often trivial) news about someone." For the purposes of this chapter, gossip is simply the sharing of news, the catching up, the verbal analog to social grooming through which we maintain relationships (see, for example, Fine 1986; Bergmann 1987/1993; Gambetta 1994; Dunbar 1996).[1]

Stories spread by word of mouth, so the social structure of people around alter is like a broadcast system transmitting information to an audience of armchair quarterbacks in vicarious game play with alter. The signal in alter behavior multiplies as it diffuses through third parties. In a game between ego and alter isolated from other people (the situation described by the baseline argument), ego plays one game with alter and receives a signal about alter's trustworthiness. Put that game in a social context of third parties, and ego receives repeated signals about alter from vicarious game play in third-party stories about alter. Thus, ego has two sources of information on alter: ego's own direct experience with alter, and ego's vicarious experience in third-party stories about alter, where the volume of stories reaching ego increases with the strength and number of ego's indirect connections to alter through third parties. For brevity, I refer to indirect connection between ego and alter through third parties as third-party ties. I discuss measures in the next section, but for the moment we can let ego's vicarious experience of alter increase as some function of third-party ties.

The Bandwidth Hypothesis

In some arguments, the information distributed through third-party ties improves ego's evaluation of alter. Assumptions about information flow in these arguments can be discussed as a bandwidth hypothesis in that third-party ties give ego better access to information on alter, so that ego can be more accurate and confident in his or her evaluation of alter. Coleman (1990, 310; cf. Coleman 1988, S104) highlights access to information in his discussion of network closure as social capital:

> An important form of social capital is the potential for information that inheres in social relations. . . . A person who is not greatly interested in current events but who is interested in being informed about important developments can save the time required to read a newspaper if he can get the information he wants from a friend who pays attention to such matters. A social scientist who is interested in being up-to-date on research in related fields can make use of everyday interactions with colleagues to do so, but only in a university in which most colleagues keep up-to-date.

The bandwidth assumption is more obvious in computer simulations of networks because simulating information flow requires a decision about closure's effect on flow. For example, Wayne Baker and Ananth Iyer (1992) illustrate with computer simulations that in markets with networks of more direct connections, improved communication between producers could stabilize prices, a central finding in Baker's (1984) analysis of a securities exchange. Werner Raub and Jeroen Weesie (1990) use simulations to describe how reputation effects could vary according to the speed with which third-party disclosures reach ego (see Yamaguchi 1994; Buskens 1998; DeCanio and Watkins 1998; Buskens and Yamaguchi 1999). Michael Macy and John Skvoretz (1998, especially figure 4) use computer simulations to describe how trust could be more likely between people in a small network of frequent interaction. The assumption that communication is enhanced by third-party ties can be justified with research or everyday anecdotes in which direct communication is more accurate than communication through intermediaries (see, for example, Gilovich 1987). Nevertheless, the effect of third-party ties on information flow and subsequent trust production remains an open empirical question.

The bandwidth hypothesis is consistent with balance theory (for example, Heider 1958; Davis 1970), with Granovetter's (1985) embeddedness argument, with Coleman's (1988, 1990) argument that network closure produces social capital, and with reputation theory in economics. (See Greif 1989, but other examples are numerous: Bradach and Eccles 1989; Nohria and Eccles 1992; Swedberg 1993; several chapters in Smelser and Swedberg 1994, especially Powell and Smith-Doerr 1994; more recently Brass, Butterfield, and Skaggs 1998; DiMaggio and Louch 1998; Gulati and Gargiulo 1999; and Buskens and Weesie 2000, for empirical evidence.)[2] The broad conclusion from these arguments is that dense networks of positive relations increase the probability of trust. Mark Mizruchi (1992, chapter 4) provides a thorough review supporting the conclusion that density needs to be distinguished from business unity, but it is more usual to see network density, or network closure more generally, cited as an antecedent to trust and cooperation.

Enforcement   An enforcement mechanism is often invoked in these arguments. The mechanism is that interconnected third parties can impose on ego a normative opinion of alter. Two prominent examples in sociology are Coleman's (1988; 1990, chapters 5, 8, 12) analysis of trust and social capital and Granovetter's (1985, 1992) discussion of trust emerging from "structural embeddedness"—that is, trust is more likely between people with mutual friends: "My mortification at cheating a friend of long standing may be substantial even when undiscovered. It may increase when the friend becomes aware of it. But it may become even more unbearable when our mutual friends uncover the deceit and tell one another" (Granovetter 1992, 44). Illustrating the trust advantage of third-party ties with rotating-credit associations, Coleman (1988, S103; 1990, 306–7) notes: "But without a high degree of trustworthiness among the members of the group, the institution could not exist—for a person who receives a payout early in the sequence of meetings could abscond and leave the others with a loss. For example, one could not imagine a rotating-credit association operating successfully in urban areas marked by a high degree of social disorganization." He summarizes: "The consequence of this closure is, as in the case of the wholesale diamond market or in other similar communities, a set of effective sanctions that can monitor and guide behavior. Reputation cannot arise in an open structure, and collective sanctions that would ensure trustworthiness cannot be applied" (Coleman 1988, S107–8). Coleman also explains educational achievement with closed networks among parents, teachers, and neighbors that facilitate cooperation in monitoring a child. Robert Putnam (1993) applies the argument to explain higher institutional performance in regional Italy with the trust, norms, and dense networks that facilitate coordinated action, and a literature has emerged on trust as an element of social capital. (See, for example, Portes 1998; see Barker 1993, for an ethnographic account of enforcement in closed networks.)

There is an analogous argument in economics. Where sociologists focus on enforcement through exclusion from current relations, economists focus on enforcement through exclusion from future relationships (for example, Tullock 1985; Kreps 1990). The argument is that mutual acquaintances make game behavior more public, thus creating an incentive for good behavior to maintain reputation within the network; good behavior decreases the risk associated with cooperation and trust between ego and alter and so increases the probability of cooperation and trust. Thus, Greif (1989) explains eleventh-century Maghribi traders benefiting from overseas agents by forming a coalition through which they could communicate and enforce reputation norms of good agent behavior. (For a similar analysis of medieval merchant guilds and the expansion of trade, which were otherwise inhibited by incentives for opportunistic behavior, see Greif, Milgrom, and Weingast 1994.) The Maghribi were middle-class Jews in North Africa whose trade by boat and caravan spanned the Mediterranean. Business was risky in that sale prices and dates were unknown at the time when a merchant invested in a shipment. Greif (1989, 860) notes: "A journey from Egypt to Sicily, for example, could take 13 to 50 days, and ships did not always reach their destination. Within the ship the goods were not well sheltered and were often damaged in transit. Furthermore, as the captain of the ship was not responsible for packing, loading, and unloading the goods, there was always the possibility that he or the crew would pilfer the goods." Greif (1993, 528) describes the system that emerged to manage the delivery and sale of goods:

> Agency relations among the Maghribis were extremely flexible, as merchants operated through several agents at the same time and even at the same trade center and seem to have been at ease initiating and canceling agency relations. . . . Agency relations enabled the Maghribi traders to reduce the cost of trade by better allocating risk through diversification, by benefiting from agents' expertise, and by shifting trade activities across trade centers, goods, and time.

With investment separated from return by a logistics nightmare, the flexible agency relations required trust because of the incentives for dishonesty. An agent could sell your shipment at a good price, then give you a fraction of your share of the profits by explaining that the arrival of another boat as he was unloading yours had lowered the price for your shipment.

Network closure might have made trust practical. Active correspondence between the Maghribi made it possible for them to monitor cooperative and abusive behavior and so to collectively exclude agents known to be abusive. Greif (1993, 530) cites an example:

> Around 1055 it became known in Fustat that Abun ben Zedaka, an agent who lived in Jerusalem, embezzled the money of a Maghribi trader. The response of the Maghribi traders was to cease any commercial relations with him. His bitter letter indicates that merchants as

far away as Sicily had ostracized him. Only after a compromise was achieved and he had compensated the offended merchant were commercial relations with him resumed.

Prediction The enforcement possible in a closed network puts pressure on ego to adopt the group opinion of alter, and ready communication within the network ensures that ego often hears the group opinion. Repetition and threat of social sanction imply that ego's opinion of alter will be polarized to extremes (see, for example, Laumann 1973, 126; Myers and Lamm 1976; Bienenstock, Bonacich, and Oliver 1990), with repetition the critical ingredient for polarization (see, for example, Isenberg 1986; Lamm 1988; Williams and Taormina 1992; Brauer, Judd, and Gliner 1995; Baron et al. 1996). *The bandwidth prediction is that ego's opinion of alter is correlated with third-party opinion, and that networks evolve toward a state of balance in which people bound by a strong relationship have similar opinions of others.*[3] If the people whom ego trusts have a positive opinion of alter, then ego is more likely to trust alter when those people share with ego the information justifying their opinions. The more positive ego's aggregate connection is to alter through third parties, the more likely it is that ego trusts alter. Conversely, the third parties' negative opinion of alter increases the odds of ego distrusting alter.[4]

Figure 2.1 illustrates how the bandwidth hypothesis extends the baseline. Above and beyond the trust predicted by the baseline hypothesis from the strength of the relationship between Henry and his contacts, this hypothesis predicts trust as a function of context. Among Henry's close contacts (1, 2, 3), trust is less likely with contact 1 because there are no third parties to the relationship. (His relation with contact 2 is embedded in a positive third-party tie through contact 3, and vice versa.) Between his weak contacts (4 and 5), Henry is less likely to trust contact 4 because there are no third parties to the relationship. Henry's relationship with contact 5 is complicated by 5's close relationship with 7, to whom Henry has a strong negative relationship, but ensured by 5's close relationship with a mutual friend, contact 2. To the extent that Henry trusts either of his negative contacts (6 and 7), it would be 7 because he has some guarantees on 7's behavior from 7 being embedded in third-party ties through contact 2, and 2's friend 5.

The Echo Hypothesis

Looking more closely at the social psychology involved when third parties pass information to ego, there is reason to question the bandwidth hypothesis in favor of what can be termed the echo hypothesis: third parties do not enhance ego's information on alter so much as they create an echo that reinforces ego's predisposition toward alter.

Etiquette   Echo results when etiquette biases the information that third parties disclose to ego. It is polite in casual conversation to go along with the flow of sentiment being shared. We tend to share in conversation those of our facts that are consistent with the perceived dispositions of the people with whom we are speaking, and facts shared are facts more likely to be remembered. The biased sample of facts shared in conversations becomes the information on, and so the reality of, the people discussed. (See, for example, Grice 1975, on cooperation in conversation; Higgins 1992, on evidence; cf. Rosen and Tesser 1970; Klayman 1995, 393–401; Backbier, Hoogstraten, and Terwogt-Kouwenhoven 1997.)

For example, Tory Higgins (1992) describes an experiment in which the subject, a college undergraduate, is given a written description of a hypothetical person, Donald. The subject is asked to describe Donald to a second student who walks into the lab. The second person is a confederate who primes the conversation by leaking his predisposition toward Donald ("kinda likes" or "kinda dislikes" Donald). The result is that subjects distort their descriptions of Donald toward the expressed predisposition. Positive predisposition elicits positive words about Donald's ambiguous characteristics and neglect of his negative concrete characteristics. Negative predisposition elicits negative words about Donald's ambiguous characteristics and neglect of his positive concrete characteristics.

Returning to ego's trust in alter, when ego implicitly or explicitly expresses a predisposition toward alter, third parties can be expected to select from their repertoire of stories about alter a story consistent with the flow of the conversation. If ego seems to trust alter, the third party relays stories of games in which alter cooperated. If ego seems to distrust alter, the third party relays stories in which alter did not cooperate. Ego's predisposition toward alter is apparent from a variety of cues ranging from the subtle nuance of a raised eyebrow, or a skeptical tone of voice when describing alter, to the blatant signal of expressing a positive or negative opinion. Having shared a story featuring certain alter behaviors, ego and the third party are thereafter more likely to think of alter in terms of the behaviors discussed.[5]

Prediction   The echo hypothesis comes in three steps. First, etiquette biases ego's third-party information on alter toward ego's prior opinion of alter, creating an echo in which third parties reinforce ego's prior opinion. Etiquette might not affect every conversation equally, but allow for a moment that it has some effect on some conversations. (I return to the question of ego and third-party motives later.) Second, as discussed under the section on the bandwidth hypothesis, strong third-party ties give ego ready exposure to alter information. In other words, stronger third-party ties create a louder echo. Third, also as discussed under the bandwidth hypothesis section, the repetition of consistent information makes ego more certain about alter, polarizing ego opinion to extremes of trust and distrust.

There is a testable distinction between the bandwidth and echo hypotheses. Both hypotheses involve ego's direct experience of alter coming together with vicarious experience. The difference is how the two kinds of experience come together. Under the bandwidth hypothesis, ego and third parties share their information on alter and so move together toward a shared opinion of alter. Under the echo hypothesis, ego and third-party opinion differences can continue unspoken because third parties are biased by etiquette to disclose to ego information consistent with what ego already knows. Echo does not depend on ego recalling the individuals from whom specific stories were heard. (Ego typically begins by saying, "I can't recall where I heard it, but I recently heard that . . .") The echo argument is only that ego hears stories consistent with his or her predisposition toward alter and becomes more certain about alter. Thus, etiquette makes it possible for gossip to vary from one relationship to the next as a function of predispositions in each; as a result, relations can develop independently such that strong positive relationships can exist next to strong negative ones. The bandwidth hypothesis's prediction of correlation between ego and third-party opinion is limited under the echo hypothesis to opinion intensity: *The echo hypothesis's prediction is that stronger third-party ties foster more intense ego opinion such that relations adjacent in a network need not be balanced in their direction (I trust friends of my friends) so much as in their intensity (I have an opinion, positive or negative, of my friends' friends).*

More specifically, to better distinguish the echo from the bandwidth hypothesis, let t_{ea} be a measure of ego's trust in alter (a trust relation from e for ego to a for alter), a variable that ranges from negative 1 if ego definitely distrusts alter, up to 1 if ego definitely trusts alter, with neutral 0 indicating that ego neither trusts nor distrusts alter. Let z_{ea} be a measure of the strength of ego's relationship with alter, a variable that ranges from negative 1 for a strong, negative ego-alter relationship, up to 1 for a strong, positive relationship, with a neutral 0 indicating no prior relationship. (See the discussion of measures in the section on illustrative evidence.) The baseline hypothesis is that t_{ea} increases with z_{ea}. The bandwidth hypothesis predicts that t_{ea} increases with $\sum_k z_{ek}z_{ka}$, $e \neq k \neq a$, the sum of ego's indirect connections to alter through third parties k; in other words, ego's positive opinion of alter increases with more positive third-party ties to alter. The echo hypothesis predicts that $|t_{ea}|$ increases with $\sum_k |z_{ek}z_{ka}|$, $e \neq k \neq a$ in other words, the intensity of ego's opinion of alter increases with the intensity of third-party ties. The trust predicted in strong relationships by the baseline hypothesis is predicted by the echo hypothesis to be more likely and intense in strong relations embedded in strong positive and negative third-party ties. The distrust predicted in weak and negative relationships by the baseline hypothesis is predicted by the echo hypothesis to be more likely and intense when the relations are embedded in strong negative and positive third-party ties.

The most powerful research strategy for testing the hypotheses is to look for situations in which third-party ties in one direction generate trust in the other direction. The bandwidth hypothesis predicts that such situations should not occur. The echo hypothesis predicts that they can.

In figure 2.1, for example, the bandwidth and echo hypotheses would be indistinguishable in predicting whom Henry trusts. The hypotheses differ at the extreme of predicting trust within Henry's negative relationships to contacts 6 and 7 (thus the box in figure 2.1 around the predictions), but the probability of trust is so low in negative relations that this would be a difficult difference to measure with available research instruments.

Distrust is more interesting. The bandwidth hypothesis predicts that Henry is more likely to distrust contact 6 than 7 because there are no third parties to his relationship with 6 and so no reputation costs to 6 for misbehavior toward Henry. The echo hypothesis predicts that Henry is more likely to distrust contact 7 because that relationship is embedded in third-party ties through contacts 2 and 5, both of whom will offer stories about contact 7 to Henry that corroborate Henry's negative relationship with 7.

Similarly for Henry's weak relationships, the bandwidth hypothesis predicts that Henry is more likely to distrust contact 4 than 5 because there are no third parties to his relationship with 4 and so no reputation costs to 4 for misbehavior toward Henry. The prediction is complicated by Henry's negative relationship with contact 7, who could be expected to tell to both Henry and contact 5 negative stories about the other so that a negative relationship develops between them consistent with the negative indirect relationship through contact 7. Cutting against that complication is 7's strong, positive connection with contacts 5 and 2 and the strong, positive third-party tie between Henry and 5 through contact 2. With positive balance of indirect connections between Henry and contact 5, and Henry's relationship with contact 4 embedded in no third-party ties, Henry is more likely to distrust 4 than 5 under the bandwidth hypothesis. The echo hypothesis reverses the bandwidth prediction. Distrust is more likely with contact 5 than 4 because the relationship with 5 is embedded in third-party ties through contacts 2 and 7. Henry's weak relationships with contacts 4 and 5 are both subject to the inevitable doubts about trusting someone with whom one has only a weak relationship, but third-party gossip is expected to amplify those doubts more with contact 5. Contact 7 would find it especially easy to be polite in reinforcing anything negative that Henry or contact 5 had to say about one another.

Motive   Workshop discussion of the etiquette mechanism often elicits three questions about motives. (1) What if ego has no predisposition toward alter and so is agnostic when soliciting alter information from third parties? (2) Why do third parties reinforce ego's predisposition regardless of their own opinion? There are individual differences in personal preference and opportunities to be with alter, so ego and third parties are likely to disagree sometimes in their evaluations despite their strong relationship with one another. For a third party displeased with alter, gossip is an opportunity to get even. (See, for example, Black 1995, 855n: "Gossip is the handling of a grievance by an informal hearing in absentia—in the absence of the alleged offender.") (3) Given the etiquette bias in third-party information, why doesn't ego discount what third parties say? These questions have to be addressed if the echo argument is to be a believable alternative to the bandwidth argument.

At minimum, the etiquette mechanism is a behavioral trait exogenous to the argument. Empirical research shows that the mechanism exists, and the echo hypothesis is an implication of its existence.

Digging deeper for more satisfying answers, begin with the question of ego's agnosticism. One answer to the question is to say that there are no such people because everyone has predispositions. Ego's predisposition could be based on no more than an image invoked by the name of a new acquaintance, or some random exogenous shock. Given a predisposition, however faint, the research question is whether predisposition is revised toward third-party opinion (bandwidth) or is reinforced under the etiquette mechanism to become ego's certain opinion (echo). Another approach is to ask what information an agnostic would hear first from third parties. Initial information will be predisposition in subsequent conversations. To the extent that bandwidth exists, the most likely opinion of alter circulating in a closed network is the group opinion, so the information most likely to be first heard would be the group opinion, whereupon etiquette's effect in subsequent conversations would be to reinforce ego's certainty in the group opinion of alter, thus creating ostensible evidence of the bandwidth hypothesis. The research implication is that ego agnostics would obscure evidence of the echo hypothesis.

Turning to the broader question of motives, it is not impossible to find reasons for the etiquette mechanism. Civility is one. Etiquette allows people of diverse backgrounds and interests to ignore social differences that would otherwise interrupt the flow of conversation.

(On the need for deception in everyday life, see Nyberg 1993; Kuran 1997.) Efficiency is another motive. In the press of other demands on the third party, corroborating ego's predisposition ends the discussion without seeming rude, and information consistent with what we already know is easier to accept. (See, for example, Ross and Anderson 1982, on attribution errors; Klayman 1995, on confirmation bias.) Identity is a third motive. People define who they are in part with stereotypes of people on the social boundary of their group (for example, Gluckman 1963; Elias and Scotson 1965/1994, chapter 7; Erikson 1966; Wittek and Wielers 1998).

Identity is at the heart of the broader motive behind gossip. Gossip is not about information. It is about creating and maintaining relationships. (See Dunbar 1996, on gossip as a verbal analogue to grooming among primates.) Relaying a story about alter consistent with ego's predisposition highlights similarity between the third party and ego with respect to other people. Moreover, there is the history of exchanges to consider. As third parties strengthen their relations with ego by offering information about alter consistent with ego's predisposition toward alter, ego strengthens his or her tie with the third party by asking for the information and responding to third-party opinion. When you and I discuss our views of John, we reinforce our relationship with one another and narrow the confidence interval around our joint opinion of John. Conversations about social structure are an integral part of building and maintaining relationships, with the primary effect of reinforcing the current structure. Ego's search for information on whether to trust alter is less often a search de novo than it is a search for a quick update on stories vaguely recalled ("Didn't you once have some trouble working with John?"). Information flow is a by-product of gossip, a by-product perceived to be unintentional and so unbiased. As Diego Gambetta (1994, 11) puts it, "Gossip does not work well if the receiver suspects ulterior motives behind the transmitter's story."

An alternative intuition is to say that ego is misled by lower-quality information in gossip. For example, Thomas Gilovich (1987) showed undergraduates a video of a person describing "something you are not too proud of," then asked subjects to describe the person on audiotape and rate his culpability for his bad behavior. A second subject then listened to the audiotape and rated the person's culpability. Evaluations by the students with secondhand knowledge from the audiotape were more extreme in blaming the person for his bad behavior. Gilovich argues that secondhand accounts elicit more extreme evaluations because the secondhand accounts leave out mitigating circumstances and situational constraints. That omission reduces the accounts to "cheap talk" that should be discounted. (See, for example, Gibbons 1992, 210ff, on cheap-talk games.) Why should ego believe a third-party account stripped of situational details? The etiquette mechanism requires less naïveté on ego's part. Third-party accounts are accurate, but not representative. Other things being equal, each third party has positive and negative stories about alter. Ego receives complete stories, but not a representative set of stories. Ego cannot know that she or he is getting a subset of information biased toward the positive (or negative) because ego does not know the scope of each third party's information on alter.

Still, ego, having been a third party in other conversations, should be aware of the etiquette mechanism and so discount information in third-party accounts. That is, unless there is no meaningful point estimate of alter's trustworthiness. The truth is that alter behaves well with some people and not with others. This truth about relationships is illustrated by two features of the colleague evaluations between bankers analyzed in the next section. First, everyone was the object of positive and negative evaluations: for each banker, two or more people said that she or he was doing a poor job, and at the same time two or more people said that she or he was doing a good job. In fact, positive and negative evaluations are correlated: the number of evaluations a banker received has a .91 correlation with the number of positive evaluations received, and a .80 correlation with the number of negative evaluations. Second, analysis of variance across the thousands of interpersonal evaluations breaks down to 25 percent of the variance being due to differences between bankers making an evaluation (some bankers gave higher evaluations on average), 13 percent being due to differences between bankers receiving an evaluation (some bankers received higher evaluations on average), and the residual 62 percent being due to qualities specific to evaluator-evaluatee pairs of bankers. In other words, evaluations are more a function of the two bankers involved than of either person individually. (See Kenny and Albright 1987, 399, for a similar result in relations between undergraduates.)

More generally, the truth about alter is for ego an evaluation with ambiguous empirical referent, an evaluation to be discussed rather than determined, and there is ample empirical evidence that such evaluations are shaped by discussion (see, for example, Festinger, Schachter, and Back 1950; Coleman, Katz, and Menzel 1966; Pfeffer, Salancik, and Leblebici 1976; Burt 1987, 1999b). If ego seems predisposed to trust alter, perhaps ego is one of the people who will get along with alter, and it is not surprising that ego's friends relay stories about alter consistent with ego's positive predisposition. On the other hand, if ego seems predisposed to distrust alter, perhaps ego is one of the people who will not get along with alter, so it is not surprising that ego's friends offer stories about alter consistent with ego's negative predisposition. Gossip is not about truth, it is about sociability (see, for example, Gambetta 1994, 13: "Plausibility is more relevant than truth. A convincing story gets repeated because of its appeal not its truthfulness"). The by-product of that sociability is that predispositions are reinforced and people become more certain in their opinions of one another.

Illustrative Evidence

I have survey network data on three study populations: a probability sample of 284 senior managers in a leading manufacturer of electronic components and computer equipment; a saturation sample of 317 staff officers in two financial companies; and a census of 345 bankers in the investment banking division of a large financial company. The senior managers are a benchmark because of published research on the network structure of their social capital. The staff officers are included for replication. Their work (human resources) differs from the work of the senior managers (primarily engineering and sales), but their network data were obtained with a questionnaire nearly identical to the senior-manager questionnaire, so evidence on the officers can be a replication of evidence on the senior managers. The bankers are included for replication and the richer network data they provide.

Baseline for Senior Managers and Staff Officers

Colleague relationships are distinguished in figure 2.2 by their relative strength. The relationships were all important in one way or another, but some were stronger than others. The managers and staff officers answered a series of sociometric questions asking them to name (a) people with whom they most often discussed important personal matters, (b) the people with whom they most often spent free time, (c) the person to whom they report, (d) their most promising subordinate, (e) their most valued contacts in the firm, (f) the people they would name as essential sources of buy-in to their replacement if they were promoted to a new job, (g) the contact most important for their continued success in the firm, (h) their most difficult contact, and (i) the people with whom they would discuss moving to a new job in another firm. The 284 senior managers cited a total of 3,015 colleague relations. The 317 staff officers cited 3,324. Respondents in both populations were asked to indicate the emotional strength of their relationship with each colleague. "Especially close" relations are labeled "strong" ties in figure 2.2, "close" relations are in the middle, while "less close" and "distant" relations are labeled "weak." Details on sampling and surveying the senior managers are available elsewhere. (See Burt 1992, 1997, 1998, 2000, on their networks as social capital; see Burt and Knez 1995, 1996, on their trust and distrust of colleagues.)[6]

As predicted by the baseline argument, trust is more likely in strong relations. (Combine the white and gray bars at the top of figure 2.2.) Among the senior managers, 39 percent of strong relationships were cited for trust, versus 4 percent of weak relationships. The difference is larger among the staff officers—67 percent of the strong relationships versus 4 percent of the weak ones. There are many indicators that could be taken as evidence of trust. Here, trusted colleagues are those few cited as someone with whom the senior manager or staff officer would discuss leaving the firm for a job elsewhere: "If you decided to find a job with another firm doing the same kind of work you do here, who are the two or three people with whom you would most likely discuss and evaluate your job options?" The element of trust is the risk associated with other people in the firm knowing that the

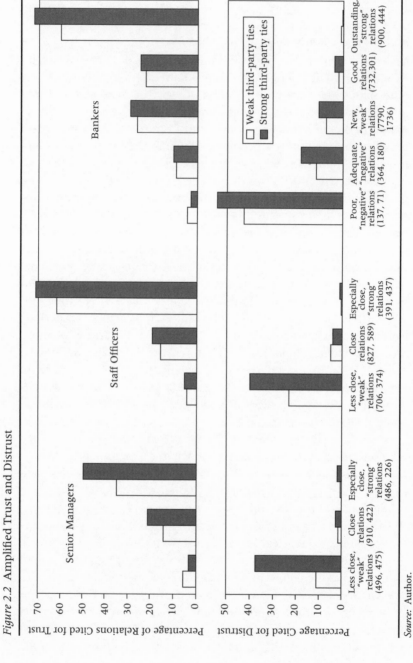

Figure 2.2 Amplified Trust and Distrust

Source: Author.

Note: The number of relations embedded in (weak, strong) third-party ties is reported in parentheses.

senior manager or staff officer was thinking of leaving. Employment is more than a contract, it is a membership. Moving to another firm repudiates membership, especially in these study populations of senior people and a loose internal structure that highlights the boundary between inside and outside as an element defining employee identities. The person threatening to leave becomes the subject, rather than a source, of the office gossip that builds solidarity among colleagues.

As predicted by the baseline argument, distrust is more likely in weak relations (bottom panel in figure 2.2). Distrust is concentrated within weak relationships; 24 percent of weak relations are cited for distrust by the senior managers, 21 percent by the staff officers. Again, there are many qualities that could be taken as evidence of distrust. Here, it is indicated by a sociometric citation for the most difficult colleague: "Of your colleagues, who has made it the most difficult for you to carry out your job responsibilities?" The citation is open to alternative interpretations since it does not ask about distrust explicitly (Krackhardt 1996). However, respondents were asked to explain why they cited the person they did, and their explanations indicate distrust in the sense of noncooperation. (See Burt and Celotto 1992; Burt 1999a, for content analysis of their explanations.)

Banker Baseline

Network data on the third study population come from an annual survey of employees within the investment banking division of a large financial organization. The respondents, whom I discuss as "bankers," include senior people responsible for making and closing deals, as well as people in administrative positions who manage bankers in lower ranks or manage analysts who service the bankers. The data are a census in that virtually all eligible employees return the survey questionnaire because responses are used as "peer evaluations" to guide promotion and bonus decisions. (See Burt 1997, 2000, on the banker networks as social capital.) Data quality is also high because the data are routinely studied by a staff of analysts looking for strategic behavior such as blackballing between cliques or inflated evaluations between friends who have little business with one another.

The results in figure 2.2 describe 345 bankers citing colleagues, in their own division and in other divisions of the organization, for a total of 12,655 important relationships.[7] For each person cited as a frequent and substantial business contact, the banker was asked for a summary evaluation of the colleague as "poor" (persons receiving multiple poor evaluations are encouraged to look for a different line of work), "adequate" (a negative evaluation akin to the grade of C in graduate school), "good," or "outstanding." (Persons receiving multiple outstanding evaluations are put on an unwritten list of "stars" for whom special efforts are to be made to prevent them from leaving the organization.) The words *poor, adequate, good,* and *outstanding* are synonyms for the words actually used in the peer evaluations.

Timing is one of the ways in which these data are richer than the data on the managers and officers. Banker evaluations of trust and distrust on the vertical axis of figure 2.2 are from this year's peer evaluations. Categories of relationship on the horizontal axis come from last year's evaluations. Strong banker relations in figure 2.2 are with colleagues cited last year as outstanding, and the weak relationships are with colleagues not cited last year. Much can happen over the span of a year in the hurly-burly of investment banking—note that most of this year's important relationships were not cited last year (9,526, or 75 percent)—but there is a qualitative difference between relationships new this year and relations sufficiently established to have been cited and evaluated in last year's survey.

A second quality for which the banker data are richer is their extension into negative relationships. The senior managers and staff officers were asked for a single negative relationship. The bankers were asked to cite all colleagues with whom they had frequent and substantial business dealings and then were allowed to offer negative evaluations of any or all. The negative banker relations on the horizontal axis in figure 2.2 are 544 relationships judged "adequate" and another 208 judged "poor."[8]

In addition to summary evaluation, bankers evaluated relations for specific qualities. Trust was one of the qualities. The trust citations at the top of figure 2.2 are to colleagues given the most positive evaluation for their cooperation in reaching collective goals and integrity in sharing information and responsibility for disappointing results. (Again, "cooperation" and "integrity" are synonyms for the terms actually used in the peer evaluations.) The distrust citations at the bottom of figure 2.2 are to colleagues whose cooperation and integrity were evaluated "adequate" or "poor." The majority of relationships fall between the extremes of trust and distrust. (Of the 12,655 cited relationships, 7,880 were cited neither for trust nor distrust.)

As predicted by the baseline hypothesis, the bars increasing from left to right for bankers at the top of figure 2.2 show that trust is more likely within stronger relationships. The bars decreasing from left to right for bankers at the bottom of figure 2.2 show that distrust is more likely within weak relationships.

Amplified Trust and Distrust

To move beyond the baseline argument, I need a measure of the third-party ties in which ego-alter relationships are embedded. Indirect connection in a network is measured as a product of direct connections (from path distance in graph theory, see, for example, Scott 1991, 71; Wasserman and Faust 1994, 144–45) and that is the measure I use: the strength of the third-party tie from respondent to colleague is the respondent's relation with a third-party k multiplied by the third party's relation with the colleague, a quantity summed across third parties k. The senior managers and staff officers were asked to describe the relationship between each pair of colleagues they cited as especially close (1.0), distant in the sense that the colleagues were total strangers or would rather not spend time together (0.0), or somewhere between the two extremes (.34, a quantitative score assigned to the middle response category from a loglinear association model of the survey network data; Burt 1992, 287–88). I assigned to the banker data arbitrary quantitative scores consistent with opinion in the organization: 1.0 for a maximum evaluation ("outstanding"), .5 for middle evaluations (.5 for "good," −.5 for "adequate"), and −1.0 for the minimum ("poor"), leaving 0 for disconnections between colleagues who do not cite one another. For the purposes of this section, I measure banker third-party ties in terms of their absolute magnitude (that is, $\sum_k |z_{ek}z_{ka}|$). (See the next section for directed ties.) The choice between direction and magnitude is a choice only in the banker networks (network data on the other two study populations describe only variably positive connections between contacts), and results on directed ties in the next section show that their relations are balanced in intensity rather than direction (figure 2.3), so absolute magnitude is the appropriate measure of third-party ties in this section.

Amplified Trust   The gray bars in figure 2.2 describe relationships embedded in strong third-party ties (the indirect connection between respondent and colleague is stronger than average for their study population), and the white bars describe relationships that are comparatively free of third parties. As predicted by both the bandwidth and echo hypotheses, the trust concentrated in strong relationships is more likely when embedded in strong third-party ties. At the top of figure 2.2, the gray bars higher than the adjacent white bars show that trust is more likely in strong relationships when they are embedded in strong third-party ties. Among the senior managers, for example, 50 percent of strong relations embedded in strong third-party ties were cited for trust (gray bar), versus 35 percent for strong relations embedded in weak third-party ties (white bar).

Statistical summary is provided by logit equations in the first three columns of table 2.1.[9] The first row of effects describes the baseline positive association between trust and relationship strength. (Standard deviations are listed in the table as a frame of reference for unit increases in the predictors.) As predicted by both the bandwidth and echo hypotheses, the trust associated with strong relationships is more likely with third parties. The effects shown in table 2.1 for the interaction with strong relationships (TP × STRONG) describe the increase in trust, which is statistically significant in all three study populations (from a 2.5 t-statistic for the senior managers to 8.8 for the bankers).[10]

Amplified Distrust   The equations in the second three columns of table 2.1 predict distrust. The first row of effects describes the baseline negative association between distrust and relationship strength. Distrust is extremely unlikely between colleagues who are emotionally close, regardless of third parties (negligible effects for TP × STRONG interactions).

As predicted by the echo hypothesis, and in contradiction to the bandwidth hypothesis, distrust is more likely in weak relationships embedded in positive third-party ties. The effect is illustrated at the

Table 2.1 Amplified Trust and Distrust

	Trust			Distrust			Standard Deviations		
	Managers	Officers	Bankers	Managers	Officers	Bankers	Managers	Officers	Bankers
Intercept	-2.983	-2.961	-1.240	1.603	.978	-2.683	—	—	—
Strength of relationship	2.966 (7.5)*	4.013 (6.7)*	1.260 (9.3)*	-5.516 (-8.4)*	-5.118 (-3.5)*	-1.7059 (-8.5)*	.294	.293	.377
Number of colleagues cited	-.033 (-1.4)	.044 (2.2)	-.005 (-1.5)	-.252 (-8.7)*	-.106 (-3.9)*	.003 (0.8)	2.471	3.554	31.874
Strength of third-party tie (TP)	-.556 (-2.1)	-3.458 (-5.5)*	-.031 (-1.4)	.322 (0.8)	-.949 (-1.0)	-.055 (-1.6)	.279	.189	3.191
TP × STRONG	4.382 (2.5)*	3.963 (7.2)*	.173 (8.8)*	6.502 (1.5)	-1.145 (-.8)	-.112 (-1.4)	.049	.227	2.223
TP × WEAK	-.541 (-1.1)	-3.539 (-1.0)	.160 (6.8)*	1.018 (3.0)*	4.095 (2.6)*	.071 (2.2)	.425	.085	3.067
TP × NEGATIVE	—	—	.043 (0.8)	—	—	.156 (2.5)*	—	—	.915
Chi-square	333.72*	358.34*	621.99*	333.72*	288.04*	461.99*	—	—	—
d.f.	5	5	6	5	5	6			

Source: Author.

Note: These are logit coefficients. (Test statistics in parentheses are z-scores adjusted for autocorrelation between relations cited by the same respondent.) Estimation is across 3,105 relationships cited by the senior managers, 3,324 cited by the staff officers, and 12,655 cited by the bankers. Relationship strengths are distinguished in figure 2.2 (and is strength last year for the bankers). Strength of third-party tie is the aggregate magnitude of indirect connections through third parties (TP = $\sum_k$ $|z_{ik}z_{kj}|$, $k \neq j$, i, where z_{ik} is the relation from i to k).

*P <.01.

bottom of figure 2.2 by the gray bars higher than the adjacent white bars over weak relationships. Among the senior managers, for example, 11 percent of weak relations embedded in weak third-party ties were cited for distrust (white bar), a figure that more than tripled to 37 percent if the third-party tie was strong (gray bar). The increase is statistically significant (3.0 test statistic in table 2.1). There is a similarly significant increase among the staff officers. Among the bankers too distrust is more likely within negative and weak relations embedded in strong third-party ties.

Frequency and Duration   Respondents with more personal experience of a colleague are predicted by the baseline hypothesis to have a more certain opinion of the colleague because they have more information on which to base their opinion. The history of interaction leading to the current strength of the relationship between respondent and colleague is held constant in table 2.1 by holding constant the current strength of the relationship. Some of that history, however, may be picked up by third-party ties. To the extent that mutual friends, enemies, and acquaintances accumulate with the time two people spend together, a stronger third-party tie between respondent and colleague would lead to the respondent having more personal experience with the colleague, so the respondent should be more certain about the colleague, not because of third-party gossip but because of having more information on the colleague.

What data I have on frequency and duration are consistent with the models in table 2.1.[11] In the study populations of managers and officers, respondents were asked about duration ("How long have you known each person?") and frequency ("On average, how often do you talk to each?"). Consistent with the baseline hypothesis, stronger relations occur between people who often talk to one another or have known one another for a long time. Regressing strength of relationship in table 2.1 across frequency and duration yields strong direct associations for the managers (respective t-tests of 18.5 and 10.5 with adjustment for autocorrelation within ego networks), as well as the staff officers (respective t-tests of 13.4 and 15.0). Nevertheless, effects in table 2.1 are robust to controls for frequency and duration. Frequency has no direct association with trust if added to the models in table 2.1

(0.7 z-score for the managers, −0.6 for the officers). Duration has a direct association with trust (3.8 z-score for the managers, 7.7 for the officers), but the key trust associations with strong ties and third parties remain: the 7.5 z-score for strong ties among the managers in table 2.1 increases to 9.1, and the 2.5 z-score for strong ties embedded in strong third-party ties increases to 3.2. The 6.7 z-score for strong ties among the officers in table 2.1 remains the same, and the 7.2 z-score for strong ties embedded in strong third-party ties is 6.3. Neither frequency nor duration has a direct association with distrust if added to table 2.1 (−0.9 and −0.2, respectively, for the managers, −1.5 and −1.0 for the officers), and the key distrust associations with weak ties and third parties remain as strong as reported in table 2.1. In sum, and consistent with the specification in table 2.1, the trust effects of frequency and duration are entirely or largely mediated through their association with relationship strength measured in terms of emotional closeness.

Balance in Intensity Rather than Direction

Figure 2.3 and table 2.2 contain evidence more discriminating in supporting the echo hypothesis over the bandwidth hypothesis. The results require data on third parties to all relationships at risk of being cited for trust or distrust, so I am limited to the banker study population. (In the other two populations, I do not have data on relations beyond each respondent's contacts.) The relations described in figure 2.3 and table 2.1 are all 118,680 possible between the bankers (345 bankers times 344 banker colleagues). Of the 118,680 relationships that could have been cited, 8,298 were (7 percent density). The other 4,357 banker citations in figure 2.2 were to colleagues elsewhere in the organization (see note 7). Owing to shared awareness of other bankers and given a higher density of cited relations within the division, relationships within the division are more likely (relative to the 4,357 relations scattered across other divisions) to show the bandwidth hypothesis's predicted balance between adjacent relationships.[12]

Relations are sorted on the horizontal axis of figure 2.3 with respect to third-party ties. In the left graph, relations vary from 0 negative third-party ties up to 10 or more. Evaluations of "poor" or "adequate" are treated as negative, and evaluations of "good" or "outstanding" as

Figure 2.3 Colleague Relationships Are Balanced in Intensity, Not Direction

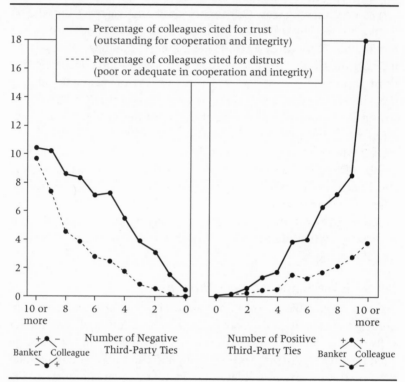

Source: Author.

positive (as in figure 2.2). As illustrated at the bottom of figure 2.3, a negative third-party tie between banker and colleague could occur in either of two ways (reported separately in table 2.2): the banker made a positive evaluation of someone who made a negative evaluation of the colleague, or the banker made a negative evaluation of someone who made a positive evaluation of the colleague. In the right graph, relations vary from 0 positive third-party ties up to 10 or more. As illustrated at the bottom of the graph, a positive third-party tie between banker and colleague could occur in either of two ways: the banker made a positive evaluation of someone who made a positive evaluation of the colleague (a friend of my friend is my friend), or the banker

Table 2.2 Trust, Distrust, and Directed Third-Party Ties

	Trust					Distrust				
	1	2	3	4	5	6	7	8	9	10
Intercept	−5.951	−4.970	−4.959	−4.955	−4.966	−6.527	−6.179	−6.217	−6.134	−6.232
Strength of relationship last year	3.077 (22.7)*	4.748 (42.1)*	3.373 (22.2)*	4.677 (39.4)*	4.609 (39.3)*	−3.069 (−11.7)*	−3.885 (−13.7)*	−4.538 (−14.9)*	−3.744 (−12.5)*	−4.559 (−15.9)*
Number of colleagues cited	−.006 (−2.3)	.015 (7.0)*	−.006 (−1.9)	.014 (5.9)*	.011 (4.8)*	−.001 (−0.2)	.012 (2.3)	.012 (3.2)*	.012 (2.3)	.013 (3.3)*
Positive third-party ties	.440 (32.2)*	—	—	—	—	—	—	—	—	—
Negative-negative	—	.124 (3.1)*	—	—	—	—	.104 (8.5)*	—	—	—
Positive-positive	—	—	.231 (18.1)*	—	—	—	—	.503 (9.7)*	—	—
Negative third-party ties	—	—	—	—	—	.442 (24.6)*	—	—	—	—
Negative-positive	—	—	—	.118 (4.1)*	—	—	—	—	.240 (4.8)*	—
Positive-negative	—	—	—	—	.210 (8.3)*	—	—	—	—	.274 (13.3)*
Chi-square	3048*	1967*	1279*	1846*	1920*	1292*	379*	550*	285*	681*
d.f	3	3	3	3	3	3	3	3	3	3

Source: Author.

Note: These are logit coefficients. (Test statistics in parentheses are z-scores adjusted for autocorrelation between relations from the same respondent.) Estimation is across all 188,680 relations among the 345 bankers. Relationship strengths are distinguished in figure 2.2. Third-party ties are counts as illustrated in figure 2.3; for example, "negative-positive" is for the banker i to banker j relationship a count of how often banker i made a negative evaluation of a colleague who made a positive evaluation of banker j.
* P < .01.

made a negative evaluation of someone who made a negative evaluation of the colleague (an enemy of my enemy is my friend).

There is evidence consistent with both the bandwidth and echo hypotheses. Lines in the graphs show how trust and distrust are associated with third parties. Logit equations in table 2.2 report the statistical significance of the associations holding constant last year's relationship and the number of third parties available to a banker as possible indirect ties to colleagues (cf. table 2.1). The solid line to the right in figure 2.3 shows the probability of trust increasing with the number of positive third-party ties. As predicted by both the bandwidth and echo hypotheses, the more mutual friends and mutual enemies a banker and colleague share, the more likely it is that the banker will cite the colleague for outstanding cooperation and integrity. Model 1 in table 2.2 shows that the increase is statistically significant. The effect exists for both kinds of positive third-party ties but is stronger with friends of friends (model 3) than with enemies of enemies (model 2).

Also, consistent with the bandwidth hypothesis, the dashed line to the left in figure 2.3 shows the probability of distrust increasing with negative third parties. The more often that banker and colleague have separate constituencies—the banker's contacts having a low opinion of the colleague, or the colleague's contacts being people of whom the banker has a low opinion—the more likely it is that the banker cited the colleague for noncooperation and low integrity. Model 6 in table 2.2 shows that the increase is statistically significant, and again, the effect exists for both kinds of negative third-party ties, though it is stronger with enemies of friends (model 10) than with friends of enemies (model 9). Not surprisingly, bankers were more affected by the opinions of third parties they admired (models 3 and 10) than of those they did not (models 2 and 9).

The striking result is the evidence that contradicts the bandwidth hypothesis in favor of the echo hypothesis: the solid line to the left in figure 2.3 shows that the probability of trust increases with negative third-party ties, and the dashed line to the right in figure 2.3 shows that the probability of distrust increases with positive third-party ties. Giving authority to the visual results in figure 2.3, statistical results in table 2.2 show significant increases in trust, and significant increases in distrust, with each kind of positive and negative third-party tie. In fact, the probability of trust within a relationship is more closely associated with total third-party ties than with the balance toward positive third-party ties, and the probability of distrust is associated more closely with the total than with a balance toward negative third-party ties.[13]

A skeptical reader might want to attribute the results in figure 2.3 to something unusual in investment banking, but the results are more likely typical of medium to large organizations. The results could seem unusual because sociometric choices in survey network data are not usually analyzed with respect to the population of relations that could have been cited. Here, the survey network data are analyzed in conjunction with a roster of people in the study population who could have been cited. Another generic feature of the results in figure 2.3 and table 2.2 is their consistency with a common finding in network analysis—relationships develop in clusters. As the number of third-party ties between two people increase, it becomes increasingly likely that the two people know about, and have an opinion of, one another. When completing their annual peer evaluations, bankers were more likely to remember work with colleagues with whom they had mutual friends, acquaintances, or enemies. More third parties increased the likelihood of remembering work with the colleague.

Central to this chapter is the empirical support for the echo hypothesis over the bandwidth hypothesis. Finding trust associated with negative third-party ties and distrust associated with positive ties is a clear contradiction to the bandwidth hypothesis's prediction of balance in adjacent relationships. It is precisely the pattern predicted by the echo hypothesis. With gossip pandering to predispositions, strong positive relations can develop next to strong negative ones. What is balanced in relationships affected by gossip is not the direction of adjacent relations, but rather their intensity. Strong third-party ties increase the volume of gossip, from which strong relationships emerge, positive and negative, depending on predispositions.

Conclusion

My purpose in this chapter has been to show how the trust association with network closure is more complex, and decidedly less salutary, than argued in closure models of social capital. A network is closed to the extent that people in it are connected by strong relationships, either directly (dense network) or indirectly through a few leaders at the center of the network (hierarchical network).

This chapter has been framed by two hypotheses describing how closure affects the flow of information in a network. The bandwidth hypothesis—presumed in closure models of social capital and in related work such as models of reputation in economics—says that network closure enhances information flow. The echo hypothesis—based on the social psychology of selective disclosure in informal conversations—says that closed networks do not enhance information flow so much as they create an echo that reinforces predispositions.

Much of the published research on trust is consistent with the bandwidth and echo hypotheses. Distrust is more likely within weak relationships, and trust is more likely within strong relationships embedded in positive third-party ties. Consistent with that evidence, I too find that distrust is more likely within weak or negative relationships, and trust is more likely in strong, positive relationships, especially when the relationships are embedded in strong third-party ties (figure 2.2).

Evidence more broadly considered supports the echo over the bandwidth hypothesis. In the past, trust research has focused on networks of positive relations, which is where both hypotheses predict that third parties increase the probability of trust. Evidence consistent with the echo hypothesis is appearing as research expands to include network effects on negative relationships. (See, for example, Burt and Knez 1995; Burt 1999a, on distrust and third parties; Labianca, Brass, and Gray 1998, on perceptions of conflict and third parties; Gulati and Westphal 1999, on third-party interlocks amplifying positive and negative predispositions to alliance between organizations.) Consistent with the emerging evidence, I too find that strong, positive third-party ties do not facilitate trust within weak relationships so much as they are associated with distrust (figure 2.2) and angry character assassination (Burt 1999a). The bandwidth hypothesis is more explicitly rejected in favor of the echo hypothesis by the fact that colleague relationships are balanced in their intensity, not their direction (figure 2.3).

The broader range of evidence calls into question the common assumption that closed networks improve information flow. Strong indirect connections between people are typically assumed to increase the probability of communication such that each knows what the other knows. The evidence presented here supports an alternative defined by the echo hypothesis: strong connection through third parties increases the probability of social reinforcement such that network closure creates echo, not accuracy. With an etiquette filter on the information that passes between people, strong connections lead to more conversations in which third parties corroborate ego's opinion so that ego hearing his or her opinion echoed becomes more certain, more intense, in his or her opinion of alter.

The bandwidth and echo hypotheses represent a fundamental choice for theoretical models of trust and its correlates. Down the bandwidth path—network closure improves information flow—lies theory in which people are better off when strongly connected to one another. Here lie stories about closed networks providing social capital and reputation (see, for example, Coleman 1988, 1990; Greif 1989; Putnam 1993). Alternatively, the path presuming the echo argument leads to theory in which perception drifts away from empirical reality, and what closed networks produce is ignorant certainty. Here lie stories about scapegoating, groupthink, and distorted reputations defined by polarized trust and distrust in closed networks. Of course, there are also positive stories about amplified trust in charismatic leaders and transcendental visions of a better future, but the positive stories are not unique to the echo hypothesis, since both the bandwidth and echo hypotheses predict amplified trust within strong relations embedded in closed networks. Still, given the evidence of amplified distrust so clearly supporting the echo hypothesis over the bandwidth hypothesis, where the two arguments contradict one another it is reasonable to ask whether the published evidence of amplified trust being consistent with both arguments is in fact due to echo, not bandwidth. This is a question for future research. Meanwhile, my summary conclusion is that network closure does not facilitate trust so much as it amplifies predispositions, creating a structural arthritis in which people cannot learn what they do not already know.

For leads into relevant literatures or editorial comment, I am grateful to Gary Becker, Sally Blount, Martin Gargiulo, Roger Gould, Chip Heath, Greg Janicik, Josh Klayman, Marc Knez, Edward Lawler, Gerry Mackie, Richard Moreland, Joel Podolny, Holly Raider, James Rauch, Sherwin Rosen, James Schrager, Toby Stuart, and Marla Tuchinsky.

Notes

1. I am excluding third parties strategically inserted between ego and alter to strengthen or weaken their relationship, such as third-party facilitators and positions of authority in a corporate or legal hierarchy (see, for example, Coleman 1990, 43–44, on complex relations; Black and Baumgartner 1983; Black 1993, chapter 6, on third parties in the legal process; and Morrill 1995, 92–140, for ethnographic illustration of the Black and Baumgartner view applied to managers). The third-party effects predicted by the bandwidth and echo hypotheses can occur with such third parties, but I put such third parties aside because adding them requires a consideration of the motives behind their presence. This chapter is about what could be termed "natural" third-party effects in casual conversations, and as Diego Gambetta (1994, 11) so nicely states the matter in his review, "Gossip does not work well if the receiver suspects ulterior motives behind the transmitter's story."

2. Edward Lawler and Jeongkoo Yoon (1993, 1998) propose a "theory of relational cohesion" that stands uniquely intermediate between what I am here discussing as baseline and bandwidth. As in the baseline, Lawler and Yoon predict that trust and commitment emerge from escalating exchanges, and they emphasize the "emotional buzz" associated with positive exchange. Beyond the baseline, certain relations develop and others do not as a function of location in the network structure. Where the structure of alternative contacts in a system of peers makes certain pairs of people more likely to have positive initial exchanges with one another, that likelihood, however slight, encourages further exchange, which can be expected to create clusters of dense, positive relations (see Feld 1981, on social foci). Bandwidth and echo extend the baseline to include the trust implications of dense third-party ties around a relationship. As Lawler and Yoon ground the baseline argument in opportunity, it could be productive to ground bandwidth and echo in the opportunity structure of a network to see whether the two arguments contradict one another in their etiology, as they do in the discussion here in their consequences.

3. Based on Fritz Heider's (1958) initial work, network balance and its extension, transitivity, was a popular application of cognitive consistency to social structure (for example, Davis 1970). Later work was primarily methodological, but balance continues to be discussed as an equilibrium in theories of consistency between adjacent elements in a network (for review, see Burt 1982, 55–60, 71–73; Scott 1991, 13–16; Wasserman and Faust 1994, chapter 14).

4. Empirical support is likely to be stronger for balance with positive rather than negative third-party ties. If the reputation advantages of treating friends well is matched by advantages from abusing enemies, then sanctions that discourage abusive behavior between colleagues with mutual friends could exist alongside sanctions that encourage abuse of people distrusted by one's friends—as is explicit in Avner Greif's (1989, 868) analysis of the Maghribi traders who felt free to cheat ostracized traders. However, the Maghribi lived within a relatively stable boundary between insiders and outsiders. To see why balance with negative third-party ties need not follow from the enforcement mechanism, consider a structure in which social boundaries are prone to change, as is typical of the boundaries between groups within an organization. A colleague capable of abusing someone today who is not "one of us" is capable of abusing you tomorrow if you are no longer considered "one of us." The more complex and dynamic an environment, the more likely that social boundaries between "us" and "them" will change. The only guaranteed result of abusive behavior is that the abuser will acquire a reputation for being someone capable of abuse. Abusive behavior, even if directed toward today's legitimate targets, has ambiguous signal value in terms of reputation. The one unambiguous prediction from the enforcement mechanism is that positive third-party ties increase the probability of cooperative behavior as ego and alter signal their cooperative predispositions to the third parties.

5. Etiquette is an element in the broader process of people defining one another as a by-product of the gossip they share (for example, Cialdini 1989; Tilly 1998). I know of no published fieldwork that offers ethnomethodological analysis of sustained conversation between senior managers, but the etiquette mechanism is a generic feature of gossip, and so it is evident in conversation at lower levels and outside the corporation, on which there are field studies. For example, Gary Fine (1986, 409) summarizes his analysis of teenager gossip:

Teenagers must present actions which are susceptible to several possible interpretations in ways which are likely to be supported by other speakers, either through ratification utterances or by story-chaining. The audience members actively or tacitly ratify the speaker's remarks, even if they disagree with the talk in principle. Interactants have techniques by which they can express their disagreement—through later contrary examples (which, too, are usually not disagreed with) or by audience role distance through joking interjections.

This is precisely the etiquette mechanism described in the text—going along with the flow of the conversation—and it implies the echo hypothesis of amplified opinion. (For example, Fine notes the exaggerated opinions in which some teenagers can "do no wrong," while others can "do no right.")

6. The staff officers are a saturation sample in the sense that all human resource employees in the two firms were mailed a network questionnaire, of whom 218 in one firm returned the questionnaire (65 percent response rate; see Burt, Jannotta, and Mahoney 1998; for results on the social capital of their networks, see Burt 2000), and 99 in the other firm returned it (40 percent response rate). Respondents were representative on various dimensions, including rank, age, salary, gender, and geography, except that employees in the senior ranks of the first firm were more likely to return the questionnaire. I combine the respondents as a single study population because their work is so similar, and so different from work in the other two study populations. There are no significant differences between the two staff officer samples in the number of colleagues cited (13.1 average in one firm, 12.4 in the other, 1.6 t-test, p = .10), or the sociometric results in table 2.1 (0.9 z-statistic for a firm dummy added to the officer trust equation, 0.03 for the distrust equation, p > .3).

7. The 12,655 cited relations are with 8,298 colleagues in the division (insiders) and with 4,357 colleagues in other divisions of the company (outsiders). Trust and distrust are similarly associated with third parties within and beyond the division. Add to the logit equation in table 2.1 predicting banker trust a dummy variable distinguishing the 4,357 relations to outsiders. The dummy variable has a positive association with trust (3.3 z-score, p < .01, indicating that the bankers acknowledge help more than disruption from people beyond their division), but there is no statistically significant effect on the incidence of trust within strong or weak embedded relations (−1.2 z-score for strong, −1.0 for weak; p > .2). Adding the outsider dummy to the logit equation for distrust shows fewer citations for distrust (−2.9 z-score, p < .01), but no signif-

icant effect on the incidence of distrust within weak or negative embedded relations (−0.7 z-score for weak, −0.4 for negative; p > .5).
Looking ahead to the next section, the insider-outsider distinction is
irrelevant to the network balance results in figure 2.3 because the results describe balance within the division.

8. As validation for the necessarily limited number of negative relations
    that can be obtained in an academic or consulting survey, it is interest-
    ing to note how few negative relations are elicited when there is no limit
    on the respondent—about two per banker (752 from 345 bankers).

9. Effects were estimated with standard errors adjusted for autocorrela-
    tion between relations described by the same respondent (for example,
    Kish and Frankel 1974) and a control for the number of colleagues
    cited. The control for the number of citations is needed for two reasons:
    (1) The senior managers and staff officers were asked for a limited
    number of trust citations and only one distrust citation, so trust and dis-
    trust are less likely from respondents citing more colleagues. (Note the
    negligible association with distrust for the bankers and significant neg-
    ative associations for senior managers and staff officers.) (2) Third-
    party ties are measured by the sum of indirect connections, which can
    be larger for respondents who make more citations. Burt and Knez
    (1995, 1996) present similar logit results on the senior managers using
    the alternative control of measuring third-party ties in terms of pro-
    portional strength relations. Another option, less useful in empirical
    research but demonstrably productive in theoretical work (Raub and
    Weesie 1990), would be to measure third-party ties by the time required
    for stories to reach ego.

10. The interaction with weak relationships in table 2.1 (TP × WEAK) is
    noteworthy with respect to reputation. The enforcement mechanism
    invoked in closure arguments is substantively important because it pur-
    ports to show the rationality of trust between people who have little or
    no history with one another. The presence of third parties ensures that
    each person can rely on the other not to be abusive because doing so
    would diminish one's reputation with the observing third parties.
    Structuring an organization to create third-party ties is thus a strategy
    for encouraging cooperation between colleagues for whom coopera-
    tion has no short-term gains. The weak relationships cited by senior
    managers and staff officers in figure 2.2 are like the negative relations
    cited by the bankers in showing little evidence of trust (and no signifi-
    cant third-party effects on trust in table 2.1). Trust is inhibited by emo-
    tional distance between respondent and colleague regardless of third

parties connecting the two people. However, the weak banker relations are weak in duration, not emotion. They are relations new to this year's peer evaluations, and as predicted by the enforcement mechanism, trust is significantly more likely in those of the new relationships embedded in strong third-party ties (6.8 t-statistic).

11. I am grateful to Martin Gargiulo for the point that third-party ties may measure respondent time with the colleague. Correlations are given below for the variables in the text. The first four are in table 2.1. Frequency distinguishes between (4) daily contact, (3) weekly, (2) monthly, or (1) less often. Duration is years known. Correlations below the diagonal are for the managers, and above are for the staff officers.

Trust	Distrust	Direct	Indirect	Frequency	Duration
—	−.196	.531	.092	.171	.372
−.123	—	−.381	−.162	−.256	−.106
.359	−.403	—	.177	.374	.293
−.037	.192	−.314	—	.205	.155
.130	−.146	.345	−.060	—	−.020
.145	−.054	.148	.019	−.143	—

12. I do not know the density of citations to other divisions because I do not know the number of colleagues at risk of being cited. However, I know that 431 colleagues were cited in other divisions. There are 148,695 possible relations from the 345 bankers to the 431 outsiders, of which 4,357 were cited, defining a 3 percent density of citations to outsiders. The 3 percent is higher than the true density because there are more than 431 colleagues in other divisions who could have been cited, but 3 percent is significantly lower than the 7 percent density among the bankers (−21.3 logit z-score, p < .001; and a −21.2 z-score if I hold constant each respondent's number of citations for the increased odds of citing insiders and outsiders).

13. This statement is based on logit models predicting trust and distrust from strength of last year's relationship and number of colleagues cited (first rows of table 2.2), then adding to the predictors the total number of third parties to the relationship (positive third-party ties plus negative third-party ties in table 2.2) and the extent to which positive third parties exceed negative ones (number of positive minus number of negative). The z-score test statistics are 19.9 and 9.9 for the third-party sum and balance, respectively, in predicting trust, and 21.9 and −4.8,

respectively, in predicting distrust. A balance toward positive third parties increases the probability of trust and decreases the probability of distrust, but both effects are weaker than the increased probability of trust and distrust with the sum of positive and negative third-party ties.

References

Backbier, Esther, Johan Hoogstraten, and Katharina Meerum Terwogt-Kouwenhoven. 1997. "Situational Determinants of the Acceptability of Telling Lies." *Journal of Applied Social Psychology* 27: 1048–62.

Baker, Wayne E. 1984. "The Social Structure of a National Securities Market." *American Journal of Sociology* 89: 775–811.

Baker, Wayne E., and Ananth Iyer. 1992. "Information Networks and Market Behavior." *Journal of Mathematical Sociology* 16: 305–32.

Barber, Bernard. 1983. *The Logic and Limits of Trust*. New Brunswick, N.J.: Rutgers University Press.

Barker, James R. 1993. "Tightening the Iron Cage: Concertive Control in Self-managing Teams." *Administrative Science Quarterly* 38: 408–37.

Baron, Robert S., Sieg I. Hoppe, Chuan Feng Kao, Bethany Brunsman, Barbara Linneweh, and Diane Rogers. 1996. "Social Corroboration and Opinion Extremity." *Journal of Experimental Social Psychology* 32: 537–60.

Bergmann, Jörg R. [1987] 1993. *Discreet Indiscretions*. Translated by John Bednarz Jr. New York: Aldine de Gruyter.

Bienenstock, Elisa Jayne, Phillip Bonacich, and Melvin Oliver. 1990. "The Effect of Network Density and Homogeneity on Attitude Polarization." *Social Networks* 12: 153–72.

Black, Donald. 1993. *The Social Structure of Right and Wrong*. New York: Academic Press.

———. 1995. "The Epistemology of Pure Sociology." *Law and Social Inquiry* 20: 829–70.

Black, Donald, and M. P. Baumgartner. 1983. "Toward a Theory of the Third Party." In *Empirical Theories About Courts,* edited by Keith O. Boyum and Lynn Mather. New York: Longman.

Blau, Peter M. 1964. *Exchange and Power in Social Life*. New York: Wiley.

———. 1968. "Interaction: Social Exchange." In *The International Encyclopedia of the Social Sciences,* vol. 7. New York: Free Press/Macmillan.

Bradach, Jeffrey L., and Robert G. Eccles. 1989. "Price, Authority, and Trust: From Ideal Types to Plural Forms." *Annual Review of Sociology* 15: 97–118.

Brass, Daniel J., Kenneth D. Butterfield, and Bruce C. Skaggs. 1998. "Relationships and Unethical Behavior: A Social Network Perspective." *Academy of Management Review* 23: 14–31.

Brauer, Markus, Charles M. Judd, and Melissa D. Gliner. 1995. "The Effects of Repeated Expressions on Attitude Polarization During Group Discussions." *Journal of Personality and Social Psychology* 68: 1014–29.

Burt, Ronald S. 1982. *Toward a Structural Theory of Action*. New York: Academic Press.

———. 1987. "Social Contagion and Innovation: Cohesion Versus Structural Equivalence." *American Journal of Sociology* 92: 1287–1335.

———. 1992. *Structural Holes*. Cambridge, Mass.: Harvard University Press.

———. 1997. "The Contingent Value of Social Capital." *Administrative Science Quarterly* 42: 339–65.

———. 1998. "The Gender of Social Capital." *Rationality and Society* 10: 5–46.

———. 1999a. "Entrepreneurs, Distrust, and Third Parties." In *Shared Cognition in Organizations*, edited by Leigh Thompson, John Levine, and David Messick. Hillsdale, N.J.: Erlbaum.

———. 1999b. "The Social Capital of Opinion Leaders." *Annals of the American Academy of Political and Social Science* 566: 37–54.

———. 2000. "The Network Structure of Social Capital." In *Research in Organizational Behavior*, vol. 22, edited by Robert I. Sutton and Barry M. Staw. Greenwich, Conn.: JAI Press.

Burt, Ronald S., and Norm Celotto. 1992. "The Network Structure of Management Roles in a Large Matrix Firm." *Evaluation and Program Planning* 15: 303–26.

Burt, Ronald S., Joseph E. Jannotta, and James T. Mahoney. 1998. "Personality Correlates of Structural Holes." *Social Networks* 20: 63–87.

Burt, Ronald S., and Marc Knez. 1995. "Kinds of Third-Party Effects on Trust." *Rationality and Society* 7: 255–92.

———. 1996. "Trust and Third-Party Gossip." In *Trust in Organizations*, edited by Roderick M. Kramer and Tom R. Tyler. Thousand Oaks, Calif.: Sage Publications.

Buskens, Vincent. 1998. "The Social Structure of Trust." *Social Networks* 20: 265–89.

Buskens, Vincent, and Jeroen Weesie. 2000. "An Experiment on the Effects of Embeddedness in Trust Situations: Buying a Used Car." *Rationality and Society* 12: 227–53.

Buskens, Vincent, and Kazuo Yamaguchi. 1999. "A New Model for Information Diffusion in Heterogeneous Social Networks." *Sociological Methodology* 29: 281–325.

Cialdini, Robert. 1989. "Indirect Tactics of Image Management: Beyond Basking." In *Impression Management in the Organization*, edited by Robert A. Giacalone and Paul Rosenfeld. Hillsdale, N.J.: Erlbaum.

Coleman, James S. 1988. "Social Capital in the Creation of Human Capital." *American Journal of Sociology* 94: S95–120.

————. 1990. *Foundations of Social Theory.* Cambridge, Mass.: Harvard University Press.

Coleman, James S., Elihu Katz, and Herbert Menzel. 1966. *Medical Innovation.* New York: Bobbs-Merrill.

Davis, James A. 1970. "Clustering and Hierarchy in Interpersonal Relations: Testing Two Graph Theoretical Models on 742 Sociograms." *American Sociological Review* 35: 843–52.

DeCanio, Stephen J., and William E. Watkins. 1998. "Information Processing and Organizational Structure." *Journal of Economic Behavior and Organization* 36: 275–94.

DiMaggio, Paul, and Hugh Louch. 1998. "Socially Embedded Consumer Transactions: For What Kinds of Purchases Do People Most Often Use Networks?" *American Sociological Review* 63: 619–37.

Dunbar, Robin. 1996. *Grooming, Gossip, and the Evolution of Language.* Cambridge, Mass.: Harvard University Press.

Elias, Norbert, and John L. Scotson. [1965] 1994. *The Established and the Outsiders.* Thousand Oaks, Calif.: Sage Publications.

Erikson, Kai T. 1966. *Wayward Puritans.* New York: Wiley.

Feld, Scott L. 1981. "The Focused Organization of Social Ties." *American Journal of Sociology* 86: 1015–35.

Festinger, Leon, Stanley Schachter, and Kurt W. Back. 1950. *Social Pressures in Informal Groups.* Stanford, Calif.: Stanford University Press.

Fine, Gary. 1986. "The Social Organization of Adolescent Gossip: The Rhetoric of Moral Education." In *Children's Worlds and Children's Language,* edited by Jenny Cook-Gumperz, William A. Corsaro, and Jürgen Streeck. New York: Mouton de Gruyter.

Gambetta, Diego. 1994. "Godfather's Gossip." *Archives Européennes de Sociologie* 35: 199–223.

Gibbons, Robert. 1992. *Game Theory for Applied Economists.* Princeton, N.J.: Princeton University Press.

Gilovich, Thomas. 1987. "Secondhand Information and Social Judgment." *Journal of Experimental Social Psychology* 23: 59–74.

Gluckman, Max. 1963. "Gossip and Scandal." *Current Anthropology* 4: 307–16.

Granovetter, Mark S. 1973. "The Strength of Weak Ties." *American Journal of Sociology* 78: 1360–80.

————. 1985. "Economic Action, Social Structure, and Embeddedness." *American Journal of Sociology* 91: 481–510.

————. 1992. "Problems of Explanation in Economic Sociology." In *Networks and Organization,* edited by Nitin Nohria and Robert G. Eccles. Boston: Harvard Business School Press.

Greif, Avner. 1989. "Reputation and Coalitions in Medieval Trade: Evidence on the Maghribi Traders." *Journal of Economic History* 49: 857–82.

————. 1993. "Contract Enforceability and Economic Institutions in Early Trade: The Maghribe Traders' Coalition." *American Economic Review* 83: 525–48.

Greif, Avner, Paul Milgrom, and Barry R. Weingast. 1994. "Coordination, Commitment, and Enforcement: The Case of the Merchant Guild." *Journal of Political Economy* 102: 745–76.

Grice, H. Paul. 1975. "Logic and Conversation." In *Syntax and Semantics,* edited by Peter Cole and Jerry L. Morgan. New York: Academic Press.

Gulati, Ranjay. 1995. "Social Structure and Alliance Formation Patterns: A Longitudinal Analysis." *Administrative Science Quarterly* 40: 619–52.

Gulati, Ranjay, and Martin Gargiulo. 1999. "Where Do Interorganizational Networks Come From?" *American Journal of Sociology* 104: 1439–93.

Gulati, Ranjay, and James D. Westphal. 1999. "Cooperative or Controlling? The Effects of CEO-Board Relations and the Content of Interlocks on the Formation of Joint Ventures." *Administrative Science Quarterly* 44: 473–506.

Heider, Fritz. 1958. *The Psychology of Interpersonal Relations.* New York: Wiley.

Higgins, E. Tory. 1992. "Achieving 'Shared Reality' in the Communication Game: A Social Action That Creates Meaning." *Journal of Language and Social Psychology* 11: 107–31.

Homans, George C. 1961. *Social Behavior.* New York: Harcourt, Brace & World.

Isenberg, Daniel J. 1986. "Group Polarization: A Critical Review and Meta-analysis." *Journal of Personality and Social Psychology* 50: 1141–51.

Kenny, David A., and Linda Albright. 1987. "Accuracy in Interpersonal Perception: A Social Relations Analysis." *Psychological Bulletin* 102: 390–402.

Kish, Leslie, and Martin R. Frankel. 1974. "Inference from Complex Samples." *Journal of the Royal Statistical Society A* 36: 1–37.

Klayman, Joshua. 1995. "Varieties of Confirmation Bias." *The Psychology of Learning and Motivation* 32: 385–418.

Kollock, Peter. 1994. "The Emergence of Exchange Structures: An Experimental Study of Uncertainty, Commitment, and Trust." *American Journal of Sociology* 100: 313–45.

Krackhardt, David. 1996. "Comment on Burt and Knez's Third-Party Effects on Trust." *Rationality and Society* 8: 113–18.

Kramer, Roderick M. 1999. "Trust and Distrust in Organizations: Emerging Perspectives, Enduring Questions." *Annual Review of Psychology* 50: 569–98.

Kreps, David M. 1990. "Corporate Culture and Economic Theory." In *Perspectives on Positive Political Economy,* edited by James E. Alt and Kenneth A. Shepsle. New York: Cambridge University Press.

Kuran, Timur. 1997. *Private Truths, Public Lies.* Cambridge, Mass.: Harvard University Press.

Labianca, Giuseppe, Daniel J. Brass, and Barbara Gray. 1998. "Social Networks and Perceptions of Intergroup Conflict: The Role of Negative Relationships and Third Parties." *Academy of Management Journal* 41: 55–67.

Laumann, Edward O. 1973. *Bonds of Pluralism*. New York: Wiley-Interscience.

Lamm, Helmut. 1988. "A Review of Our Research on Group Polarization: Eleven Experiments on the Effects of Group Discussion on Risk Acceptance, Probability Estimation, and Negotiation Positions." *Psychological Reports* 62: 807–13.

Lawler, Edward J., and Jeongkoo Yoon. 1993. "Power and the Emergence of Commitment Behavior in Negotiated Exchange." *American Sociological Review* 58: 465–81.

———. 1998. "Network Structure and Emotion in Exchange Relations." *American Sociological Review* 63: 871–94.

Macaulay, Stewart. 1963. "Noncontractual Relations in Business: A Preliminary Study." *American Sociological Review* 28: 55–67.

Macy, Michael W., and John Skvoretz. 1998. "Trust and Cooperation Between Strangers." *American Sociological Review* 63: 638–60.

Mizruchi, Mark S. 1992. *The Structure of Corporate Political Action*. Cambridge, Mass.: Harvard University Press.

Morrill, Calvin. 1995. *The Executive Way*. Chicago: University of Chicago Press.

Myers, David G., and Helmut Lamm. 1976. "The Group Polarization Phenomenon." *Psychological Bulletin* 83: 602–27.

Nohria, Nitin, and Robert G. Eccles, eds. 1992. *Networks and Organizations*. Boston: Harvard Business School Press.

Nyberg, David. 1993. *The Varnished Truth*. Chicago: University of Chicago Press.

Pfeffer, Jeffrey, Gerald R. Salancik, and H. Leblebici. 1976. "The Effect of Uncertainty on the Use of Social Influence in Organization Decision-making." *Administrative Science Quarterly* 21: 227–45.

Portes, Alejandro. 1998. "Social Capital: Its Origins and Applications in Modern Sociology." *Annual Review of Sociology* 24: 1–24.

Powell, Walter W., and Laurel Smith-Doerr. 1994. "Networks and Economic Life." In *The Handbook of Economic Sociology*, edited by Neil J. Smelser and Richard Swedberg. Princeton, N.J.: Princeton University Press.

Putnam, Robert D. 1993. *Making Democracy Work*. Princeton, N.J.: Princeton University Press.

Raub, Werner, and Jeroen Weesie. 1990. "Reputation and Efficiency in Social Interactions: An Example of Network Effects." *American Journal of Sociology* 96: 626–54.

Rosen, Sidney, and Abraham Tesser. 1970. "On Reluctance to Communicate Undesirable Information: The MUM Effect." *Sociometry* 33: 253–63.

Rosnow, Ralph L., and Gary Alan Fine. 1976. *Rumor and Gossip*. New York: Elsevier.

Ross, Lee, and Craig A. Anderson. 1982. "Shortcomings in the Attribution Process: On the Origins and Maintenance of Erroneous Social Assessments." In *Judgment Under Uncertainty*, edited by Daniel Kahneman, Paul Slovic, and Amos Tversky. New York: Cambridge University Press.

Scott, John. 1991. *Social Network Analysis*. Thousand Oaks, Calif.: Sage Publications.

Smelser, Neil J., and Richard Swedberg, eds. 1994. *The Handbook of Economic Sociology*. Princeton, N.J.: Princeton University Press.

Snijders, Chris, and Werner Raub. 1998. "Revolution and Risk: Paradoxical Consequences of Risk Aversion in Interdependent Situations." *Rationality and Society* 10: 405–25.

Staw, Barry M., and Jerry Ross. 1987. "Behavior in Escalation Situations: Antecedents, Prototypes, and Solutions." In *Research in Organizational Behavior*, vol. 9, edited by L. Cummings and Barry M. Staw. Greenwich, Conn.: JAI Press.

Stinchcombe, Arthur L. 1990. *Information and Organizations*. Berkeley: University of California Press.

Swedberg, Richard., ed. 1993. *Explorations in Economic Sociology*. New York: Russell Sage Foundation.

Tilly, Charles. 1998. "Contentious Conversation." *Social Research* 65: 491–510.

Tullock, Gordon. 1985. "Adam Smith and the Prisoner's Dilemma." *Quarterly Journal of Economics* 100: 1073–81.

Uzzi, Brian. 1996. "The Sources and Consequences of Embeddedness for the Economic Performance of Organizations: The Network Effect." *American Sociological Review* 61: 674–98.

Wasserman, Stanley, and Katherine Faust. 1994. *Social Network Analysis*. New York: Cambridge University Press.

Williams, Steve, and Robert J. Taormina. 1992. "Group Polarization in Business Decisions in Singapore." *Journal of Social Psychology* 132: 265–67.

Wittek, Rafael, and Rudi Wielers. 1998. "Gossip in Organizations." *Computational and Mathematical Organization Theory* 4: 189–204.

Yamaguchi, Kazuo. 1994. "The Flow of Information Through Social Networks: Diagonal-free Measures of Inefficiency and the Structural Determinants of Inefficiency." *Social Networks* 16: 57–86.

Zucker, Lynne G. 1986. "Production of Trust: Institutional Sources of Economic Structure, 1840–1920." In *Research in Organizational Behavior*, edited by Larry Cummings and Barry M. Staw. Greenwich, Conn.: JAI Press.

Discussion

Another View of Trust and Gossip

Joel Sobel

My task is to describe how an economic theorist might model the issues raised by Ronald S. Burt in chapter 2, "Bandwidth and Echo:
Trust, Information, and Gossip in Social Networks." I focus my discussion on a stylized argument that plays a central role in the chapter. The two steps of the argument are:

1. Information from closely connected third parties tends to confirm
   prior information (etiquette).

2. The availability of a dense network of close third parties increases
   the information available to a manager (bandwidth).

Burt concludes that managers with close third-party connections
tend to become more confident of their judgments (he calls this amplification). He then argues that close third-party ties tend to weaken
weak relationships. Burt claims that his argument helps us to understand why managers with strong-tie networks perform worse than
managers with weak-tie networks.

Economists treat agents as goal-oriented actors who make choices
that maximize their utility subject to constraints. Viewed using this
narrow notion of rationality, one wonders what motivates the managers to behave as Burt assumes they do. If a manager knows that
closely connected third parties always provide information that echoes
his prior beliefs, then he would not waste resources collecting this

information. If the information a manager receives from third-party connections is predictable, then it should neither increase his information nor influence his decisions.

Burt supports his story with empirical evidence and grounds it in convincing anecdotal evidence. He tempts an economist to ask: Why would a manager seek out information from close ties? Why should this information tend to confirm prior beliefs? And why should the information nevertheless tend to amplify prior biases?[1]

In this discussion, I describe a model that is broadly consistent with Burt's arguments. I cannot assert that this is the "right" model. Still, the exercise has several uses. It represents how one economist would approach Burt's problem. It demonstrates that Burt's observations can be consistent with rational behavior. (That is, it is not necessary to appeal directly to social or psychological considerations in order to explain the behavior.) It highlights the importance of incentives, a factor not emphasized by Burt that may influence behavior. A focus on incentives opens up the possibility that the design of the work environment helps to determine how people seek out and use third-party information.

The model is not consistent with Burt's story in two respects. First, the justifications provided for the two steps of the argument follow for reasons that are different from Burt's. Second, Burt's conclusions about the disadvantages of close ties do not necessarily follow from my assumptions.

A Model of Communication in Networks

The manager must decide whether to trust a worker.[2] He has prior information, possibly based on experience, on the reliability of the worker. The manager controls the level at which he trusts the worker. If he has complete confidence that the worker is reliable, then he will take an extreme action. For example, he may completely delegate important decisionmaking authority or permit the worker to do a sensitive job without supervision. If the manager is certain that the worker is unreliable, then he may fire the worker. Lacking complete information, the manager prefers to take less extreme actions.

The manager begins with an imprecise estimate of the reliability of the worker. The manager can supplement the information by asking a third party. (I describe later what happens when there are multiple third parties.) The third party also has information about the worker. Sometimes the third party is perfectly informed. Other times her information is less precise (but still valuable to the manager). The third party wants the manager to take a decisive action. That is, if she believes that the worker is more likely to be reliable than not, she prefers total rather than partial trust.[3]

What distinguishes a close third-party connection from a distant tie (in my story) is what the third party knows about the manager's information. Close third parties are aware of the manager's prior disposition. Distant third parties are not. The manager can distinguish between close and distant third parties.

The process of information collection and decisionmaking follows this sequence: the manager acquires his own information about the worker; the third party communicates with the manager;[4] and finally, based on all of the information that he has received, the manager decides the extent to which he will trust the worker.

I have described a game. The strategy of the third party is a recommendation to the manager (as a function of her information about the worker). The strategy of the manager is an action, which describes the extent to which he will trust the worker (as a function of the third party's recommendation). One would like to make a prediction about how the manager and the third party will behave. It is conventional (in economics) to assume that they play equilibrium strategies. In equilibrium, the manager draws the correct inference about the third party's information from her message and acts accordingly; the third party correctly predicts how the manager will respond to anything she might say and says the thing that leads to the action she most prefers.

Whether the third party is a close or a distant connection, the game has an equilibrium in which the manager ignores the third party's recommendation and makes a decision based exclusively on his prior information. The manager decides that third-party reports supply no useful information and resolves to ignore them. At the same time, the third party, realizing that nothing she says influences the manager's decision, makes uninformative statements. Although this "babbling" equilibrium is surprisingly robust (and could be descriptive of communication breakdowns that do arise), it is apparent that substantive communication is in the best interests of both the manager and the third party. I thus concentrate on those equilibria in which there is effective communication.[5]

Assume that the manager's personal information is favorable to the worker. Hence, without additional information, he would be inclined to trust the worker; because his information is imprecise, however, he would not trust the worker completely. What the third party says could influence the manager's decision. Assume that the third party can make only two statements: "I think that the worker is reliable," or, "I think that the worker is unreliable."[6] In equilibrium, the manager takes the third party's statement into account and is more inclined to trust the worker after a favorable report.

When will the third party provide a favorable report? There are two different situations to consider. First, assume that the manager and the third party have a distant association. The third party does not know that the manager is inclined to trust the worker. She has only her private information and will announce that the worker is reliable if and only if she has favorable information about the worker.

Now consider a third party with a close tie to the manager. She knows that the manager has prior information that is favorable to the worker. Recall that the third party either obtains information that conclusively reveals the worker's reliability or weaker information. When the third party takes into account both her information and the manager's, she is willing to trust the worker if her private information suggests that the worker is reliable or if her private information weakly suggests that the worker is unreliable.

In the first case, all signals indicate that the worker is reliable. In the second case, knowledge that the manager is favorably disposed outweighs the third party's private information.[7] Only if the third party has definitive information that the worker is unreliable will she recommend against trusting the worker.

This analysis permits a comparison between the interaction of a manager with a close tie to that of a manager with a distant tie. In both settings, a favorable recommendation increases the manager's confidence that the worker is reliable and increases the extent to which the manager trusts the worker. An unfavorable recommendation leads to less trust. In both settings, information that confirms prior beliefs amplifies these beliefs and leads the manager to take a more extreme action. As Burt suggests, the manager is more likely to receive confirming information from a close tie than from a distant tie. It is for precisely this reason that confirming information from a close tie has less influence than confirming information from a distant tie. In the game-theoretic equilibrium, the manager takes into account that his close third party will say, "I think that the worker is reliable," unless she is certain the worker is unreliable. Hearing this recommendation makes the manager more confident in the worker's reliability because it rules out the possibility that the third party has extremely damaging information about the worker. Hearing the same recommendation from a distant informant is less expected and even more reassuring, however, because it also rules out the possibility that the third party has mildly damaging information about the worker.

With high probability, the manager receives recommendations from close ties that confirm his prior beliefs. (It is natural to assume that it is rare for the third party to obtain definitive unfavorable information.) When the manager receives a recommendation that confirms his prior beliefs, his beliefs are amplified and he takes an action that is more extreme than the action he would take without prior information. In my story, the third party provides confirming information not out of etiquette but out of self-interest. Still, the prediction of the model is consistent with Burt's argument.

Although the basic model provides conclusions that correspond to Burt's, there are significant differences between the model and Burt's story. First, the mechanism that leads third parties to reinforce beliefs is self-interest, not etiquette. Second, though information amplifies beliefs, when the manager is inclined to trust the worker without third-party information, favorable information provided by distant contacts amplifies beliefs more strongly than favorable information provided by close contacts. Close contacts provide amplification more often than do distant contacts. When a distant contact does provide confirmatory information, however, it has a stronger effect on beliefs than when the information comes from a close contact. Analysis of a model with multiple third parties helps to reconcile these differences.

Suppose that there are many third-party informants whom the manager consults independently. Assume that information received by these third parties is like the model described here: distant connections do not know what the manager knows, and close connections do. Each third party receives either definitive information or a weak signal about the reliability of the worker. These signals provide supplementary information about the reliability of the worker. To simplify, assume that the manager consults only distant third parties or only close third parties.

Ignore the equilibrium in which the manager does not listen to the recommendations of third parties. In the other equilibrium outcome, a distant contact will state that the worker is reliable if her private information leads her to believe that the worker is reliable. The more third parties there are who supply favorable reports, the more trust the manager will have in the worker. When the third parties are close ties, an equilibrium in which they provide unfavorable reports only when they have definitive information that the worker is unreliable exists under conditions that I describe shortly. Given this behavior, the manager infers (accurately) that the worker is totally unreliable if at least one of his informants makes a negative recommendation. In effect, any close third party has the ability to cause the manager to discontinue the relationship with the worker. If all of the third parties state that the worker is reliable, then the manager's trust in the worker will be amplified.

Equilibrium requires a coordination of beliefs. In general, an informant behaves differently depending on what she expects other informants to do and how she expects the manager to respond to her recommendation. One can interpret etiquette as an expectation that close associates will provide confirming information as frequently as possible consistent with self-interest. Etiquette then creates the expectation that a negative recommendation is a sign that the informant has truly bad news. Under these expectations, the manager responds to recommendations in only two ways. If all of the third parties submit favorable reports, he becomes more confident that the worker is reliable. If one or more of the third parties supplies negative information, the manager becomes convinced that the worker is completely unreliable. These actions and beliefs can be part of an equilibrium under two conditions. First, all agents must believe that everyone else follows the rule of etiquette. This is a condition about the behavior of other agents. Second, the manager must believe that the worker is reliable if none of the third parties has strongly negative information about the worker. This is a restriction on the parameters of the model. Under these two conditions, a third party knows that her message to the manager will influence his decision only if all of the other third parties made favorable reports. Otherwise, the worker will be fired no matter what the third party says. So in deciding what to tell the manager, the third party can assume that none of the other informants had strongly negative information. Taking this inference into account, she would confirm the reliability of the worker unless her information was strongly negative.

When third parties are close ties, the etiquette equilibrium (in which all recommendations confirm the manager's prior belief unless the third party is sure that the worker is unreliable) may exist even when the third party's private information is always more precise than the manager's information. To exist, the etiquette equilibrium requires the much weaker condition that one third party's imprecise information does not outweigh the aggregate information of the other third parties and the manager. When the second condition fails, there is a "direct" equilibrium in which third parties make a positive recommendation if and only if their private information is positive. This is the equilibrium that results when third parties are distant contacts.[8]

Adding additional third parties leaves the principal conclusions unchanged. Again, information from close ties is much more likely to confirm the bias of the manager, and confirming information leads to amplification of beliefs. When there are many third parties, the amplification obtained from close ties is frequently greater than the amplification obtained from distant informants. Except in the unlikely event that one of the third parties has definitive information, all close third parties provide positive recommendations. On the other hand, it is likely that some distant informants supply information that is counter to the manager's bias; this information would moderate beliefs formed from third-party communication in loose networks.

When there are multiple third parties, the manager with a network of close contacts may not do as well as the manager with a network of distant contacts. Aggregating information obtained from many distant sources can provide a more accurate picture of the worker's reliability. Intuitively, when the manager relies on information from distant parties, he changes his relationship with the worker depending on the number of favorable recommendations he receives. When the information comes from close ties, multiple negative appraisals are redundant. This observation supports Burt's conclusion that managers with weak networks outperform managers with strong networks.

Throughout this discussion I have assumed that the manager's private information biased him in favor of the worker. When the manager's private information is negative, again, recommendations from close third-party sources tend to confirm and amplify this negative bias. A single favorable recommendation from a close tie, however, will lead the manager to trust the worker.[9] Hence, information provided by dense networks of informants amplifies distrust with high probability but also creates a small probability of decisively reversing a negative bias.

Conclusion

Burt wishes to distinguish relationships depending on the source of third-party information. Relative to information supplied by distant contacts, Burt argues that when the manager is predisposed to distrust the worker, close third-party informants tend to make trust more difficult to establish, and that consequently managers without close third-party ties perform better than those who do have such ties. I provide a model in which information supplied by close third-party ties reinforces a predisposition to distrust the worker more often than information supplied by distant ties. There is, however, a small probability that information provided by close third parties will cause the manager to reverse his prior position and place a great deal of trust in the worker.

Burt and I predict the same qualitative behavior—most of the time. We differ in our explanations of what causes the behavior. My approach suggests that empirical studies should look for the (rare) occasions on which close associates do not confirm their boss's preconceptions. If managers are free to select their informants from close or distant ties, I cannot reconcile (within the simple rational-actor framework I have presented) managerial consultation with closely connected third parties with the conclusion that managers with weak ties perform better than managers with strong ties. There may be situations in which the manager is better off obtaining information from distant ties. If the manager maximizes his utility and is free to select his informants, however, he would choose to get information from distant contacts in these situations.

The conflict between my approach and Burt's can be resolved in several ways. The most decisive resolution would be to abandon the notion that the manager acts to maximize his utility (at least as it is defined in my model). Although this approach may be the most sensible, a conventional economic analysis reexamines other assumptions instead. For example, the network of available third parties may be fixed, so that the manager in a dense network cannot seek out information from distant sources. The manager would also tend to look first to close ties if these contacts were easier to locate, or if there were costs associated with leaving them out of the decisionmaking process.

On the other hand, one does not need to demonstrate that strong ties are worse for the manager to conclude that agents who fill structural holes are more successful than agents who do not fill them. First, managers who fill many holes but have weaker ties could be more valuable than those with fewer ties even if they do less well in each situation—because they have more opportunities to succeed. Second, the ability to fill a structural hole might be the key characteristic for a higher-level manager. Good performance in a low-level job is not necessarily the best predictor of good performance in a higher-level job.

In my model, managers without weak ties may do badly in an etiquette equilibrium in which their informants rarely supplement private information. Under these circumstances, a smart manager would do things differently. He might try to hide his inclinations (or prior information). He might try to manipulate the incentives of the third-party informants.[10] An economist would like to know more about the incentives that prevail in the environments studied by Burt.

I thank Jim Rauch and participants at the 1999 Manresa Conference on Networks and Coalitions for comments and the National Science Foundation and the Center for Advanced Study in the Behavioral Sciences for financial support. An extended version of this discussion containing an explicit description of the formal model and results is available.

Notes

1. Rabin and Schrag (1999) study the implications of a model in which decisionmakers systematically misinterpret information opposed to their prior opinion. Amplification arises naturally in their framework.

2. I use "manager" in place of Burt's "ego," and "worker" in place of "alter."

3. Prendergast and Stole (1996) provide an explicit model that provides reasons why some agents may behave as if they have a preference for extreme or "impetuous" actions. For simplicity, I make the assumption without behavioral justification.

4. It is reasonable to interpret statements made by the third party as "gossip" in that no one can verify the truth of these statements. It is consistent with the model to imagine that the third party's information consists of a set of anecdotes, some favorable and some unfavorable, and that what she communicates to the manager is a selection from these anecdotes.

5. Since the ordinal preferences of the third party and the manager coincide, one could also invoke Grice's (1989) Cooperative Principle to justify effective communication.

6. The assumption that the third party has extreme preferences implies that, in equilibrium, there are at most two distinct actions that the manager will take after consulting with the third party. Hence, the assumption that the third party makes one of two statements can be made without loss of generality.

7. This conclusion depends on the assumption that the manager's information is more informative than weak information received by the third party. This assumption can be replaced by a much less restrictive assumption when there are many third parties.

8. For some parameter values, both etiquette and direct equilibria exist.

9. My intuition suggests that it is more likely for a single negative recommendation to destroy trust than for a single positive recommendation

to create trust. The model would provide this kind of asymmetric conclusion if one assumes that third parties never receive information that unambiguously demonstrates that the worker is reliable.

10. Several recent papers by economists develop these arguments. Prendergast (1993) demonstrates a tendency for informants to confirm the manager's prior information under some incentive schemes. Levitt and Snyder (1997) discuss situations in which agents may suppress negative information and devise schemes to induce more complete revelation. Banerjee and Somanathan (2001), Bernheim (1994), Loury (1994), and Morris (forthcoming) present analyses of strategic settings in which agents may misrepresent their tastes or information to conform to the expectations of others. Krishna and Morgan (forthcoming) study a model in which a decisionmaker must balance the information obtained from two informants with possibly differing biases.

References

Banerjee, Abhijit, and Rohini Somanathan. 2001. "A Simple Model of Voice." *Quarterly Journal of Economics* 116(1): 189–227.

Bernheim, B. Douglas. 1994. "A Theory of Conformity." *Journal of Political Economy* 102: 841–77.

Grice, H. Paul. 1989. "Logic and Conversation." In *Studies in the Way of Words*. Cambridge, Mass.: Harvard University Press.

Krishna, Vijay, and John Morgan. 2001. "A Model of Expertise." *Quarterly Journal of Economics*.

Levitt, Steven, and Christopher Snyder. 1997. "Is No News Bad News?: Information Transmission and the Role of 'Early Warning' in the Principal-Agent Model." *Rand Journal of Economics* 28: 641–61.

Loury, Glenn. 1994. "Self-Censorship in Public Discourse: A Theory of 'Political Correctness' and Related Phenomena." *Rationality and Society* 6: 428–61.

Morris, Stephen. 2001. "Political Correctness." *Journal of Political Economy* 2(109): 231–65.

Prendergast, Canice. 1993. "A Theory of Yes Men." *American Economic Review* 83: 757–70.

Prendergast, Canice, and Lars Stole. 1996. "Impetuous Youngsters and Jaded Old-timers: Acquiring a Reputation for Learning." *Journal of Political Economy* 104: 1105–34.

Rabin, Matthew, and Joel Schrag. 1999. "First Impressions Matter: A Model of Confirmatory Bias." *Quarterly Journal of Economics* 114: 37–82.

Chapter 3

The Organization of the Taiwanese and South Korean Economies: A Comparative Equilibrium Analysis

Robert C. Feenstra, Gary G. Hamilton, and
Deng-Shing Huang

Most specialists recognize that business networks are widespread in Asia. The dominance of the keiretsu in Japan and the chaebol in South Korea is common knowledge. In recent years, many scholars and journalists have also written about the importance of Chinese business networks in all the Chinese-dominated economies (for example, mainland China, Taiwan, Hong Kong, and several Southeast Asian countries, including Thailand and Malaysia). Despite the recognition that Asian business networks are commonplace, there has been surprisingly little effort to analyze the organization and performance of these networks. In fact, most writers dismiss the importance of business networks as a result of either market failures or state directives, and hence as entities that have no independent effects on the economy in their own right. Such writers would conclude that differences in the organization of business networks do not make a difference.

In this chapter, we argue that business networks are important, that they are not simply reflections of market or state forces, and that organizational differences between networks do make a difference. Our key questions address these differences. How and why does economic organization differ across countries, and does it matter? These questions are, of course, rather general and abstract. To tie down our research empirically, we ask these questions of two East Asian countries, Taiwan and South Korea. Most specialists in Asian development (Amsden 1985, 1989; Gold 1986; Wade 1990; Evans 1995) view the economies of Taiwan and South Korea as being organized in essentially the same way. Our research (Orrû, Biggart, and Hamilton 1997; Hamilton and Feenstra 1995) and that of others (Fields 1995; H.-R. Kim 1993, 1994; E. M. Kim 1997) have shown, however, that the two economies are organized very differently. The rapid growth common to these two countries hides the very substantial, and we believe important, differences in how their firms interact.

This chapter describes the organizational differences between the two economies. Simply put, the predominant organizational features of the Korean economy are the very large, vertically integrated business groups called chaebol. Of particular significance are the five largest of these groups, which together account for a substantial share of the export output of the Korean economy. In contrast, the most important features of Taiwan's economy are the small and medium-sized firms, which dominate export production, and the large business groups, which are on average much smaller than the chaebol and mainly supply intermediate goods and services for the small and medium-sized firm sector. Using a highly stylized model to represent the pricing decisions of firms in general equilibrium, we ask whether the organizational differences between the two economies can be explained in terms of simple economic reasoning. Our results show that *multiple equilibria* of interfirm organization are possible. In other words, several configurations of interfirm networks represent stable outcomes of cross-market pricing decisions, and furthermore, two of these outcomes approximate the South Korean and Taiwanese economies in organization.

One stable configuration is for firms to create enterprise groups in which firms buy intermediate goods and services from other firms in their own group and refuse to sell the same goods and services to competing groups. This configuration, which we call "V-group" (for vertical integration), resembles the organization of the South Korean economy. The model even predicts a division between a stable set of mega-groups and an unstable set of smaller groups. The logic here is that, in a vertically integrated economy, there is only so much profit to be made in manufacturing similar products. The larger and more heavily internalized groups have a competitive advantage over smaller groups. This division resembles what has occurred in South Korea, where the large chaebol have been extremely successful, but a second tier of chaebol have struggled mightily.

A second stable configuration of firms predicted from the model consists of a relatively large number of enterprise groups producing intermediate goods to sell at a profit to other firms utilizing those goods in the manufacture of final products. This configuration, which we call "U-group" (for upstream), resembles the economic organization of the Taiwanese economy. In other work, Hamilton (1997) has used the metaphor of a gold rush to describe this kind of economic organization. In a gold rush, although a few miners strike it rich, the largest and most successful firms are those that sell goods and services to miners. By analogy, as long as the small and medium-sized firms compete with each other to manufacture products for the global market, they create demand for the goods and services that the larger upstream business groups provide. It is important to note that the model predicts that the U-group enterprise networks occur only at fairly low levels of vertical integration. In other words, it does not necessarily make good sense for a manufacturer of shovels to hire miners to use the shovels they produce for mining gold. This logic has counterparts in the Taiwanese economy. Large Taiwanese producers of textiles have not integrated forward to make garments, and large producers of plastics (such as Formosa) have not made toys; instead, the upstream groups have relied on the abundant number of small and medium-sized firms downstream to utilize their inputs and produce the final goods.

Our equilibrium model shows that, in principle, both V-groups and U-groups represent stable solutions to mutually determined pricing decisions reached by firms in an environment of other firms. Our empirical research suggests that the model roughly approximates the organizational dynamics of the Korean and Taiwanese economies. However, even if we assume that the model tells us something about the current organization of those economies, it tells us nothing about how they got that way. The model does not predict which stable alternative trajectory a society will take. We conclude with a brief discussion of the factors that may account for the different paths taken, and of what our model has to say about the recent financial crisis in Asia, with its differential impact in South Korea and Taiwan.

A Stylized Model of Business Groups

A business group is one example of a network structure between firms, and in general, networks can affect production and trade in a number of ways. The potential advantages to being within a network include: information flows between firms and customers (Egan and Mody 1992; Rauch 1999), information flows on production techniques between firms and suppliers (Aoki 1990), financial insurance provided by a bank within a group (Aoki and Patrick 1994; Hoshi, Kashyap, and Sharfstein 1990, 1991; Lincoln, Gerlach, and Ahmadjian 1994), and externalities between firms that reduce costs within the group (Friedman and Fung 1996). Our focus is on the preferential access to intermediate inputs sold by member firms to other firms in the group. This is clearly a highly stylized description that abstracts from many of the actual features of South Korea and Taiwan but nevertheless is sufficient to generate outcomes similar to those observed in each country. A mathematical model along these lines is developed in Feenstra, Huang, and Hamilton (1997); here we summarize the essential features and results from that model.

In this stylized setting, let us divide the economy into two sectors: an upstream sector producing intermediate inputs from some primary factors, and a downstream sector using these intermediate inputs (along with primary factors) to produce final consumer goods. Suppose that both sectors are characterized by product differentiation, so that each firm retains some limited monopoly power by virtue of the uniqueness of its product and therefore charges a price that is above its marginal cost of production. As usual under monopolistic competition, we allow for the free entry of firms in both the upstream and downstream sectors, to the point where economic profits are driven to zero. (By zero economic profits we mean that the groups are earning only a "normal" rate of return on capital.) Thus, the profits earned by firms by charging prices above marginal cost go to cover their fixed costs of production, where these fixed costs represent those of research, development, marketing, or any other lump-sum costs associated with having a differentiated product.

In contrast to conventional treatments of monopolistic competition, we also allow firms to integrate across markets when this is advantageous. In particular, there is an incentive to integrate both upstream and downstream, because in the absence of any such integration, the market prices for intermediate inputs are above marginal cost, a sure sign that agents could do better by internalizing the sale and pricing the input at exactly its marginal cost of production. By internalizing the sale in this manner, the groups located in both upstream and downstream markets obtain higher joint profits than unaffiliated firms simply trading the intermediate input at its market price. Our definition of a business group is a set of firms in the upstream and downstream markets that maximize their joint profits. In the same way that we allow for the free entry of individual firms, we also allow for the free entry of business groups. We are, of course, abstracting for the moment from the many political and social factors that influence the configuration of business groups in any setting. Here we simply ask what outcomes we might expect from the pure economics, focusing on the pricing decisions of the firms in general equilibrium.

The economy we have in mind is pictured in figure 3.1. The upstream sector produces a range of products indicated by the dots at the top of the diagram. These are used in the production of the downstream products, indicated by the dots in the bottom of the diagram. A group produces a range of both upstream products and downstream products, choosing the number of each to produce so as to maximize group profits. Alternatively, unaffiliated firms can produce individual upstream and downstream products. The equilibrium conditions are that the groups maximize profits, as do unaffiliated firms, and in addition there is free entry of both groups and unaffiliated firms. This means that in equilibrium the profits of both groups and unaffiliated firms must be forced down to zero, so that business groups are not earning any more or less than unaffiliated firms.

Business groups sell the intermediate inputs to their own firms at marginal cost and to unaffiliated firms at marginal cost plus a markup. Because these business groups are thus inherently more efficient in their production than a combination of upstream and downstream un-

Figure 3.1 Model of Business Groups

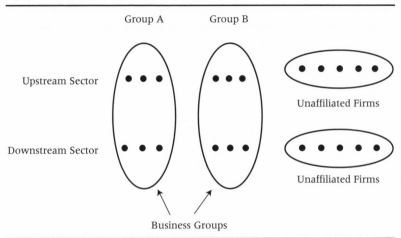

Source: Authors.

affiliated firms, an incentive arises for these groups to form. It should be stressed, however, that efficiency within a group (due to selling intermediate inputs at marginal cost) does not necessarily translate into efficiency for the economy overall. Business groups have an incentive to withhold their intermediate inputs from other groups because they do not want the competing groups to enjoy the same production efficiency that comes from having access to the specialized intermediate inputs. Business groups withhold intermediate inputs by charging high prices for them—possibly even an infinite price, so that the intermediate inputs are not sold to competing groups at all. This is a clear sign of inefficiency for the economy overall, because groups are not sharing access to their proprietary inputs with other groups. We will have to investigate the extent to which this occurs in equilibrium.

Before describing the possible equilibria, we need to ask: What prevents business groups from being so efficient that they dominate the economy entirely? We introduce into the model "governance costs," which represent the costs of monitoring and coordinating the activities of firms within the group. These costs are borne only by groups, not by the unaffiliated firms. There is a special reason within the model for such agency costs to arise. Because the inputs produced within a group are sold internally at marginal cost, these firms are not covering their fixed costs of production and therefore need to receive a financial transfer from the rest of the group. The size of this transfer depends on the extent of the fixed costs (such as research and development) that are devoted to the creation of new product varieties. Since this is normally the private information of the firm involved, it is difficult to implement this financial transfer without leading to some inefficiency. For example, the guarantee of the group to cover the fixed costs of the upstream firms could induce the managers of these firms to expend less effort. We do not model these agency costs in any detail but simply assume that the groups have a fixed governance cost, over and above the costs of unaffiliated firms.

Although governance costs act as a check on the business groups, we think it is realistic to assume that these costs are small. This assumption has strong implications for the ability of unaffiliated firms to exist. Since a business group is otherwise more efficient than a set of unaffiliated upstream and downstream firms, when free entry drives the profits of the groups down to zero, it must be that the profits of some unaffiliated firms are even lower. This means that a zero-profit equilibrium involving the business groups, as well as the upstream and downstream firms, cannot occur: either the upstream or the downstream unaffiliated firms (or both) are driven out of existence by the free entry of business groups.

Thus, for sufficiently small governance costs, the equilibrium organization of this stylized economy can have only three possible configurations: business groups dominate in the upstream sector (U-groups) and are vertically integrated downstream but also compete with some unaffiliated downstream firms; business groups dominate in the downstream sector (D-groups) while purchasing some inputs internally and others from unaffiliated upstream firms; or business groups drive out unaffiliated producers in both the upstream and downstream sectors and are therefore strongly vertically integrated (V-groups). These three configurations are illustrated in figure 3.2. The first panel shows a U-group selling to unaffiliated firms, and the second shows a D-group buying from unaffiliated firms.[1] In the final panel, we display two V-groups that can optimally choose whether to sell inputs to each other or not.

Figure 3.2 Types of Business Groups

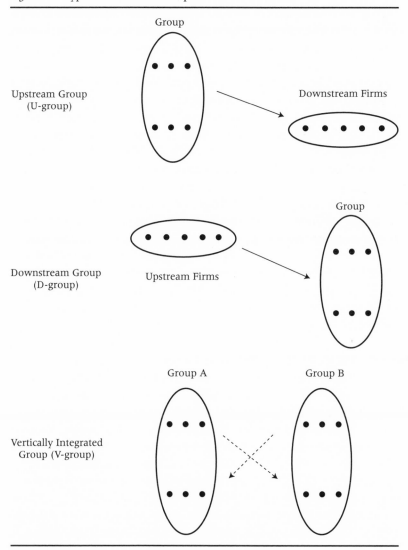

Source: Authors.

The purpose of a mathematical model is to determine which of the configurations shown in figure 3.2 can arise in equilibrium; that is, in a situation where all firms are maximizing profits, there is free entry of both groups and firms, and there is full employment of the economy's resources. (For simplicity, our model has just a single resource, called labor.) Before describing the results, it is worth outlining how the model is solved. Our key simplifying assumption is that *all groups are the same size.* (This assumption also holds for unaffiliated firms in each of the upstream and downstream markets.) Thus, when a business group determines its optimal strategy, it does so knowing that all other groups have the same number of firms producing inputs, and the same number of firms producing final goods, with similar prices in each sector. Each group must then determine whether it is profitable to *deviate* from the choices made by other groups. The economy is in equilibrium when no group (and no unaffiliated firm) has any incentive to deviate from the similar choices made by others. We use the model to determine what the number and size of groups in the economy must be in equilibrium, allowing for the possibility that more than one configuration of groups may be consistent with no single group wanting to deviate from the common pattern.

When Will Groups Sell Inputs to Each Other?

Our first question is: When will the groups sell inputs to each other? For convenience, we focus initially on the V-groups, supposing that any unaffiliated firms find it unprofitable to enter. A key choice variable of the business groups is the *price that groups charge for the intermediate inputs sold to other groups.* This variable reflects the competition that groups perceive that they face with each other. If group A believes that selling an input to group B confers a substantial advantage to group B, in the sense that group B can produce the downstream good at lower cost and therefore compete more aggressively downstream, then group A could decide *not* to sell this input even at a very high price. We are interested in knowing when this type of outcome occurs.

To begin, we review some well-known results from economics. An unaffiliated firm finds it most profitable to set the price for a good it is selling in inverse relation to its "elasticity" of demand; this is called the

Lerner pricing rule. The elasticity measures the extent to which buyers can substitute away from a good if its price goes up. A good with high elasticity (many substitutes) should therefore be priced close to marginal cost; a good with low elasticity (few substitutes) can be priced much higher than marginal cost, earning substantial profits. When the elasticity approaches unity, then the firm loses no sales revenue at all from increasing the price, so it sets its price arbitrarily high. Since infinite prices do not make any sense, this leads to the well-known result that the elasticity of demand for any firm with some ability to set its price must be greater than unity.

Now consider how the Lerner pricing rule changes when a group is selling the intermediate input to another group. We expect that the competition in the downstream market leads the group to price higher than would an unaffiliated firm. That is, the group wants not only to maximize its profits from selling the intermediate input (as would an unaffiliated firm) but also to ensure that it does not give a cost advantage to the purchasing group from having that input available, since these groups also compete in the downstream market. How intense is this competition? That depends on how many groups are in the economy. If there are only a small number, say two, then each group is supplying one-half of the entire downstream market (since we are assuming there are no unaffiliated firms). Each group is therefore a large player in this market, and concerned about protecting its profits downstream. For this reason, we expect to find that the smaller the number of business groups competing "head to head" downstream, the higher the prices of the intermediate inputs become.

We can now answer the question of when a group would want to sell to other groups at all. Sales do not occur if the optimal price for the intermediate input is arbitrarily high, approaching infinity. In conventional models, infinite prices do not make any sense, but in our model these prices apply only to external sales; internal sales still occur at marginal cost. We find that the external prices are infinite—so that the groups do not sell to each other—whenever the elasticity of demand is less than or equal to $G/(G-1)$, where G is the number of business groups. For example, with just two groups, the groups do not sell to each other for any elasticities less than 2; with three groups, this occurs for elasticities less than 1.5, and so forth. We still suppose that the

Figure 3.3 Regions Where Groups Sell Inputs or Not

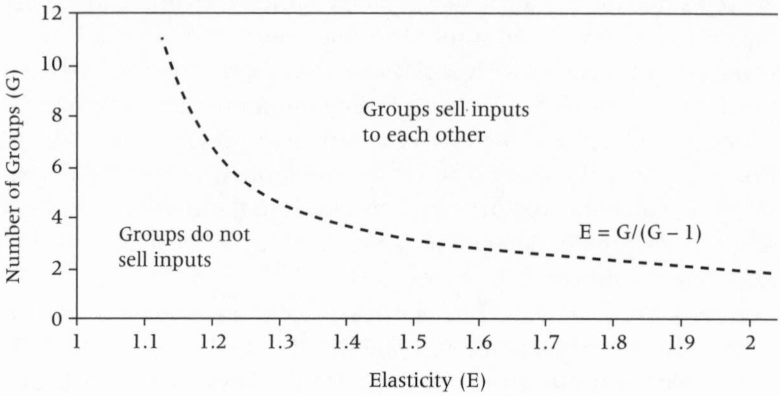

Source: Authors.

elasticity is greater than unity, so that for elasticities in the range between unity and $G/(G-1)$, sales of the inputs are only internal.

These results are illustrated in figure 3.3, where we show the number of groups G on the vertical axis, and the elasticity of demand (exceeding unity) on the horizontal axis. The dashed line along which the elasticity E equals $G/(G-1)$ is labeled as such. Whenever the number of groups or elasticity lies below this line, there are no external sales: each group is entirely self-sufficient. This is an extreme form of the "one-setism" (the desire to grow ever larger, expanding into the whole range of upstream and downstream products) that characterizes South Korean business groups. In contrast, when either the number of groups or elasticity lies above the line $E = G/(G-1)$, then the groups are willing to sell their inputs to each other (or unaffiliated firms). This is more characteristic of the vertically oriented groups in Japan, where, for example, a supplier to Toyota may also sell its products to other automobile groups.

Our goal now is to fill in the regions of figure 3.3 with equilibria from the theoretical model. To do so, we pick a value for the elasticity of demand for inputs (E). In our model, we suppose that this same value applies to all possible inputs in the economy. (Another value of the elasticity applies to all final goods.)[2] We then solve for an equilibrium, satisfying profit maximization and free entry of all business groups (later we also add unaffiliated firms) and full employment of resources in the economy. This allows us to determine the number of groups (G) in equilibrium; that number will be plotted in figure 3.3 above the elasticity with which we started. This exercise is then repeated for every other value of the elasticity: in each case, we find the number of groups, and their prices charged for inputs and final goods. In this way, we obtain a plot of various equilibria of the economy, depending on the value of the elasticity. Obviously, the precise position of this plot depends on details of the model, such as consumer tastes and resource endowments. Our interest, therefore, is in the more general features of the equilibria obtained, and in particular, whether for each elasticity there is a unique number of groups or several group configurations that are consistent with equilibrium.

Equilibria with Vertically Integrated Groups

We have found so far that an equilibrium of the economy with only V-groups can take one of two forms: either the groups do not sell to each other, or they choose to do so at some optimal price. Let us focus initially on the case where no sales occur between the groups. The question then is: How many groups will choose to enter, so that the profits of each are bid down to zero? The answer to this question clearly depends on how large the economy is, as measured by its resource endowments. For a given size, however, we find in the model that the number of business groups is uniquely determined. That is, with all groups choosing to expand into as many upstream and downstream products as they find optimal, and with free entry of groups of this same size, none of whom are selling to each other, there is room only for a certain number of groups in a given economy.

This result is illustrated in figure 3.4, where, as in figure 3.3, we show the number of groups G on the vertical axis and the elasticity of demand E for the intermediate input on the horizontal axis. The line along which $E = G/(G-1)$ is shown. For each value of the elasticity, we solve for the number of groups consistent with equilibrium, and this value of G is plotted as a triangle. We see that for elasticities less than about 2.5, the equilibrium number of groups is small enough that the plotted points lie below the line $E = G/(G-1)$; in other words, the groups do not sell any intermediate inputs to each other. Furthermore,

Figure 3.4 Number of V-Groups

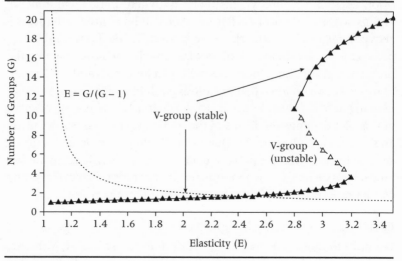

Source: Authors.

in this region the equilibrium number of groups is uniquely determined once we specify the elasticity and other parameters of the economy (such as its size): for each elasticity, there are a certain number of
V-groups consistent with equilibrium.

Now consider values of the elasticity exceeding 2.5. This moves us
into the region above the line E = G/(G − 1), where groups begin selling inputs to each other. What, then, is the equilibrium number of
groups in the economy? It would appear that this depends on the price
charged for the intermediate inputs: if this price is high, it prevents
business groups (and unaffiliated firms) from entering; if it is low,
more groups want to enter. But we have already argued that the equilibrium price of the intermediate inputs depends on the number of
business groups: when there are fewer groups, they each have a larger
share of the downstream market and want to charge a higher price for
the intermediate inputs used by their rivals. So now there is a circu-
larity in the argument: the equilibrium number of groups depends on
the price of the intermediate input, but the price charged for these inputs depends on the number of groups. This kind of circular reasoning is precisely what gives rise to multiple equilibria in any economic

model, and our stylized economy is no exception. We therefore expect to observe two types of equilibria: those with a small number of business groups and a high price for the intermediate inputs, and those with a large number of groups and a lower price for the intermediate input.

This line of reasoning is confirmed when we solve for the equilibria. For elasticities just slightly greater than 2.5, there is still a unique number of groups G consistent with equilibrium. However, for elasticities between about 2.8 and 3.2 we find that there are three equilibria, giving the S-shaped curve shown in figure 3.4. The idea that equilibria come in odd numbers is a characteristic feature of many economic and physical models. Just as an egg standing upright either balances where it is or falls to the left or right with the slightest bump, the "middle" equilibrium is often unstable while those on either side are stable. We have checked the stability of the V-group equilibria by slightly increasing the number of groups beyond the equilibrium number and computing whether the profits of the groups rise or fall: if profits fall, the number of groups returns to its equilibrium number, so the equilibrium is stable; if the profits rise, however, even more groups want to enter, and the equilibrium is unstable.

The stable V-group equilibria are illustrated with solid triangles in figure 3.4, and the unstable are illustrated with open triangles. To further understand how these multiple equilibria arise, in figure 3.5 we plot the optimal price for the intermediate input.[3] For values of the elasticity less than 2.5, the business groups do not sell to each other, that is, the price of the inputs is infinite. For slightly higher values of the elasticity, the price begins to fall, and when the elasticity reaches 2.8, there appear multiple equilibria, with high and low prices. The high-priced equilibria support a small number of business groups, and the low-priced equilibria support a larger number of groups, with an intermediate case in between. The intermediate case is unstable, while both the high-priced and low-priced equilibria are stable.

To summarize our results thus far, computing the equilibria of our stylized model with V-groups confirms our expectation that there are multiple equilibria. The price system itself imposes some structure on the organization of the economy but, equally important, does not fully determine which of these equilibria will arise. In principle,

Figure 3.5 Pricing of Inputs with V-groups

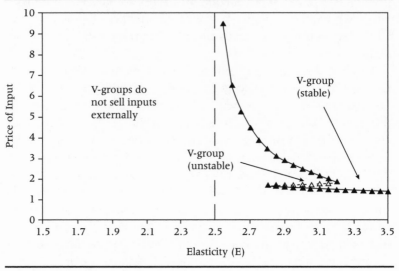

an economy with the same underlying conditions (such as resource endowments and consumer tastes) could give rise to more than one equilibrium organization. We have confirmed that two of these multiple equilibria are stable—that is, once they are established, there is no reason for them to change, even as the economy experiences some degree of change in underlying conditions.

Upstream and Downstream Business Groups

We now add the possibility of unaffiliated firms locating in the upstream or downstream markets. Because there is free entry of these firms, they choose to enter whenever the profits available cover the fixed costs of entry; entry continues until profits are driven down to zero. Although we allow entry into both the upstream and downstream markets, we do not expect to see both to occur simultaneously, since the business groups are inherently more efficient than a like-sized combination of upstream and downstream firms. Recall that we have offset the efficiency advantage of the groups by giving them small governance costs (the additional fixed cost that each group bears). In our model, we adjust the governance cost so that upstream or downstream firms are profitable in at least some equilibria. That is, we intentionally choose the governance cost so as to obtain a wide range of equilibrium configurations.[4]

To determine whether the unaffiliated firms enter, we first need to check the V-group equilibria illustrated in figure 3.4. For many of these equilibria, we find that the profits that could be earned by either unaffiliated upstream or downstream firms are not sufficient to cover their fixed costs, so entry does not occur. This is not the case, however, for the low-priced equilibria with a correspondingly large number of V-groups that occur at the top of the S-shape in figure 3.4. For values of the elasticity exceeding 2.8, these equilibria allow for profitable entry of downstream unaffiliated firms. Accordingly, we allow these firms to enter until the profitable opportunities are exhausted, and we recompute the number of business groups in the equilibrium. Since these groups compete with the downstream firms, they are dominant only in the upstream market and are therefore referred to as U-groups.

In figure 3.6, we show the equilibrium number of U-groups as squares, for elasticities exceeding 2.8. We have confirmed that these equilibria are stable, in the sense that a small increase in the number of business groups leads to lower profits for all of them, and therefore some groups will exit. The low prices charged by the U-groups for the intermediate inputs are optimal because each group has only a small share of the downstream market and is not that concerned over the cost advantage it gives to rivals by selling them inputs. This configuration of the economy can be thought of as similar to the economy of Taiwan, where business groups dominate in the upstream markets, such as chemicals, but supply intermediate inputs at competitive prices to a great number of downstream firms.

Next, we check for the equilibrium configuration in which there are unaffiliated upstream firms, so that the business groups dominate in the downstream market. These "D-groups" are plotted as circles at the top of figure 3.6, for elasticities between 1.8 and 2.8. These equilibria are all stable, though there are other unstable D-group equilibria that we have not plotted. The prices charged by the D-groups for the intermediate inputs are low, despite the fact that most of these

Figure 3.6 Number of Business Groups

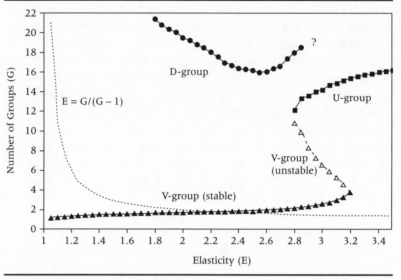

Source: Authors.

equilibria occur in the range of elasticities where the V-groups would not sell the inputs externally. The D-groups charge a low price for inputs partly because there are many of them in downstream markets, so that each group has only a small fraction of the market, but also because they face competition from other unaffiliated upstream producers. Thus, in the same way that we have multiple stable equilibria for elasticities exceeding 2.8, with the U-groups pricing low and the V-groups pricing high, we also have multiple stable equilibria for elasticities in the range from 1.8 to 2.6, with the D-groups pricing low and the V-groups pricing high (often at infinity).

At the top of figure 3.6, the right end of the D-group of equilibria is labeled with a question mark. These are initially solved as D-group equilibria, allowing for the entry of upstream, unaffiliated firms. However, when we check for the profitability of downstream unaffiliated firms, it turns out that they also want to enter. Therefore, in this range we evidently have an equilibrium configuration with business groups, and upstream and downstream firms. The same situation applies at the other end of the D-group equilibria, for elasticities below 1.8. We have not fully solved for this case in our model, but logic certainly suggests that it is a possible outcome, and we find that it implies an even larger number of business groups, of smaller size, than those equilibria shown in figure 3.6.

High-Concentration and Low-Concentration Equilibria

Given the complexity of the equilibria in figure 3.6, it is useful to summarize the general features of this diagram. Recall that our method of solving for the equilibria has been to pick each value of the elasticity and then determine the equilibrium number of groups and their prices; this is repeated for all elasticities between unity and 3.5. For most of the elasticities, we have found two stable equilibria. For example, for elasticities between 1.8 and 2.6, we have either the D-groups or the tightly integrated V-groups, which do not sell inputs to each other. For elasticities between about 2.8 and 3.2, we have either U-groups or V-groups. Beyond elasticities of 3.2, there is a unique type of equilibrium with U-groups.[5] These unique equilibria extend beyond the elasticity of 3.5 shown in figure 3.6, up to an elasticity of about 6.6, after which we no longer find profitable business groups for the governance costs we have assumed in the model.

We argue that some of the equilibria we have found bear a resemblance to the group structure in Korea, and other equilibria resemble that found in Taiwan. To make this precise, we need some criterion for selecting between equilibria. Since we think of different elasticities as applying to different types of goods, it would not make any sense to say, for example, that Korea has low elasticities while Taiwan has high elasticities. On the contrary, we will suppose that any value of the elasticity can apply in either country, and we shall focus on all values between 1.8 and 6.6 (at intervals of 0.05).[6] Then, for each elasticity, we choose the equilibrium with the *large* number of business groups and say that it belongs to the *low-concentration* set, while we choose the equilibrium with the *small* number of business groups and say that it belongs to the *high-concentration* set. In this way, we identify two generic types of equilibria, distinguished by the degree of concentration of the business groups, over the whole range of elasticities being considered.

Specifically, in figure 3.6 the high-concentration equilibria include the stable V-group at the bottom of the figure, for all elasticities up to

3.2, followed by the U-group equilibria for elasticities above 3.2. For completeness, we also include the unstable V-group equilibria when graphing this path, as a reminder of what lies in between the V-group and U-group equilibria. The low-concentration equilibria form a path at the top of the figure and include the D-group equilibria for elasticities up to 2.8, followed by the U-group equilibria for elasticities above 2.8. When there is a unique equilibrium, as for the U-groups with elasticities above 3.2, then it belongs to both the high-concentration and low-concentration sets.

Our goal for the rest of the chapter is to characterize the high-concentration and low-concentration equilibria in terms of some variables that can be measured in practice, and then to compare these theoretical results with actual business groups in South Korea and Taiwan.

We argue that the chaebol in Korea seem to conform to features of the high-concentration equilibria, and particularly that the largest chaebol in Korea are similar to the V-groups in our model. In contrast, the business groups in Taiwan bear a resemblance to the low-concentration equilibria, and especially to the U-groups in our model. We make the connection between the simulated equilibria from the model and the actual business group data, using both diagrams and simple summary statistics. We focus on three variables to compare the simulated equilibria and actual data: sales, vertical integration, and horizontal diversification.

Vertical Integration

We measure the vertical integration of the groups using the ratio of their internal sales to total sales. Recall that the internal sales of inputs occur at marginal cost, while total sales are measured as internal plus external sales of inputs, plus external sales of the final goods. These can be quite readily constructed in each of the simulated equilibria. In figures 3.7 and 3.8, we plot the internal sales ratio against the sales of the business group, for the high-concentration and low-concentration equilibria, respectively. Notice that the sales axis is plotted as a logarithmic scale; we have deliberately kept this scale the same in each graph, to emphasize that the high-concentration V-groups are so much

Figure 3.7 Internal Sales in High-Concentration Equilibria

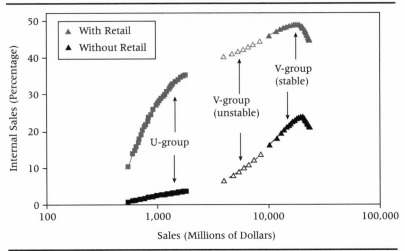

Source: Authors.

Figure 3.8 Internal Sales in Low-Concentration Equilibria

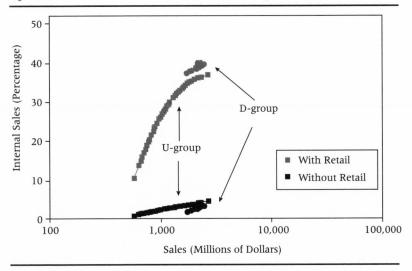

Source: Authors.

bigger. In fact, the largest V-group plotted in figure 3.7 has sales of nearly $24 billion, whereas the smallest U-group in either figure 3.7 or 3.8 has sales of about $500 million. We have intentionally chosen the size of the labor force in the model so that the sales of the V-groups in figure 3.7 roughly match the actual sales (in dollars) of the largest groups in Korea, but the *relative size* of the different types of business groups in the model is not affected at all by the choice of the labor force. Rather, the relative size of the groups reflects the different outcomes of the model across the high-concentration versus low-concentration equilibria, and across the range of elasticities for the intermediate input being considered (all those from 1.8 to 6.6).

The internal sales ratio constructed from the model is plotted in black and labeled "without retail sales."[7] It is apparent that the internal sales of the V-groups are much larger than those of the U-groups or D-groups. When we compare the simulated equilibria to the actual group data, in the next section, we compute the internal sales ratios over all firms in the group, both including and excluding the internal purchases of trading companies and other wholesale and retail firms. We make this computation because, in the actual group data, including the transactions of trading companies biases the internal sales ratios upward. Our model does not incorporate any of the informational considerations that would give rise to trading companies, but it does contain a rudimentary distinction between manufacturing and retailing activities. The upstream sector in the model produces and sells intermediate inputs, while the downstream sector assembles and sells the final products. We can conceptually split the downstream sector into its two parts—assembly and retail sales—and treat these as distinct activities. If we suppose that the sales are done by firms other than those engaged in assembly activity but belonging to the same group, then the purchases of the retail firms can be either included within the internal sales ratio or excluded. These two calculations differ only in an accounting sense in the model and correspond to how the internal sales ratios are computed for the actual group data.

In figures 3.7 and 3.8, the gray points indicate internal sales ratios that are computed inclusive of the retailing activity of each group and are labeled "with retail sales."[8] Naturally, the internal sales ratios are higher when the retail purchases are included. We see in figure 3.7

that the internal sales ratios for the V-groups are still higher than those for the U-groups, whether retail sales are included or not. In figure 3.8, where we plot the low-concentration path, the D-groups have internal sales of around 40 percent, and the largest U-groups slightly less than this, when retail sales are included. This is still less than the large V-groups in figure 3.7, where the internal sales are between 45 and 50 percent when retail sales are included. Thus, we conclude that whether retail sales are included or not, the large V-groups have internal sales that exceed not only the remaining U-groups in the high-concentration equilibria but also any of the groups found in the low-concentration equilibria.

Horizontal Diversification

A second way that we contrast the high-concentration and low-concentration equilibria is in the range of varieties of the intermediate input, and the final good, that each group produces. A conventional measure of horizontal diversification is the Herfindahl index. Defined over the share of sales s_i that the group makes in different sectors i, the Herfindahl index equals $1 - \sum_i s_i^2$, where a value closer to unity indicates greater product diversification. In our model, and when we look at the actual groups in Korea and Taiwan, we can measure the Herfindahl index over all sales of a group or over internal sales only, and over all products sold or over intermediate inputs only. We report the results from two alternatives: the broadest case, where the Herfindahl index is defined over all sales and products; and the narrowest case, where the Herfindahl index is defined over just intermediate inputs sold internally to the group.[9]

In figures 3.9 and 3.10, we plot the two Herfindahl indexes for the high-concentration and low-concentration equilibria, respectively. The sales axis is again measured logarithmically. In figure 3.9, the Herfindahl indexes for either all sales (in gray) or internal inputs only (in black) approach unity for the largest V-groups. In contrast, the highest value of the Herfindahl index for the U-groups in the high-concentration equilibrium is about 0.6 for all sales, and 0.4 for internal inputs, indicating much less product variety; these indexes fall to zero for the smallest U-groups.[10] The low-concentration equilibria, shown in figure 3.10, include both the D-groups and U-groups. When

Figure 3.9 Variety per Group in High-Concentration Equilibria

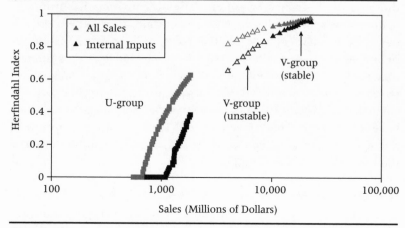

Source: Authors.

Figure 3.10 Variety per Group in Low-Concentration Equilibria

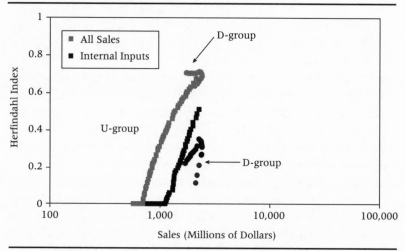

Source: Authors.

the Herfindahl index is computed over all sales, the D-groups have product diversity between 0.6 and 0.7, while the U-group index ranges from 0.0 to 0.7. Product variety is somewhat less when measured for internal inputs only, where the D-group index ranges from 0.1 to 0.4, while the U-group index ranges from 0.0 to 0.6.

We conclude that the V-groups in the high-concentration equilibria have the greatest product diversity, exceeding that of U-groups and D-groups regardless of how the index is measured. This conclusion reflects in part the very large size of V-groups, as well as the economies of scope that come with size: since any new input is sold to a large number of downstream firms within the V-group, there is a strong incentive to develop more input varieties. From this result we should not conclude, however, that the high-concentration equilibria produce greater product variety for the economy overall. On the contrary, our model predicts that a high-concentration equilibrium with V-groups produces *less* variety in final products for the economy overall than a low-concentration equilibrium evaluated at the same elasticity (and for like values of the other parameters, such as the size of the labor force). This reduced variety of the final goods translates into lower consumer welfare (holding fixed the number of final product varieties available through imports). This illustrates a point we made when introducing our stylized economy: the inherent efficiency of the business groups (because they sell inputs internally at marginal cost) does not necessarily translate into efficiency for the economy overall.

To understand why the economywide variety of final products is reduced by V-groups, note that the large input variety in each group, combined with marginal-cost pricing of inputs internally, results in low downstream costs. This gives the V-groups an incentive to produce a higher *quantity* of any final product than other types of groups or unaffiliated firms would have, with corresponding higher sales. But now we need to appeal to the resource constraint for the economy. With the V-groups selling more of each final good than would other types of groups, it is impossible for the economy to also produce more final varieties; on the contrary, with the same labor force available, a low-concentration equilibrium with either U-groups or D-groups must have *higher variety of final goods* than a high-concentration equilibrium with V-groups. Put simply, the focus of the V-groups on high sales for each final product rules out the possibility that the economy also produces a wide range of final consumer goods. A good example is provided by the focus of many of the South Korean groups on a narrow range of products, such as cars (the Hyundai) or microwave ovens; in contrast, Taiwan supplies a vast array of differentiated products to retailers in the United States and elsewhere, customizing each product to the buyer's specification. We find that the focus on a narrow range of varieties is a characteristic feature of the high-concentration V-group equilibria, whereas a broad range of final products in the economy comes from either the U-groups or D-groups.[11]

The Organization of Business Groups in South Korea and Taiwan

To compare our theoretical analysis with data on business groups, we have created a database of forty-four business groups for South Korea in 1989, and eighty groups for Taiwan in 1994. For both countries we are able to construct a *transaction matrix* for the major business groups. This matrix specifies the sales to other member firms within the group, as well as total sales and other information for each firm. Thus, the transaction matrices can be used to construct measures of the vertical integration for each business group. We first report detailed results for the Korean groups, and then we describe the Taiwanese groups. The comparison vividly illustrates the differences in both their size and vertical integration: the largest groups in Korea are huge by comparison with other groups found in Korea or Taiwan and are integrated through the entire production chain.

Korean Business Groups, 1989

The primary source for the 1989 Korean data is the volume *1990 Chaebol Analysis Report (Chaebol Boon Suk Bo Go Seo)*, published by Korea Investors Service. This volume provides information on the fifty largest business groups (measured in terms of assets) in South Korea, but for six of these groups the data on internal transactions are missing. Thus, the 1989 database for Korea includes only forty-four groups, with 499 firms. Data on financial and insurance companies belonging to the groups are excluded from the database, since their sales cannot be accurately measured. In table 3.1, we show summary information for each of these forty-four groups.

The largest groups have become well-known names in the United States. Samsung and Hyundai, for example, each had total sales exceeding $25 billion in 1989, while the forty-four groups combined had sales of $152.5 billion.[12] This magnitude is sometimes compared to Korean GDP ($219.5 billion in 1989) to conclude that the business groups control the majority of the domestic economy. Such a comparison is incorrect, of course, because GDP is a value-added concept, reflecting the contribution made by each firm over and above its cost of materials. The *1990 Chaebol Analysis Report* provides the value-added calculations for each group; included in the database, these totaled $32.2 billion over the forty-four groups. Thus, these groups account for about 15 percent of Korean GDP in 1989.

Of principal interest is the extent to which business groups' sales go to other firms in the group, or equivalently, the extent to which each group relies on its own firms for intermediate inputs. We refer to this as the "internalization" of a group, and it can be measured by the ratio of the sales to firms in the same group relative to total group sales.[13] The internal sales ratio for each group is shown in the third column of table 3.1. It is apparent that larger groups have rather high internalization, exceeding 30 percent in several cases, and that internalization is correlated with the size of the group. This can be observed in the simple and weighted averages reported at the bottom of table 3.1: the simple average of the internal sales ratio is 11.3 percent, but the sales weighted average is about twice as large, at 22.1 percent. Nevertheless, some smaller groups have very high internalization, such as the Sammi steel group, with an internal sales ratio of 36.6 percent.[14]

One feature of the internalization ratio is somewhat misleading, and that is the fact that it includes the trading companies of most groups. These are companies that act as intermediaries in transactions between firms in the group and also sell to and buy from firms outside the group. Including these firms can artificially increase the internalization ratio when, for instance, the trading companies are simply transferring products between firms in the group. Twenty-seven out of the forty-four groups in Korea—or about 60 percent—have trading companies.

Table 3.1 Business Groups in Korea, 1989

Business Group	1989 Sales (Millions of Dollars)	Number of Firms	Internal Sales Ratio (Percentage)	Internal Sales (No Retail)	Herfindahl Index (All Sales)	Internal Sales (Internal Manufacturing)
Samsung	26,175	32*	31.9	18.8	0.70	0.35
Hyundai	25,500	30*	33.0	19.8	0.80	0.78
Lucky-Goldstar	18,807	45*	26.0	12.5	0.74	0.46
Daewoo	13,837	24*	23.5	9.7	0.68	0.66
Sunkyong	8,910	16*	20.6	10.3	0.69	0.42
Ssangyong	5,777	15*	14.8	11.6	0.75	0.63
Hyosung	4,697	20*	7.4	3.3	0.20	0.04
Kia	4,602	9*	25.6	6.6	0.80	0.64
Lotte	3,900	23*	9.2	7.7	0.25	0.12
Han Jin	3,895	11*	2.7	2.2	0.63	0.43
Korea Explosives	3,172	19*	7.7	4.7	0.80	0.58
Doosan	2,417	17*	13.3	11.5	0.84	0.77
Kolon	2,218	14*	10.6	4.0	0.65	0.00
Dongbu	1,978	7*	26.1	17.3	0.50	0.12
Daelim	1,951	12*	4.4	0.6	0.38	0.27
Dongkuk Steel Mill	1,886	10*	5.4	3.4	0.27	0.01
Dong Ah Construction	1,866	12*	1.1	0.7	0.39	0.00
Sammi	1,696	5*	36.6	27.0	0.51	0.00
Kumho	1,430	8*	3.3	0.4	0.64	0.00
Hanil	1,296	12*	7.1	7.1	0.61	0.39
Miwon	1,295	13*	12.5	6.4	0.65	0.26

Halla	1,262	7	10.2	10.2	0.62	0.51
Kangwon Industries	1,256	12*	33.5	11.4	0.74	0.31
Samyang	1,038	5	1.6	1.6	0.41	0.63
Kohap	1,016	6*	18.2	12.5	0.53	0.37
Poongsan	941	6	3.3	3.3	0.36	0.08
Woosung Construction	834	6	2.0	2.0	0.47	0.00
Kukdong Oil	812	3	19.3	0.0	0.39	0.00
Dongkuk Corporation	689	7*	11.3	1.1	0.55	0.00
Tongil	685	10	4.4	4.4	0.74	0.08
Tong Yang	672	5*	9.3	9.3	0.49	0.33
Byucksan	661	17	0.6	0.6	0.75	0.50
Taejon Leather	627	7	1.6	1.6	0.61	0.11
Daesung Industries	589	8	2.0	2.0	0.55	0.55
Anam Industrial	537	5	8.7	8.7	0.28	0.00
Oriental Chemical	528	9	8.9	8.9	0.40	0.48
Jinro	490	40	2.6	2.6	0.63	0.14
Taihan Electric Wire	490	3	3.0	3.0	0.12	0.00
Kyesung Paper	437	5	17.3	17.3	0.28	0.00
Han Yang	436	4*	6.6	0.7	0.22	0.00
Hanbo	420	3	2.6	2.6	0.35	0.44
You One Construction	281	2*	0.3	0.0	0.41	0.00
Kuk Dong Construction	247	4	0.1	0.1	0.10	0.00
Life Construction	211	4	3.5	3.5	0.48	0.00
Average	3,441	11.3	11.3	6.7	0.52	0.26
Weighted average	—	23.9	22.1	12.2	0.66	0.45

Source: Authors.

* A business group with trading companies.

To correct for the presence of the trading companies, two questions need to be addressed. The first is: How do we distinguish trading companies? In the Korean database, we relied on three criteria. First, we made telephone calls to the Korean business groups to find out whether each group had a trading company. Second, we used the company descriptions in the *Yearbook on the Korean Economy and Business, 1991–1992*, published by Business Korea. If a company was described as a trading arm of its business group, it was counted as a trading company. Third, along with the company description, if a company was largely involved in the group's internal transactions, it was counted as a trading company. Most of the trading companies are classified in wholesale and retail trade, though only a subset of firms in that sector are designated as trading companies.

The second question is: How do we correct for the presence of these companies when measuring the degree of internalization? Consider a trading company that purchases from firm A and sells that product to firm B, both in the same business group. Since this firm is simply acting as an intermediary in the transactions, it would be double-counting to include both the purchase and sale. But since the product was transferred from A to B, it would be incorrect to exclude both transactions as well. Instead, we should ignore either the purchase or the sale by the trading company. We decided to ignore the purchases of the trading companies from other firms within the group.[15] Thus, when a trading company buys from an outside firm and sells to another firm within the group, the sale is counted as an internal transaction. But when a group firm sells to a trading company, which then sells outside the group, no internal transaction is counted at all. We use the phrase "without trading companies" ("no TC") to mean that we are consistently ignoring the purchases of trading companies from within the group. We have recomputed the internal sales ratio for each of the business groups, without trading companies.[16] This reduces the average internalization of all forty-four groups from 11.3 percent to 8.2 percent, and the weighted average from 22.1 percent to 13.8 percent.

Since most of the trading companies are engaged in wholesale and retail trade, by excluding their purchases we are moving toward a measure of the business groups' vertical integration within just man-

ufacturing activities. To properly measure manufacturing integration, we also need to exclude the purchases of all other firms within
each group that are classified as within wholesale and retailing. There
are some differences between the trading companies and other firms
classified as in that sector. Many of the trading companies are actively
involved in seeking overseas customers and therefore play an informational role within the business group. In contrast, the other
wholesale and retailing firms are engaged in marketing the products
domestically, through establishments owned by the group. This distinction is not hard and fast, however, and there is considerable overlap in their activities.

As a natural extension to omitting the purchases of trading companies, in the fourth column of table 3.1 we report the internal sales
ratio while omitting both the purchases of trading companies and all
other firms in the wholesale and retail sector within each group.[17] As
compared to the original calculation, omitting trading companies and
other wholesale and retailing firms reduces the average internalization ratio from 11.3 percent to 6.7 percent, and the weighted average
from 22.1 percent to 12.2 percent. The internalization of some of the
largest business groups is reduced by roughly one-half, through avoiding the double-counting of goods transferred between firms within a
group. We regard this calculation as a more accurate measure of vertical integration.

Turning to horizontal diversification, the chaebol in Korea are
sometimes criticized for "one-setism," that is, for spanning so many
activities in different sectors. We can measure the diversification of
the groups across different sectors using the Herfindahl index, defined
as $1 - \sum_i s_i^2$, where s_i is the share of total sales in each sector i. To implement this index we divided the entire economy into thirty-one sectors, with twenty-two in manufacturing and seven in services. We
identified each firm in a group as selling in one of these sectors by its
major product category, and then computed the Herfindahl index for
each group. We considered four different calculations: using all sales
or internal sales only; and using all products or manufacturing only.
In the final columns of table 3.1, we report the results from two alternatives: the broadest case, where the Herfindahl index is defined
over all sales and all products; and the narrowest case, where the

Herfindahl index is defined over just manufacturing inputs sold internally to the group.

The simple average of the Herfindahl index over all sales is 0.52, and the weighted average is 0.66, indicating that the larger groups are more diverse in their sectoral sales. This remains true if instead we consider the internal sales of manufacturing goods, where the simple average is 0.26 and the weighted average is 0.45. Focusing on manufacturing sales in the top five groups, Hyundai has multiple firms producing in primary metals, metal products, machinery, electronic equipment, shipbuilding, and motor vehicles. These firms are supplying their products to the other firms located downstream and ultimately marketing the finished goods to consumers using their trading companies. The Daewoo group has a similar range of activities. An even greater spread is shown by Samsung, which includes firms within textiles, supplying to garments and apparel; pulp and paper, supplying to printing and publishing; chemical materials supplying to plastics; and machinery and electronic equipment, supplying to motor vehicles. Lucky-Goldstar shows a dominant concentration in electronic products, with nearly half of its firms in that sector, but it still maintains a presence in chemical and plastics, metals, and other sectors. These examples illustrate the one-setism that characterizes the largest groups, but even among the smaller groups there are many with a high degree of product diversification.

Taiwanese Business Groups, 1994

We relied on two primary sources for the 1994 Taiwan data: *Business Groups in Taiwan, 1996–1997,* published by the China Credit Information Service (CCIS), and company annual reports to the Taiwan stock exchange, for 1994, collected by the CCIS and supplemented by interviews with selected firms. *Business Groups in Taiwan, 1996–1997,* provides information on 115 business groups in Taiwan. For the largest eighty of these groups, data on sales to and purchases from other firms in the groups were collected from their annual reports. As with the Korean database, the sales of firms in some service sectors are incomplete. As a result, one of the largest Taiwanese groups, the Linden group (which owns Cathay Insurance), is not included in the database; also missing from the database is the Evergreen group (a shipping company). Using the information available, the 1994 database for Taiwan includes eighty groups, with 797 firms, as listed in table 3.2.

The largest groups in Taiwan are considerably smaller than their counterparts in Korea, and the total sales of the Taiwan groups is $76.3 billion, or about half as much as the Korean groups.[18] To do a comparison with Taiwanese GDP ($241 billion in 1994), we need to have a value-added figure for the groups. This was not provided in any of the source materials, but a rough estimate can be obtained by noting that the ratio of value-added to total sales for all the Korean groups is 21.2 percent. If we apply this same ratio to the total sales of the Taiwanese group, we obtain an estimated value-added of $16.2 billion, so that the eighty groups account for 6.7 percent of Taiwan GDP. The average number of firms in each group, shown at the bottom of column 2, is also smaller than for Korea.

In the third column of table 3.2, we report the internal sales ratio for the Taiwanese groups. In contrast to the Korean groups, it does not appear that the internalization ratios for Taiwanese business groups are significantly correlated with the size of the group. Thus, the largest group—Formosa Plastics—has an internalization ratio of 15.8 percent, no larger than the internalization ratio for a number of other groups of varying size. This can also be seen from the averages reported at the bottom of table 3.2. The average for the internal sales ratio is 7.0 percent and 9.5 percent, computed as simple and weighted, respectively. Both the size and difference between these are much smaller than they were for the Korean groups. Thus, the groups in Taiwan have less vertical integration on average, and also less difference between groups of various sizes.

We have corrected for the presence of trading companies in the business groups of Taiwan. Two criteria were used to select trading companies: whether the name of the firm from *Business Groups in Taiwan, 1996–1997,* included the words "trading company," and whether the description of products from that source indicated "buying and selling" as a primary activity. The trading companies in most cases belong to the input-output sectors called domestic wholesale trade, domestic retail trade, and import and export trade, though only a subset of the firms with these sector classifications are designated as trading companies.

Table 3.2 Business Groups in Taiwan, 1994

Business Group	1994 Sales (Millions of Dollars)	Number of Firms	Internal Sales Ratio (Percentage)	Internal Sales (No Retail)	Herfindahl Index (All Sales)	Internal Sales (Internal Manufacturing)
Formosa Plastics	6,654	16	15.8	15.8	0.54	0.58
Shin Kong	5,724	25*	0.4	0.4	0.40	0.22
Wei Chuan Ho Tai	4,889	23*	28.1	0.4	0.55	0.02
Far Eastern	4,291	26	0.7	0.5	0.53	0.05
Yulon	4,264	23*	26.6	5.2	0.77	0.26
President	3,932	31*	6.4	4.5	0.70	0.29
Tatung	3,634	36	8.3	6.3	0.38	0.18
Acer	3,243	9*	3.5	2.4	0.62	0.01
Chinfon	2,986	16*	24.1	1.1	0.19	0.00
Hualon	2,517	9*	16.4	4.7	0.70	0.00
Ho Hsin	2,104	15*	0.2	0.2	0.50	
Tuntex	1,831	16*	8.1	7.9	0.78	0.38
Teco Electric & Machinery	1,474	17*	2.6	2.6	0.60	0.15
Chi Mei	1,268	6*	0.3	0.3	0.25	0.09
Rebar	1,221	9*	1.4	0.9	0.72	0.00
Pacific Cable	1,214	26	3.2	3.2	0.54	0.05
Sampo	1,096	11	12.5	12.5	0.26	0.00
Tainan Spining	1,075	17	2.1	2.1	0.71	0.00
Pacific Construction	1,032	15	2.8	2.7	0.63	0.46
Yuen Foong Yu	1,000	8*	18.5	4.5	0.46	0.13

Ruentex	997	25*	0.7	0.0	0.51	0.00
Taiwan Cement	997	16	3.6	3.6	0.48	0.39
Lien Hwa Mitac	900	12*	2.8	2.7	0.53	0.00
Walsin Lihwa	881	8	0.1	0.1	0.02	0.06
Lite-On	875	10	0.5	0.5	0.71	0.50
Kwang Yang	855	7*	6.3	6.3	0.20	0.18
Cheng Loong	823	7*	16.3	16.2	0.08	0.00
Shih Lin Paper	766	5	0.1	0.1	0.20	0.00
United Microelectronics	673	4	8.5	8.5	0.00	0.00
Chung Shing Textile	668	5	6.6	6.1	0.50	0.00
Yeang Der	618	14	1.0	0.1	0.37	0.02
China General Plastics	598	5	12.6	12.6	0.67	0.00
Chun Yuan Steel	528	5	4.7	4.7	0.36	0.00
Adi	484	9	0.7	0.3	0.22	0.00
Shinlee	456	12*	0.4	0.4	0.52	0.00
Umax Elitegroup	436	8*	7.2	7.2	0.00	0.00
Pou Chen Industrial	434	3	4.5	4.5	0.49	0.50
Aurora	406	7*	17.5	8.6	0.09	0.00
Ase	404	5*	10.5	1.3	0.35	0.00
Great Wall	375	12	21.1	20.7	0.31	0.17
Ho Cheng	375	8*	14.5	14.5	0.26	0.00
Taiwan Glass	350	9*	2.6	0.6	0.00	0.00
Tung Ho Steel	350	4	0.6	0.6	0.25	0.09
Lealea	335	7	9.4	9.4	0.17	0.00
Vedan	327	8*	8.1	7.5	0.04	0.00
Chia Hsin Cement	303	7*	7.0	7.0	0.00	0.00

(Table continues on p. 120.)

Table 3.2 (Continued)

Business Group	1994 Sales (Millions of Dollars)	Number of Firms	Internal Sales Ratio (Percentage)	Internal Sales (No Retail)	Herfindahl Index (All Sales)	Internal Sales (internal Manufacturing)
Hwa Eng Cable	303	3	8.9	8.9	0.51	0.00
Lily Textile	301	7	0.7	0.7	0.04	0.00
Chia Her	293	5	1.6	1.6	0.38	0.00
Sun Moon Star	287	5*	7.1	3.8	0.49	0.00
Ta Ya Cable	276	6	4.0	4.0	0.10	0.21
Shing Nung	256	13*	6.2	5.9	0.42	0.22
Tah Tong Textile	235	13*	4.5	0.7	0.55	0.39
Dahin	231	5*	12.3	9.9	0.51	0.21
Chicony Electronics	217	3	4.3	4.3	0.00	0.00
Kenda Industrial	211	8	0.5	0.5	0.49	0.00
Lee Tah Farm Industrial	204	5	11.6	11.6	0.19	0.50
Fwu Sow Industrial	200	7*	7.1	7.0	0.01	0.00
Asia Chemical	180	13*	4.6	2.7	0.10	0.00
Men Yi	170	4	1.0	1.0	0.00	0.00
China Unique	166	4	2.8	2.8	0.22	0.00
Ve Wong	161	3	10.0	10.0	0.00	0.00
Hong Ho Precision Textile	159	6*	3.4	3.4	0.10	0.00

Chun Yu	158	7*	6.1	5.3	0.45	0.50
Ability	157	11	2.2	2.2	0.26	0.38
Far Eastern Machinery	156	7	0.3	0.3	0.20	0.00
UB	139	8	7.4	7.4	0.48	0.00
Chien Shing Stainless Steel	137	6	8.4	8.4	0.17	0.00
South East Cement	134	5	8.0	8.0	0.12	0.46
Bomy	116	9	29.5	0.0	0.48	0.00
Taiwan Everlight Chemical	104	5*	14.2	3.5	0.30	0.00
Ching Kuang Chemical	104	3	10.6	10.6	0.26	0.00
Nan Pao Resins	104	3	8.4	8.4	0.22	0.00
Victor Machinery	101	12*	1.2	1.2	0.16	0.00
Ren Hou (Chih Lien)	83	10*	0.0	0.0	0.51	0.00
Yung Shin Pharmaceutical	78	8*	2.7	1.8	0.05	0.00
Fu I Industrial	77	5*	5.1	5.1	0.30	0.00
San Wu Textile	53	3	2.7	2.7	0.57	0.05
Fong Kuo	48	4	6.5	6.5	0.34	0.10
Tong Hsing	35	4*	2.8	2.0	0.57	0.00
Average	954	10.0	7.0	4.7	0.35	0.10
Weighted average	—	16.9	9.5	4.5	0.48	0.16

Source: Authors.
* A business group with trading companies.

Of the eighty business groups, thirty-nine, or roughly one-half, were found to have trading companies, but there were recorded purchases between only twenty-three of these trading companies and other firms in the group.[19] Taiwan trading companies are considerably less involved in the internal transactions of their groups than their counterparts in Korea. When the trading companies are excluded from the calculation of the internal sales ratio, then average internalization falls from 7 percent to 6 percent, or from 9.5 percent to 8.5 percent calculated as a weighted average. This is much smaller than the corresponding reduction for Korea. One reason for this smaller reduction is that a number of groups with high internalization (more than 15 percent) do not have trading companies but still have high domestic retail sales. Three of these groups are very large producers of motor vehicles: Wei Chuan Ho Tai, with sales of $4.9 billion; Yulon, with sales of $4.3 billion; and Chinfon, with sales of $3.0 billion. These groups sell to a domestic market protected by tariffs and domestic content requirements.[20] The fourth group, Bomy, a smaller producer of fruit and vegetable juices, also sells domestically.

To determine the impact of excluding these wholesale and retail sales from groups' internalization, in the fourth column of table 3.2 we recompute the internal sales ratio while omitting the purchases of trading companies and all other firms classified as in the sectors of domestic wholesale trade, domestic retail trade, or import and export trade. The internalization of the three large groups in autos, and the Bomy group in beverages, falls dramatically, though the internalization of Formosa Plastics does not change at all. The average internal sales ratio now becomes 4.7 percent, while the weighted average is 4.5 percent. There is evidently no relation between sales and internalization once the retail sales of the three large automotive groups are excluded. The corresponding internalization rates computed without retail sales for Korea were 6.7 percent (simple average) and 12.2 percent (weighted average). The weighted average in particular is considerably higher than that for Taiwan, indicating the tendency of the largest groups in Korea to have high vertical integration, even after trading companies and other retail firms are excluded.

Business groups in the two countries also differ in the extent of their horizontal diversification, as measured by the Herfindahl indexes. In the final columns of table 3.2, we report the Herfindahl indexes for Taiwan, in the broad case, defined over all sales and all products, and the narrow case, defined over just manufacturing inputs sold internally to the group. The simple average of the Herfindahl index over all sales is 0.35, and the weighted average is 0.48, as compared to 0.52 and 0.66 for Korea. Thus, the Korean groups have greater product diversity, though in both countries there is some tendency for larger groups to be more diverse in their sectoral sales.

When we consider the internal sales of manufacturing goods, the Herfindahl indexes fall substantially to 0.10 (simple average) and 0.16 (weighted average), as compared to 0.26 and 0.45 for Korea. The largest group, Formosa Plastics, still has a high value of 0.58 for the Herfindahl index, comparable to the level of the largest groups in Korea. However, there is an important difference in the diversification of Formosa Plastics and the Korean groups: Formosa has its largest sales in only a few upstream sectors—chemicals and plastics and heavy machinery—with high internal sales between them, and a smaller presence in textiles. Generally, the Taiwanese groups tend to be focused on a narrower range of activities, diversifying across one or two areas in addition to their major sector. As examples, Shin King and Far Eastern both have their major presence in textiles, with diversification to chemicals, plastics, and nonmetallic minerals. In these cases, the dominant sector is located upstream, and the linkages between that sector and others where the group has diversified are quite limited. This pattern is typical of the Taiwanese business groups and contrasts with the much larger and more diversified groups in Korea.

Cross-Country Comparison

An initial comparison of the groups in South Korea and Taiwan can be obtained by looking at the sector sales of the firms involved. For each country, the sales of business group firms are classified according to the input-output sector of their primary product. These sales are then aggregated to twenty-two broad manufacturing sectors, as shown in table 3.3. The group sales are expressed as a percentage of total sales of all manufacturing firms in these sectors. For Korea we show values constructed for 1983 and 1989, while for Taiwan we show values for

Table 3.3 Group Sales in South Korea and Taiwan

Sector	Korea, 1983, Group Sales–Sector Sales	Korea, 1989, Group Sales–Sector Sales	Taiwan, 1983, Group Sales–Sector Sales	Taiwan, 1994, Group Sales–Sector Sales
Primary products				
Agriculture, forestry, fisheries	n.a.	0.3	n.a.	2.9
Mining	10.6	12.8	0.0	0.0
Manufactured products				
Food products	33.7	23.8	26.3	13.9
Beverages and tobacco	27.6	47.3	3.8	1.4
Textiles	38.4	32.5	50.7	45.3
Garments and apparel	12.6	0.9	12.0	0.4
Leather products	15.2	7.6	9.1	—[a]
Lumber and wood products	31.5	13.4	4.0	1.1
Pulp and paper products	6.7	15.4	20.1	20.8
Printing and publishing	—[b]	9.2	—[b]	0.0
Chemical materials	54.3	37.5	42.4	35.3
Chemical products	24.0	26.9	8.4	2.2

Petroleum and coal products	91.9	100	0.0	4.25
Rubber products	76.8	21.9	13.0	1.2
Plastic products	—[c]	38.8	5.4	5.0
Nonmetallic mineral products	44.6	28.0	47.6	37.6
Primary metals	28.0	34.3	7.8	2.8
Metal products	26.7	25.8	6.0	22.5
Machinery	34.9	33.9	3.6	12.3
Electronic products	50.9	64.3	22.7	24.4
Motor vehicles and shipbuilding	79.0	80.4	23.6	34.9
Precision instruments	14.0	11.1	0.0	0.0
Miscellaneous industrial products	5.2	2.88	10.7	0.12
Total manufacturing	45.4	40.7	19.0	16.4
Nonmanufactured products				
Utilities	n.a.	3.6	n.a.	1.2
Construction	66.0	31.7	5.6	8.4
Transportation, communications, and storage	23.1	23.6	1.8	3.0

Source: Authors.

[a] Leather products for Taiwan for 1994 are included with garments and apparel.

[b] Printing and publishing for 1983 is included with pulp and paper products.

[c] Plastic products for Korea in 1983 are included with chemical materials.

1983 and 1994. Overall there is a substantial degree of conformity in the sales of the groups between the earlier and later years. The principal change is that groups in both countries have been moving out of several sectors, including garments and apparel, rubber, and non-metallic mineral products (stone, clay, and glass items).

About one-half of the Korean sectors have business group sales that account for more than 25 percent of total sales, and in several cases the business group sales account for more than 50 percent of total sales, including petroleum and coal, electronic products, motor vehicles, and shipbuilding. The groups have a strong presence in both upstream and downstream sectors. Overall, the forty-three business groups account for 41 percent of manufacturing output in 1989, together with 13 percent in mining, 32 percent in utilities, and 24 percent in transportation, communication, and storage.

In Taiwan, by contrast, the business groups dominate in only a selected number of upstream sectors. Thus, in textiles the business groups account for nearly one-half of total manufacturing sales. These groups are selling downstream to the garment and apparel sector, where business groups are almost nonexistent. This pattern can also be seen from the strong group presence in pulp and paper products, chemical materials, nonmetallic minerals, and metal products. In comparison, business groups have a weak presence in downstream sectors such as wood products, chemical products, rubber and plastic products, as well as beverages and tobacco. Overall, the groups account for only 16 percent of total manufacturing output in 1994, along with small shares outside of manufacturing. We feel that the lower share of business groups in Taiwan matches neatly with the presence of unaffiliated firms in the low-concentration equilibria.

In nearly every sector where Taiwanese groups have a significant share of sectoral sales, the Korean groups account for even more. In addition, Korean groups are dominant in heavy industries such as petroleum and coal, basic and nonferrous metals, and shipbuilding. With the exception of only a small number of sectors (notably garments and apparel), business groups in Korea spread across nearly the entire manufacturing sector, but this is not true in Taiwan, where groups are principally found in upstream sectors. This difference between the two countries in sectoral allocation is consistent with the higher degree of

Figure 3.11 Internal Sales of Korean Groups, 1989

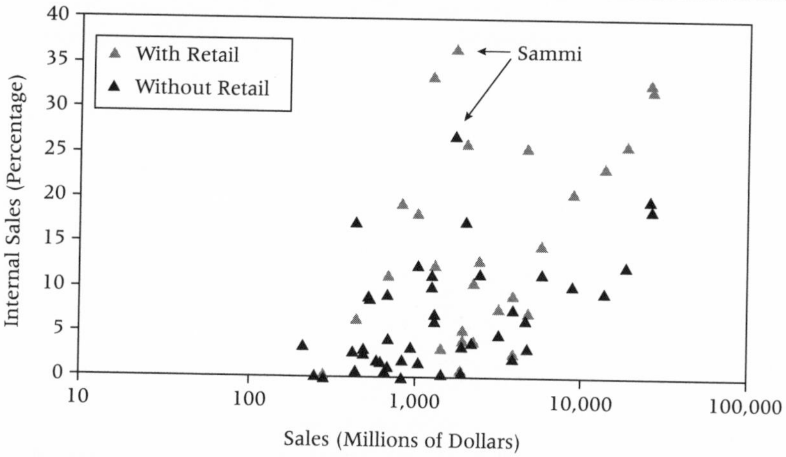

Source: Authors.

internalization found in Korean business groups, since these groups integrate forward and backward to span the production process.

Vertical Integration

Further evidence on the vertical integration of the groups can be taken from the internalization ratios, reported in tables 3.1 and 3.2. In figures 3.11 and 3.12, we plot the internalization ratios against the sales of each group, for Korea and Taiwan, respectively. Sales on the horizontal axis are measured in millions of dollars, with a logarithmic scale, which we have intentionally kept the same in both figures. The gray points are the internal sales ratios, while the black points are the internal sales ratios calculated without the internal purchases of trading companies or other retail firms.

The top five groups for Korea stand out on the right-hand side of figure 3.11, being dramatically larger with sales from $9 billion to $26 billion, and also having higher internalization as compared to many (though not all) of the others. The remaining groups have sales between $500 million and $5 billion, and internalization ratios mostly less than 20 percent (computed without the retail firms). The groups for Taiwan in figure 3.12 display much the same pattern as the

Figure 3.12 Internal Sales of Taiwanese Groups, 1994

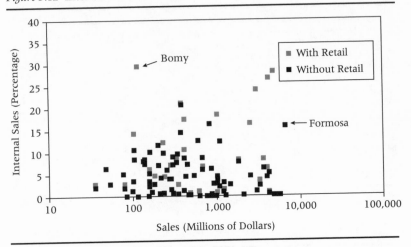

Source: Authors.

remaining Korean groups. The largest group for Taiwan, Formosa Plastics, stands out somewhat with sales exceeding $5 billion and an internalization of 15.8 percent, whether trading companies and other retail firms are excluded or not. But for nearly all other groups with high internalization ratios (above 20 percent), they are reduced substantially when the purchases of retail firms are excluded. There are also more very small groups in Taiwan than in Korea.

We invite the reader to compare figures 3.11 and 3.12 with the results from our theoretical model in figures 3.7 and 3.8, which display the high-concentration and low-concentration equilibria, respectively. The presence of the large and highly integrated groups is strikingly similar in Korea (figure 3.11) and the high-concentration equilibria (figure 3.7). Conversely, Taiwan (figure 3.12) and the low-concentration equilibria (figure 3.8) have groups that are smaller, and internalization that is not strongly correlated with sales. Clearly, the actual data for Korea and Taiwan are much more dispersed than the simulated equilibria, as we discuss later. Our primary interest is to compare the mean values of the actual and simulated data, as reported in table 3.4 for the Korean groups and the high-concentration equilibria and in table 3.5 for the Taiwanese groups and the low-concentration equilibria.

Table 3.4 Comparison of Korean Groups with Simulated High-Concentration Equilibria

Included Groups	Statistic	Sales (Millions of Dollars)	Internal Sales Ratio (Percentage)[a]	Internal Sales Ratio (No Retail)[b]	Herfindahl Index (All Sales)[c]	Herfindahl Index (Internal Inputs)[d]
Korean Groups, 1989						
All forty-four	Average	3,441	11.3	6.7	0.52	0.26
	St. Dev./√N[e]	917	1.6	1.0	0.03	0.04
Top five	Average	18,645	27.0	14.3	0.72	0.54
	St. Dev./√N	3,329	2.4	2.1	0.02	0.08
Other thirty-nine	Average	1,492	9.2	5.7	0.50	0.23
	St. Dev./√N	212	1.4	0.9	0.03	0.04
Stable High-Concentration Equilibria						
All	Average	6,236	32.3	8.1	0.51	0.34
	St. Dev.	8,072	11.1	9.0	0.34	0.41
V-groups[f]	Average	18,412	46.9	21.7	0.96	0.95
	St. Dev.	2,704	1.9	1.8	0.01	0.03
U-groups[g]	Average	1,119	26.1	2.3	0.32	0.08
	St. Dev.	365	6.7	0.8	0.20	0.12

Source: Authors.

[a] Computed as the ratio of sales between firms in each group to total sales of the group.

[b] "No retail" means that the internal sales ratio is calculated without including the purchases of any trading companies or other wholesale or retail firms from within the group.

[c] The Herfindahl index equals $1 - \sum_i s_i^2$, where s_i is the share of total sales in each sector i.

[d] The Herfindahl index is computed over internal sales of manufacturing inputs only.

[e] Standard deviation divided by the square root of the number of observations.

[f] The V-groups consist of those equilibria with elasticities between 1.8 and 3.2.

[g] The U-groups consist of those equilibria with elasticities between 3.2 and 6.6.

Table 3.5 Comparison of Taiwan Business Groups with Simulated Low-Concentration Equilibria

Included Groups	Statistic	Sales (Millions of Dollars)	Internal Sales Ratio (Percentage)[a]	Internal Sales Ratio (No Retail)[b]	Herfindahl Index (All Sales)[c]	Herfindahl Index (Internal Inputs)[d]
Taiwan, 1994						
All eighty	Average	954	7.0	4.7	0.35	0.10
	St. Dev./√N[e]	154	0.8	0.5	0.03	0.02
Top five	Average	5,164	14.3	4.5	0.56	0.23
	St. Dev./√N	457	6.0	3.0	0.06	0.10
Other seventy-five	Average	673	6.5	4.7	0.33	0.09
	St. Dev./√N	96	0.7	0.5	0.03	0.02
Stable Low-Concentration Equilibria						
All	Average	1432	29.3	2.54	0.42	0.15
	St. Dev.	598	7.8	0.8	0.24	0.15

Large U-group[f]	Average	2,116	35.9	3.9	0.66	0.45
	St. Dev.	131	0.3	0.2	0.02	0.04
Small U-group[g]	Average	1,119	26.1	2.3	0.32	0.08
	St. Dev.	365	6.7	0.8	0.20	0.12
D-group[h]	Average	2,193	38.7	2.6	0.70	0.29
	St. Dev.	240	0.9	0.5	0.01	0.04

Source: Authors.

a Computed as the ratio of sales between firms in each group to total sales of the group.

b "No retail" means that the internal sales ratio is calculated without including the purchases of any trading companies or other wholesale or retail firms from within the group.

c The Herfindahl index equals $1 - \sum_i s_i^2$, where s_i is the share of total sales in each sector i.

d The Herfindahl index is computed over internal sales of manufacturing inputs only.

e Standard deviation divided by the square root of the number of observations.

f The large U-groups consist of those equilibria with elasticities between 2.8 and 3.2.

g The small U-groups consist of those equilibria with elasticities between 3.2 and 6.6.

h The D-groups consist of those equilibria with elasticities between 1.8 and 2.8.

From table 3.4, we see that the top five groups for Korea have 1989 sales averaging $18.6 billion, while the remaining thirty-nine groups have sales averaging $1.5 billion. In our model, we have chosen the size of the labor force so that the average simulated sales of the V-groups are $18.4 million, similar to the sales of the top five Korean groups. Holding the labor force at this same value, we then find that the remaining U-groups in the high-concentration equilibria have average sales of $1.1 billion, or roughly the same as average sales for the remaining groups in Korea. This is a remarkable similarity of the mean sales for the largest and remaining groups in the Korean data and in the simulated high-concentration equilibria. Notice that the figure for mean sales for all Korean groups, $3.4 billion, is quite different from that from the model, $6.2 billion. Average simulated sales tend to be "pulled up" because we have simulated many V-group equilibria, but include only five actual groups in the top-five comparison.

Turning to the internal sales ratios, these range from 27 percent for the top five Korean groups, or 14.3 percent when trading and retail companies are excluded, to 9.2 percent and 5.7 percent for the other thirty-nine groups. Thus, the internalization of the top five groups is about three times larger than it is for the remaining groups. In our simulated high-concentration equilibria, the V-groups have internalization of 46.9 percent, or 21.7 percent when retail sales are excluded, as compared to 26.1 percent and 2.3 percent for the remaining U-groups. Thus, the model predicts internal sales in the large V-groups that are between two and ten times larger than for the remaining groups. Using the business group data for Korea, we found that the top five groups had *three times* the internalization of the remaining groups, so the theoretical range includes our actual finding from the group data. While the internalization figures in the model and the Korean data do not match exactly, they are still quite similar.

In table 3.5, we repeat this comparison for Taiwan and the low-concentration equilibria. The largest five Taiwanese groups have average 1994 sales of $5.2 billion, which is eight times larger than the average sales for the other seventy-five groups of $673 million. In our model, the low-concentration equilibria include both U-groups and D-groups. We divide the former into those that are larger (for elasticities between 2.8 and 3.2) and those that are smaller (for elasticities exceeding 3.2). The large U-groups have average sales of $2.1 billion, or twice the average sales of $1.1 billion for the smaller U-groups. The same difference is obtained between the D-groups, with average sales of $2.2 billion, and the smaller U-groups, with sales of $1.1 billion. So the Taiwanese data and the low-concentration equilibria both display a contrast between the largest groups and those remaining, though this contrast is more marked in the actual data than in the simulated equilibria. Although we feel that the large groups in Taiwan, such as Formosa Plastics, are best described as U-groups, the low-concentration equilibria in our model also include large D-groups. Perhaps this configuration is appropriate for some of the Taiwanese groups that have large retail sales, such as the automotive groups described earlier, or the Acer group. So while the comparison of Taiwan with the low-concentration equilibria is not as exact as we obtained for Korea, we feel that it is still highly suggestive.

The internal sales ratios range from 14.3 percent for the top five Taiwanese groups, or 4.5 percent when trading and retail companies are excluded, to 6.5 percent and 4.7 percent for the other seventy-five groups. Thus, the largest groups have internalization between one and two times greater than that of the remaining groups. In the low-concentration equilibria, we can compare the internalization of the largest U-groups, which is 35.9 percent or 3.9 percent, depending on whether retail sales are included, to that of the smaller U-groups, which is 26.1 percent or 2.3 percent. Thus, the internalization of the larger groups is about one and a half times higher than for the remaining U-groups, which is roughly similar to that found in the Taiwanese data. Focusing on the internalization while omitting retail sales, the simulated low-concentration equilibria have lower average values than the simulated high-concentration equilibria, as we also find when comparing across Taiwan and Korea.

Horizontal Diversification

The comparison of the actual data with simulated equilibria can also be made for horizontal diversification, as measured by the Herfindahl

Figure 3.13 Product Variety of Korean Groups, 1989

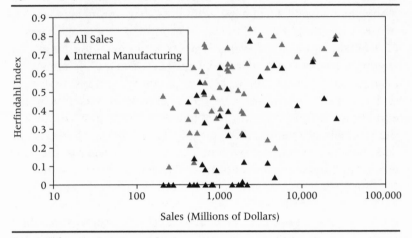

Source: Authors.

Figure 3.14 Product Variety of Taiwanese Groups, 1994

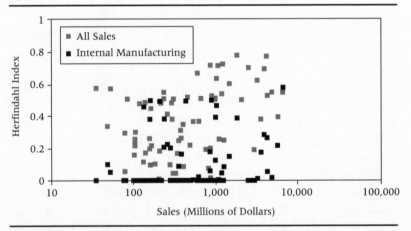

Source: Authors.

indexes. In figures 3.13 and 3.14, we plot these indexes for Korea and Taiwan, respectively, with the index computed over all sales shown in gray and that computed over internal manufacturing sales only shown in black. These figures display a great deal of dispersion: the largest groups in Korea tend to have higher product diversification, but there is little or no such tendency in Taiwan.

The group data in figures 3.13 and 3.14 can be compared with the simulated high- and low-concentration equilibria in figures 3.9 and 3.10, respectively. Again, we feel that there is some similarity in the pairs of diagrams, especially the largest groups in Korea and the high-concentration equilibria, which have the greatest product diversity. This is confirmed by comparing the means values from the group data and simulated equilibria, as reported in the final columns of tables 3.4 and 3.5.

In table 3.4, the top five groups for Korea have product diversity that is one and a half to two times greater than that of the remaining groups, depending on which measure of the Herfindahl index is used. Similarly, in the simulated high-concentration equilibria, we find that the V-group equilibria have product diversity exceeding that of the U-groups, though this difference is exaggerated in the simulated equilibria: product diversity for the V-groups is between three and twelve times greater than it is for the remaining U-groups. Notice that the overall mean level of product diversity is quite comparable in the Korean economy and the high-concentration equilibria. This similarity of the overall means also holds for Taiwan and the low-concentration equilibria, as shown in table 3.5. The large U-groups have product variety exceeding that of the small U-groups, as also observed between the largest and remaining groups for Taiwan, though again, the differences are exaggerated in the simulated data. So while the actual and simulated levels of product diversity do not match exactly, we feel that the essential features of horizontal diversification in the two countries are well represented by the simulated equilibria.

Standard Deviations of Simulated and Actual Data

In addition to mean values, it is also of interest to compute standard deviations in the actual and simulated data. A quick comparison of figures 3.7, 3.8, 3.9, and 3.10 with figures 3.11, 3.12, 3.13, and 3.14 confirms that the actual group data are much more dispersed than the simulated equilibria. On reflection, this is to be expected. Recall that each of the simulated equilibria is computed for a given value of the elasticity of demand for intermediate inputs; repeating this calculation over the whole range of elasticities gives us the plots in figures 3.7 to 3.10. The equilibrium at each of the elasticities represents an *entire* economy, where we have assumed that the business groups in each economy are the same size, which then equals their mean size. So the plots in figures 3.7 to 3.10 should be thought of as a series of economies that show how the mean size and internal sales of the groups vary across each. The dispersion in these points can therefore be interpreted as a standard deviation of the mean sales, or internal sales, across economies.

We contrast this with the plots of the actual group data for Korea and Taiwan, shown in figures 3.11 to 3.14. Each point in these figures represents the sales, and internal sales, for a *single* business group, so the whole set of points taken together represents the situation in one economy. The wide dispersion of points shown represents the standard deviation of sales and internal sales across the various business groups. If instead we want to measure the standard deviation of mean sales, or internal sales, as we have argued is done in the model, then we should compute the standard deviation of the sample divided by the square root of the number of observations. These values are reported in the top panels of tables 3.4 and 3.5, for the actual Korean and Taiwanese data, while in the bottom panel we report the standard deviation over all simulated equilibria, with no adjustment for the number of observations. In summary, because the simulated equilibria have business groups of equal size in each economy, we feel that the standard deviation of these equilibria is most appropriately compared to the standard deviation of the *mean* in our actual data, which is computed by dividing by the square root of the number of observations.

Some of the standard deviations in the actual data and the simulated equilibria are quite close. For example, the sales and internal sales of the top five groups in Korea and the V-groups in the high-concentration equilibria have standard deviations that are very close. Although we could hardly expect this pattern to appear consistently, it reinforces our finding that the high- and low-concentration equilibria are able to replicate features found in two such different economies as Korea and Taiwan.

Conclusions

How did South Korea and Taiwan start down such different paths? Some would argue that, for Korea at least, the state created the "historical moment" when the chaebol became the leading edge of industrial development (Woo 1991). Others (for example, Biggart 1990) argue that Korea's large firm economy had historical and institutional roots. To understand how these two economies work today, it makes no difference which view is correct. What is important is that they started organizationally in different places, for whatever reasons, and went on from there. The interaction of firms in the period of development after World War II and the Korean War created an emergent, self-maintaining system of production whose impact today is different from, and more extensive than, the factors that led to its development in the first place.

These impacts were especially evident in the wake of the Asian business crisis of 1997 to 1999. The organizational differences between South Korea and Taiwan were reflected perhaps more clearly than at any other period of time in the divergent outcomes of the crisis that they experienced. The financial crisis had disastrous consequences in Korea because so much indebtedness had been incurred in creating and maintaining one-setism. These groups are further endangered by their heavy reliance on a very few products for the majority of their profits, which they in turn subtly redistribute among upstream firms, usually in the form of low-cost loans. At the same time that capital markets reevaluated the exchange rates during the crisis, global commodity prices also fell. As a consequence of the double squeeze—the rising cost of money and the falling price of products—the chaebol entered into a period of extreme crisis, and a substantial number of them went bankrupt. Keun Lee (1999) cites twenty-three groups from the largest sixty chaebol that went bankrupt in the first year of the crisis. As predicted by the unstable equilibria in our model, the chaebol that went bankrupt immediately were not among the five largest chaebol but rather were concentrated among the intermediate-sized chaebol (ranked sixth through thirtieth in assets). Two years later, in 1999, Daewoo, one of the top five chaebol, still had not recovered from the financial shock and appeared headed for dissolution.

By contrast, the only crisis that Taiwan faced during the 1997 to 1999 period was falling demand in Asia for its products. The crisis did not endanger Taiwan's most export-oriented sector, because Taiwan's small and medium-sized firms continue to carry very low levels of debt. Many in Taiwan argued, in fact, that the crisis elsewhere presented Taiwanese businesses with an opportunity to capture greater shares of product markets and to upgrade production, strategies that the heavily indebted firms elsewhere could not afford to adopt. By 1999 Taiwan had passed Korea as the third largest global producer of high-technology products, as measured by total value, a lead that expanded the following year.

As we have demonstrated in this chapter, the organization of interfirm relations generates its own momentum and produces effects that are both independent of state officials and macroeconomic factors and influence them. In another paper, we (Hamilton, Choe, Kim, and Lim 1999) argue that state officials, as well as entrepreneurs, become encased in an increasingly institutionalized system of firms, creating a distinct economic world, which they can neither ignore nor easily reform. Once the emergent economic organization becomes a going concern, the viable options for the state's economic policies become progressively narrowed. Only those policies that conform to the organization of the economy have a real chance of success, and other policies may languish or fail miserably. As Haeran Lim (1998) shows, the Korean state's many economic initiatives encouraging the growth of small and medium-sized firms have had very limited, if any, success. And as Karl Fields (1995) shows for Taiwan, state officials failed in their efforts to create large Japanese- and Korean-style trading firms to handle the links between small and medium-sized producers and global buyers. Also, on several different occasions, economic planners in Taiwan tried to promote an export automobile industry, but never with any success. For state officials and entrepreneurs alike, once economic organization develops its own internal momentum, it is like the proverbial tiger: once you begin riding it, you cannot get off.

Notes

1. We have illustrated a single business group just for convenience in the drawing. In equilibrium, there are generally a number of groups, which we assume are all of the same size.
2. Initially, we used an elasticity of demand for final goods equal to 5. Although we found both V-group and U-group equilibria at this value,

it was difficult to find D-group equilibria in which the unaffiliated downstream firms had no incentive to enter. To limit this incentive, it was necessary to use lower values for the final demand elasticity, especially when the elasticity of demand for inputs itself was low. Accordingly, all our equilibria are computed with an elasticity of demand for final goods equal to 5 for $E \geq 2.65$, and equal to $1.9E$ for $E \leq 2.60$.

3. Note that the marginal cost of intermediate inputs has been set at unity in the model, which equals the internal price within a group.

4. Actually, we introduce two types of governance costs into the model: a fixed cost borne by each group, and a fixed cost for each new input or final good developed (due to research and development, and marketing, for example). The latter fixed cost is borne by both unaffiliated firms and groups, but we assume that it is slightly higher for the groups. In other words, the unaffiliated firms are assumed to be slightly better at creating new products, in either the upstream or downstream market. This assumption is needed to offset the efficiency advantage that the business groups have. In addition, this assumption helps limit the incentive of the business groups to take over the unaffiliated firms. We suppose that if such a takeover occurs, the fixed costs of each product are raised slightly when the unaffiliated firm is merged with the group. So the group will not necessarily want to pursue such a takeover, even if the unaffiliated firm is profitable.

5. Beyond elasticities of 3.2, there is a unique U-group equilibrium, shown in figure 3.6. Recall from our previous discussion, however, that there is another type of equilibrium in which all three types of firms enter (unaffiliated upstream, unaffiliated downstream, and business groups); this was indicated by the question mark at the top of figure 3.6. So there might be multiple equilibria even for elasticities exceeding 3.2: an equilibrium of the U-group type and another with all three types of firms. Since we did not solve for this equilibrium, we cannot include it in our analysis.

6. Below elasticities of 1.8, we show only a single equilibrium in figure 3.6, with the tightly integrated V-groups. However, we have also found that for elasticities in this range there is likely to be an alternative equilibrium, involving the simultaneous entry of business groups, and upstream and downstream firms. Because we have not been able to solve for this equilibrium in detail, we do not consider elasticities below 1.8.

7. Specifically, the internal sales ratio excluding retail sales equals $A/(A + B + C)$, where A equals sales of inputs within the group, evaluated at their marginal cost; B equals group sales of inputs to other groups or unaffiliated firms; and C equals group sales of final goods.

8. The internal sales ratio including retail sales equals $(A + D)/(A + B + C + D)$, where A, B, and C are defined as in note 7, and D equals group sales

of final goods, evaluated at their marginal cost. We imagine that the transactions D are made to a group trading company, which then sells the goods to consumers for the amount C. For clarity in figures 3.7 and 3.8, both internal sales ratios are plotted against total sales measured as $(A + B + C + D)$.

9. In our model, each group sells internally the same amount of each input variety produced, so the narrow measure of the Herfindahl index becomes $[1 - (1/\text{the number of input varieties})]$. The broad measure of the Herfindahl index combines both the input varieties and output varieties and measures the sales of each relative to total sales $(A + B + C + D)$, as defined in notes 7 and 8.

10. Because our model allows the number of varieties produced to be less than unity, the Herfindahl index can become negative. We plot these observations as zero values.

11. This hypothesis is confirmed empirically when we compare the product variety of exports from Korea and Taiwan to the United States in Feenstra, Yang, and Hamilton (1999).

12. The dollar values for Korea have been converted from the Korea won using the exchange rate of 679.6 won per dollar, at the end of 1989.

13. That is, the internalization ratio is calculated as (internal sales within a group)/(internal sales within a group plus all external sales to other firms or consumers).

14. Sammi is one of the groups that went bankrupt during the financial crisis in Korea of 1997 to 1998.

15. All of the trading companies made purchases from other firms in their group, and most also made sales.

16. The purchases of the trading companies are excluded from both the numerator and denominator of the internal sales ratio. Thus, the internal sales ratio calculated without the trading companies equals (all internal sales within a group, except those made to trading companies)/(all internal sales within a group, except those made to trading companies, plus all external sales to other firms or consumers).

17. This internal sales ratio is calculated as (all internal sales within a group, except those made to trading companies or other wholesale and retail firms)/(all internal sales within a group, except those made to trading companies or other wholesale and retail firms, plus all group sales to external firms or consumers).

18. The U.S. dollar values for Taiwan have been converted using the exchange rate of 26.24 New Taiwan dollars per U.S. dollar at the end of 1994.

19. There may be some other cases of internal purchases that we are not aware of, owing to missing data.

20. Taiwan has had a 30 percent tariff on imported autos, and also a domestic content requirement that 50 percent of parts and components for sedans be made in Taiwan. Until 1994 it also banned imports from Japan. Despite these restrictions, auto imports accounted for one-third of total sales in 1994, with the largest imports coming from Japanese automobiles produced in the United States.

References

Amsden, Alice H. 1985. "The State and Taiwan's Economic Development." In *Bringing the State Back In*, edited by Peter B. Evans, Dietrich Rueschemeyer, and Theda Skocpol. Cambridge: Cambridge University Press.

———. 1989. *Asia's Next Giant: South Korea and Late Industrialization*. New York: Oxford University Press.

Aoki, Masahiko. 1990. "Towards an Economic Model of the Japanese Firm." *Journal of Economic Literature* 28(1): 1–27.

Aoki, Masahiko, and Hugh Patrick. 1994. *The Japanese Main Bank System*. Oxford and New York: Oxford University Press.

Biggart, Nicole Woolsey. 1990. "Institutionalized Patrimonialism in Korean Business." *Comparative Social Research* 12: 113–33.

Egan, Mary Lou, and Ashoka Mody. 1992. "Buyer-Seller Links in Export Development." *World Development* 20(3): 321–34.

Evans, Peter B. 1995. *Embedded Autonomy: States and Industrial Transformation*. Princeton, N.J.: Princeton University Press.

Feenstra, Robert C., Deng-Shing Huang, and Gary G. Hamilton. 1997. "Business Groups and Trade in East Asia: Part 1, Networked Equilibria." Working paper 5886. Cambridge, Mass.: National Bureau of Economic Research (January).

Feenstra, Robert C., Tzu-Han Yang, and Gary G. Hamilton. 1999. "Business Groups and Product Variety in Trade: Evidence from South Korea, Taiwan and Japan." *Journal of International Economics* 48(1): 71–101.

Fields, Karl J. 1995. *Enterprise and the State in Korea and Taiwan*. Ithaca, N.Y.: Cornell University Press.

Friedman, Daniel, and K. C. Fung. 1996. "International Trade and the Internal Organization of Firms: An Evolutionary Approach." *Journal of International Economics* 41(1–2): 113–37.

Gold, Thomas B. 1986. *State and Society in the Taiwan Miracle*. Armonk, N.Y.: M. E. Sharpe.

Hamilton, Gary G. 1997. "Organization and Market Processes in Taiwan's Capitalist Economy." In *The Economic Organization of East Asian Capitalism*, edited by Marco Orrù, Nicole Woolsey Biggart, and Gary G. Hamilton. Thousand Hills, Calif.: Sage Publications.

Hamilton, Gary G., and Robert Feenstra. 1995. "Varieties of Hierarchies and Markets." *Industrial and Corporate Change* 4(1): 93–130.

Hamilton, Gary G., Wongi Choe, Chung Ku Kim, and Eun Mie Lim. 1999. "Riding the Tiger's Back: A Reassessment of the Asian Development State." Paper presented at the annual meeting of the American Sociological Association, Chicago, 1999.

Hoshi, Takeo, Anil Kashyap, and David Sharfstein. 1990. "The Role of Banks in Reducing the Costs of Financial Distress in Japan." *Journal of Financial Economics* 27: 67–88.

———. 1991. "Corporate Structure, Liquidity, and Investment: Evidence from Japanese Industrial Groups." *Quarterly Journal of Economics* 106(1): 33–60.

Kim, Eun Mee. 1997. *Big Business, Strong State: Collusion and Conflict in South Korean Development, 1960–1990*. Albany, N.Y.: State University of New York Press.

Kim, Hyuk-Rae. 1993. "Divergent Organizational Paths of Industrialization in East Asia." *Asian Perspective* 17: 105–35.

———. 1994. "The State and Economic Organization in a Comparative Perspective: The Organizing Model of the East Asian Political Economy." *Korean Social Science Journal* 20: 91–120.

Lee, Keun. 1999. "Corporate Governance and Growth in the Korean Chaebols: A Microeconomic Foundation for the 1997 Crisis." Unpublished paper. Seoul National University, Seoul.

Lim, Haeran. 1998. *Korea's Growth and Industrial Transformation*. New York: St. Martin's Press.

Lincoln, James R., Michael L. Gerlach, and Christina L. Ahmadjian. 1994. "Keiretsu Networks and Corporate Performance in Japan." Unpublished paper. Haas School of Business, University of California at Berkeley (December).

Orrù, Marco, Nicole Woolsey Biggart, and Gary G. Hamilton, eds. 1997. *The Economic Organization of East Asian Capitalism*. Thousand Hills, Calif.: Sage Publications.

Rauch, James. 1999. "Networks Versus Markets in International Trade." *Journal of International Economics* 48(1): 7–37.

Wade, Robert. 1990. *Governing the Market: Economic Theory and the Role of Government in East Asian Industrialization*. Princeton, N.J.: Princeton University Press.

Woo, Jung-en. 1991. *Race to the Swift: State and Finance in Korean Industrialization*. New York: Columbia University Press.

Discussion

Stability, Efficiency, and the National Organization of Production

Neil Fligstein

Robert Feenstra, Gary Hamilton, and Deng-Shing Huang raise one of the deepest questions for economics and economic sociology: If market processes select efficient systems of social organization, how do we account for the persistent differences we observe in the social organization of national capitalisms? There are at least three ways to answer this question. One could argue that these social relationships do not matter for firm survival and that it is important only to have basic factors in place like economies of scale and scope (Chandler, Amatori, and Hikino 1997). One could also argue that the persistence of differences across societies results from the fact that firms are not directly competing, and therefore not experiencing similar selection pressures (Fligstein 1997). Their ability to maintain different forms of social organization may result from a lack of market integration or the use of trade barriers of various kinds to prevent integration.

Finally, one could argue that there is in fact more than one way to organize to attain profit-maximizing outcomes in a given market. This is the approach that Feenstra and his colleagues favor. They use standard tools and assumptions in the economics of industrial organization to consider why this might be the case. The model they present considers the decisions of firms to integrate to form business groups. Although they never define business groups, they appear to be referring to how family-owned firms in the Korean and Taiwanese societies draw the boundaries of their firms by deciding what products to produce.

They suggest that groups may form in one of three ways: they may integrate around upstream production (in their terminology, U-groups) and sell to many wholesalers and retailers; they may integrate in downstream production (D-groups) and use a large number of suppliers of raw materials; or they may choose to vertically integrate (V-groups) the firm from the beginning of the production chain to the end. The model that informs this decision to form groups starts with the idea that the decision is based on how much profit can be captured by integration. If there is free entry in markets for firms and groups, then the gains to integration will end at the point at which the profits gained from integration go to zero.

The interesting twist in the model is the assertion that there may be more than one equilibrium solution to the integration problem (that is, the degree to which it makes sense for groups to integrate). The authors demonstrate this possibility by showing how, at different elasticities of substitution for intermediate products, different numbers of groups with different integration strategies manage to capture the profits. The model assumes that firms face different elasticities because of what their competitors do. Thus, if a given set of competitors integrate, they can charge a given firm higher prices for their needed inputs. All firms therefore have to integrate or risk having inputs priced too high. The authors use the model to show that fewer highly integrated groups exist at a given equilibrium, while a larger number of less integrated groups exist at another equilibrium for the same parameters. They also use the model to show that highly integrated groups have a higher percentage of internal sales and tend to be larger than groups that are integrated on upstream or downstream products only.

The point of this exercise is to suggest why Taiwanese business groups and Korean business groups, which, the authors argue, exhibit very different structures of integration, may both be rational responses to market conditions. The argument can be made that both types of business groups may be able to capture gains from coordination, but that they have pursued different strategies to do so. Feenstra and his colleagues present data on both societies' major business groups to illustrate this point. They claim to demonstrate that Taiwanese business groups generally are not highly integrated and tend to be relatively small. Korean firms either follow the Taiwanese pattern or, if they do sell a substantial part of their production internally, are very large. There are few intermediate cases, as the model would predict.

I am impressed by the fact that a model motivated by economic assumptions is able to produce arguments for multiple equilibria in drawing the boundaries of the firm. This suggests that the plethora of social arrangements we observe across societies can be plausibly thought of as equally efficiency-enhancing, or at least profit-maximizing. This is not a problem for sociologists who are prepared to believe that there is more than one way to organize capitalist markets for firms.

For sociologists, however, this modeling strategy of producing multiple equilibria does present empirical problems. That a certain set of empirical distributions of firms is roughly consistent with a given model is not enough evidence to conclude that the arrangements are optimal, because the alternative hypotheses about what might cause these social relations (such as political control over trade, regulatory control over a given industry, or a general lack of competitive integration across markets located in different geographical locations) are not directly evaluated. In this case, one is left assuming that both the chaebol and the Taiwanese strategies are efficient under certain conditions.

This criticism is even more important if the model predicts the existence of multiple equilibria. As sociologists always expect about economic models, if one can easily develop a model for two equilibria, then theoretically a model can be developed to describe any situation that persists as profit-maximizing. If one reasons back from existing arrangements to theoretic accounts, one is always going to end up with an argument that they are profit-maximizing. If one starts with the view that multiple equilibria are possible in the same industry or market, then every arrangement may theoretically be shown to be profit-maximizing under the right conditions.[1]

I would like to take up three issues. First, I want to be more critical of the model and take issue with how well it fits the data. Second,

I want to consider an alternative account of what these data mean. Finally, I want to return to the uneasy problem of profit maximization and effectiveness.

What Do the Data Really Show?

I want to question the empirical characterization of what is distinctive about the Korean and Taiwanese firms. I disagree with Feenstra and his colleagues that the most important feature of these business groups is their degree of integration. Indeed, the average level of integration (using internal sales as a measure) in firms is only 11.3 percent in Korea (table 3.1) and 7.0 percent in Taiwan (table 3.2). If one eliminates retail trade, this average level is only 6.7 percent in Korea and 4.7 percent in Taiwan. Korean firms are more integrated than their Taiwanese counterparts, but these averages are hardly very different. Indeed, almost 93 percent of the activities of both Korean and Taiwanese firms do not feed into one another. Although there is vertical integration, it does not appear to be the main focus of firm strategy.

I think the most obvious counterinterpretation focuses not on the issue of vertical integration but on diversification of products, as the authors note. A Herfindahl index of the degree to which firms are diversified shows Korean firms with an index of .52, compared to .35 for the Taiwanese. Korean firms are also much larger and, as the authors note, put out many more kinds of products than their Taiwanese counterparts. This appears to be the real difference between Korean and Taiwanese firms that needs explaining, not their degree of vertical integration.

A More Sociological Account

What would account for the higher level of product diversification of Korean firms? Sociological theories of firms and markets often start with the problem of uncertainty and view managers as trying to control or reduce the effect of uncertainty on outcomes. The nature of the uncertainty that managers and owners may face is determined by the particular economic and political situation in which they find themselves. Thus, if raising capital is the main source of resource dependence, firms find ways of co-opting or, if that fails, managing their dependence on lenders. If state managers allow them financing only if they undertake certain kinds of economic projects that are deemed in society's interest, then managers are likely to follow the rules to get financing and to make the investments they have been asked to make.

Sociological theories of organization emphasize that organizational actors are interested in the survival of their firm. This is what is meant by "effectiveness" in the organizational literature (Fligstein 1996). Sociologists see firm survival as dependent not only on the buyers and sellers in the markets in which they operate but on states, workers, and suppliers; in a given situation, these other groups may prove pivotal to firm survival. To ensure firm survival, managers and owners must stabilize their social relations with these important actors in their world. One way to ensure survival may be to deploy your capital efficiently enough to attain economies of scale and scope. But this is not the only strategy available to managers and owners. They can use their power and influence to create stable understandings and social relationships between themselves, governments, competitors, and workers. I have called these stable understandings and the social structures they help create in particular markets "conceptions of control" (1996).

A sociologist analyzing Taiwan and Korea would turn to history in order to understand the evolution of institutional arrangements and how these produced the distinctive social structures that characterize large firms in these societies. The sociologist's interest would be in understanding the nature of the uncertainties that managers and owners faced and in asking why firms diversified as a result. Sociological analyses of Taiwan and Korea would focus on the rapid transition into capitalism since 1950, preexisting authority structures and organizations, and the political alignments of elites and workers (Hamilton and Biggart 1988; Fligstein 1996). War and imperialism have both played important parts in shaping the institutions of Asian societies. Once those societies began to industrialize, their governments and economic elites fixed on a set of rules, practices, and arrangements that subsequently structured what was possible (Steinmo, Thelen, and Longstreth 1992).

The Korean chaebol were a product of the pre-war Japanese occupation and the post–Korean War political situation. Families controlled businesses in a manner based on the Zaibatsu model prevalent in pre–World War II Japan. The chaebol form has its roots in the pre–Korean War era (Song 1997). South Korea emerged from the Korean War with a devastated economy. The South Korean government had a strongly centralized and bureaucratic structure that came to direct the economy by controlling the financial sector and influencing firms' investment decisions (Amsden 1989).

The government decided to use the chaebol as the private-sector agents that would guide the development project. The family owners of the chaebol created integrated conglomerates to enter markets deemed essential by the government. Governments helped reduce their uncertainty and help guarantee chaebol survival in two ways. First, the chaebol received capital from the government. Second, the government guaranteed them labor peace by cracking down on unions. This hierarchic relationship with the government stabilized firms and allowed them to make profits. The families who owned the firms gave up some autonomy over what they would produce, but gained political stability and stable labor relations in return.

The Taiwanese case played out quite differently. The postwar government in Taiwan was the exiled Chiang Kai-shek regime. The existing firms in Taiwan were organized as traditional Chinese family businesses. These firms were small and internally financed. Taiwanese development was less directly led by the government, although the government did play a role in building infrastructure and controlling the financial sector (Gold 1986). There was not as much direct state control over financial markets, however, as in Korea. Firms were made to compete in free markets internally and for exports.

The industrial groups that formed in Taiwan were the unintended result of the Taiwanese modernization project. Although there were many opportunities for family-owned firms to make money, there was no well-developed capital market. Taiwanese businesses started out smaller, less diversified, and owned by extended families (Gold 1986; Wade 1990). To take advantage of new economic opportunities, Taiwanese family-owned firms would spin off new firms to family members. A firm would supply capital to start a new business run by a relative. The main sources of uncertainty were the lack of capital and the low level of development. These problems were solved by families keeping tight control over their main operations. Instead of building highly diversified firms, Taiwanese families were more likely to help other family members by loaning them money to start new enterprises.

For Feenstra and his colleagues, these processes produced the vertically integrated chaebol in Korea and the less integrated, smaller Taiwanese firms. They do not disagree with this story. (Indeed, it is the one they tell in the introduction and conclusion to their chapter.) Their point is that these were successful strategies because the chaebol maximized profits by vertically integrating while the Taiwanese firms maximized profits by remaining smaller and less integrated. Both types of business groups worked at one of the authors' equilibria.

From a more sociological perspective, these structures are not profit-maximizing, but effective. The owners and managers of firms used already existing organizational vehicles to manage their most severe uncertainties. The most successful of these firms were the ones that did this most effectively. The formation of business groups in Asia, from this perspective, is about the attempt to produce stability for the entire group. (For a similar economic argument about Japanese keiretsu, see Aoki 1988.)

The most interesting features of the firms under study here are their varied approaches to ownership and the diversity of the products they produce. Both the chaebol and Taiwanese firms are run mainly by families. But in Korea, families have chosen a tightly integrated structure that produces many products and looks a lot like a diversified American corporation. In Taiwan, families have chosen to keep their firms small and to invest in other family members' enterprises. They have not created large integrated structures but are happy to influence the family group through more informal mechanisms.

From a sociological point of view, these differences are the product of the initial organization of production and the political projects that produced the development projects. Families with capital began with a set of institutional blueprints and took what their political system gave them. They managed to build extremely successful business empires that have grown large and brought prosperity to their societies along quite different lines.

The Question of Efficiency and the Asian Financial Crisis

The economic account proposed by Feenstra and his colleagues and the more sociological account (what I would call a political-cultural approach) are both attempts to make sense of the diversity of social arrangements that exist in market societies. At one level, they are very different theories and cannot be easily "tested" against one another because they rely on quite different explanatory mechanisms to explain the same outcomes.

It is my view that one of the main differences between economics and sociology is epistemological. Sociologists are strongly committed to the empirical world because they believe it is "real" and that it is what one should be trying to understand directly. Actors make decisions in real contexts, and their decisions are shaped by their cognitive processes, their current understandings of their situations, their relative ability to frame actions given their understanding, and, of course, their real structural position. This decisionmaking becomes even more complex when one considers that decisionmakers rarely act alone or without the cooperation and active participation of others. So managers and owners must take others in their organizations into account, and their actions must ensure the positive participation of others.

One aspect of this fundamental difference between sociology and economics is that sociologists care about what actors think and what they mean and how others interpret their actions. Sociologists note that what actors pay attention to can differ across situations, and that who they are attempting to co-opt may differ as well. For these reasons, sociologists who study economic processes within and between firms are open to spotting the nuances of social situations and how they differ across contexts. They are also attuned to how these differences play out in and around organizations.

Since owners and managers generally are dealing with uncertainty and bounded rationality, they simplify their worlds to promote the survival of their firms. Thus, managers pay attention to more than just their customers. Sociologists find it natural for owners and managers to worry about where their capital is coming from, what their competitors are doing, how governments affect their businesses, and how to secure worker cooperation (particularly in developing societies).

Sociologists are prepared to accept that there is more than one way to produce a given set of goods and services. Working toward the use of economies of scale and scope is one strategy to do this, but it is only part of the story. I think both sides can learn from one another in the following sense. It is, of course, possible that in some circumstances the price system (or agency or transaction costs) can drive firms toward single forms of social organization. It is also the case that such mechanisms can even be shown to be compatible with multiple equilibria, as Feenstra and his colleagues have suggested. But the political, cultural, and organizational factors I have suggested are mechanisms by which market structures appear as well. Careful empirical work is necessary to understand why and under what conditions different mechanisms predominate.

I want to use these different perspectives to comment briefly on the crisis of the Asian economies in the late 1990s. In their conclusion, Feenstra and his colleagues suggest that while these downturns were particularly difficult for Korea, the Korean model appears to be recovering and remains successful (that is, some of the chaebol have disappeared, but the form survives). The authors seem to hedge their point as to why this is so. On the one hand, if these forms are profit-maximizing, then they should survive the downturns that were mainly induced by poorly executed macroeconomic policies. But the authors also seem to imply that these forms are highly institutionalized and weathered this crisis because they are the organizational vehicles by which the largest and most important firms in these societies are organized. This is a sociological explanation that emphasizes the interests of economic and political elites in the given status order.

Critics of Asian capitalism have decried the group arrangements discussed here as "crony capitalism." If the economic model presented by these authors has any validity, this perspective makes no sense. If business groups are in fact capturing profits by using integration, then it is difficult to argue that these relations are forms of rent-seeking.

The sociological view is more sympathetic to the crony capitalism critique. If the social organizations of both Taiwanese and Korean firms are political projects that stem from the desires of their firm owners to produce stable worlds and are based on their relations to governments, then they clearly are open to rent-seeking. This would seem particularly true of the chaebol, which are much more dependent on government. But the sociological approach would want to ask the question in a more empirical fashion. Is this crisis caused by the business groups inefficiently allocating capital and choking off competition, as suggested by the crony capitalism thesis?

The evidence does not seem to point in this direction. The huge devaluation in currency set off a large-scale crisis in Korea because of the chaebol's dependence on dollar-denominated loans (as Feenstra and his colleagues suggest). The Taiwanese firms, which relied more on internal financing, were less vulnerable to currency devaluation because it did not affect their ability to raise capital. These crises are more about the dependence of firms on foreign capital than about the social organization of production. It would seem that the chaebol as a way of organizing capital to make profit in the context of government-led development will continue to be successful if they can solve their financial problems.

For a sociologist, this kind of empirical question is pivotal to making sense of the causes of stability and instability in accounting for differences in national styles of business. The chaebol might disappear only if the entire business structure and its relation to the government were in crisis. Their disappearance would not reflect their efficiency in an "economies of scale and scope" sense, but the general legitimacy of state-business relations as a whole.

Here is how I envision the possible transformation of the chaebol. Under the impetus of this financial crisis and the pressure applied by international authorities in the International Monetary Fund (IMF), the government could privatize the banking system and stop directing development. Then the families who run the chaebol would have to decide which of their businesses to keep and which to sell off. I would predict that the biggest and best managed of the chaebol would survive as diversified firms. But because their relationship to their government would be radically altered, they would be a different kind of firm. Instead of depending on the government for loans and industrial policy, managers and owners would come to more closely resemble their American and European counterparts in how they made strategic decisions. This huge reorganization would have nothing to do with capturing gains in integration and quite a bit to do with trying to find a new way to create a stable world for the firm.

I would like to thank James Rauch and an outside reviewer for their helpful comments.

Note

1. There is at least one unrealistic assumption in the model. The model assumes that the integration of a particular market is a closed system. The vertically integrated firms could not coexist with firms that were less integrated. In practice, this would mean that Taiwanese and Korean firms were never competing in the same market. Given that both countries are very export-oriented and produce many of the same products (such as textiles, consumer electronics, computer equipment, and automobile parts), this assumption is certainly violated. This means that in practice Korean chaebol are competing with small-scale Taiwanese firms.

References

Amsden, Alice. 1989. *Asia's Next Giant: South Korea and Late Development*. New York: Oxford University Press.

Aoki, Masahiko. 1988. *Information, Incentives, and Bargaining in the Japanese Economy*. Cambridge: Cambridge University Press.

Chandler, Alfred, Franco Amatori, and Takashi Hikino. 1997. *Big Business and the Wealth of Nations*. Cambridge: Cambridge University Press.

Fligstein, Neil. 1996. "Markets as Politics: A Political-Cultural Approach to Market Institutions." *American Sociological Review* 61: 656–73.

———. 1997. *Markets, Politics, and Globalization*. Uppsala, Sweden: Uppsala University Press.

Gold, Thomas. 1986. *State and Society in the Taiwan Miracle*. Armonk, N.Y.: M. E. Sharpe.

Hamilton, Gary G., and Nicole Woolsey Biggart.1988. "Market Culture and Authority." *American Journal of Sociology* 94: S52–94.

Song, Byong-Nak. 1997. *The Rise of the Korean Economy*. New York: Oxford University Press.

Steinmo, Sven, Kathy Thelen, and Frederic Longstreth. 1992. *Structuring Politics*. Cambridge: Cambridge University Press.

Wade, Robert. 1990. *Governing the Market*. Princeton, N.J.: Princeton University Press.

Chapter 4

Market Organization and Individual Behavior: Evidence from Fish Markets

Alan Kirman

Markets, their organization, and the relationships that develop within them have long held a fascination for historians, anthropologists, and sociologists. Economists have, despite the work of Douglass North and others, tended to take some specific model of market organization as given and then to examine the aggregate behavior of the market. The intricacies of particular forms of market organization are not considered relevant to the aggregate outcome. Frequently the individuals are thought of as acting independently of each other and linked only through the price system. In this case, the market is generally assumed to behave like an individual. Alternatively, one can think of a market as a game and model a situation in which every agent is consciously and strategically interacting with every other agent. This approach produces two difficulties. First, it is difficult to characterize the equilibrium behavior, and second, such a vision ignores the specific intricate trading and relational networks that develop and influence market outcomes. Agents may well interact strategically, but there are few markets where they do so with all the other agents. In this chapter, I look at a very special type of market, fish markets, which present a special interest for economists partly for historical reasons and partly because the perishability of fish eliminates any physical link between successive markets. Complicated considerations of inventories are eliminated.

The theme of this chapter is that the aggregate behavior of a market may well present clear regularities that can be thought of as representing some sort of collective rationality. However, these features should not be thought of as corresponding to individual rationality. The process of aggregation itself may lead to more regular behavior on the aggregate level. Finally, the relationship between the behavior of the individual participants and the market as a whole is mediated by the way in which the market is organized.

I argue, using data for a particular market—the wholesale fish market in Marseille—that, while a fish market may behave at an aggregate level in the way that economists might expect, this is an artifact of the aggregation of a complicated interactive system, not the reflection of simple, conventional individual behavior. "Nice" aggregate behavior may appear in a situation where individuals are clearly not acting in isolation and where the market framework is very different from that described in the standard competitive model.

If I am to claim that market structure influences aggregate outcomes, then I must show how some particular feature of aggregate behavior is related to the details of the organization of the market. One such feature of the market used here as an example that may contribute to the regularity of the aggregate outcomes is the existence of specific and durable trading relationships. In the second section of the chapter, I suggest an economic explanation for the emergence of the trading relationships in this sort of market. I argue that the sort of features suggested by the theory developed there are consistent with the empirical evidence. This theory is based on learning from experience rather than on optimizing behavior. However, to go beyond the simplest market situation one must resort to simulations that, fortunately, show that the features of the theoretical model are preserved in more complicated versions.

Finally, I develop an approach to modeling these rather complicated markets using even simpler learning rules for the traders, and I show how these models are capable of generating specific features very similar to those observed in the real market, particularly those involving price dispersion and the type of relationships observed between buyers and sellers.

Fish Markets: Background

The long history of fish markets includes both descriptions of how they function and economic analysis. An important feature of Mediterranean life, the fish market was one of the first markets to develop, and thus it is not surprising that there have been many accounts of its functioning, from the time of the Greeks until the present.

A detailed account of the functioning of the surprisingly sophisticated main fish market in Rome is given by Claire De Ruyt (1983). The first market "bubble" is probably that for red mullet, a Mediterranean fish that became highly prized at the time of the Romans. Cicero, Horace, Juvenal, Martial, Pliny, Seneca, and Suetonius all discuss in detail the price of this fish, which they considered to be unreasonable and based on a fad. The price of large red mullet specimens rose to extraordinary levels during the Roman Empire, and at one point three specimens fetched 30,000 sesterces ($300). Even allowing for the problems of converting to modern prices, this was out of proportion to other consumption goods. As a result, the emperor Tiberius was moved to impose a sumptuary tax on the fish market. The bubble burst, and Macrobius noted later that prices had become "reasonable" again.

Fish markets are particularly interesting to economists because they exhibit two features that make them a natural subject of economic analysis. First, as has already been mentioned, fish is a perishable good; since stocks cannot be carried over, formal analysis of this market is simpler. Second, the organization of such markets varies from location to location, for little obvious reason. In Iceland, for example, there are thirty-two auctions, eighteen of which are English ("rising price") and fourteen of which are Dutch ("descending price"). At Lorient in France, fish is sold through a combination of pairwise trading and auction, while at Sète it is sold by Dutch auction, and at nearby Marseille by pairwise trading. The fish market in Sydney, Australia, is conducted as two simultaneous Dutch auctions. The comparison of different outcomes under different forms of organization is an obvious research topic, but one that has received little attention to date.

Fish Markets: Previous Economic Analysis

Fish markets have a long tradition in the economic literature. They were the subject of a debate between John Stuart Mill (1869/1967) and William Thornton (1870) over the nature of the prices charged for the same type of fish during auctions. Mill argued that there were either several possible equilibria or no equilibrium prices at all, while Thornton took the opposing view that what were observed were out-of-equilibrium or disequilibrium prices. This debate was reopened by Negishi (1986) and was followed by a discussion by Ekelund and Thommesen (1989) and a reply by Negishi (1989). What emerged as the central issue of that debate is relevant to this chapter: How do we interpret the notion of equilibrium in markets such as the fish market?

Since fish is perishable, markets such as Marseille can be considered as ones in which stocks are fixed and prices are used as a strategic variable in each period.[1] This view depends, of course, on the sort of market organization under consideration. In auction markets such as Sète, the stocks are indeed fixed, but the prices can hardly be thought of as strategic variables since they are set through the auctioneer. However, in a market such as Marseille, the prices are set by pairwise negotiation. No prices are posted, and total stocks are not common knowledge at the beginning of the day.

Most economists who have studied fish markets in the past (see Gorman 1959; Barten and Bettendorf 1989) have not taken note of the particular organization of the fish market but have simply analyzed it in terms of a standard competitive market and estimated a demand system for it.

The Marseille Fish Market

The wholesale fish market for Marseille, situated at Saumaty on the coast at the northern edge of Marseille, is open every day of the year from 2:00 A.M. to 6:00 A.M.[2] More than five hundred buyers and forty-five sellers come together (although not all are present every day) and transact more than 130 types of fish.[3] Prices are not posted, and all transactions are pairwise. There is little negotiation, and prices can reasonably be regarded as take-it-or-leave-it prices given by the seller. The data set consists of the details of every individual transaction made over a period of three years. The data are systematically collected and recorded by the Chambre de Commerce de Marseille, which manages the market. The following information is provided for each transaction:

1. The name of the buyer

2. The name of the seller

3. The type of fish

4. The weight of the lot

5. The price per kilo at which the lot was sold

6. The order of the transaction in the daily sales of the seller.

The data run from January 1, 1988, to June 30, 1991. The total number of transactions for which we have data is 237,162.

When the market was being reorganized, provision was made for the establishment of an auction. Since neither buyers nor sellers were favorable to this development, however, the market has remained organized as before. Given the number of agents involved in the same place at the same time on a regular basis, one might be led to expect that at any given moment the same type of fish would be sold at essentially the same price. This, as will be seen, is far from the case. Furthermore, one might expect to see evidence of the standard assertion that, as the day progresses, prices diminish. This is again not true.

Market Properties and Individual Behavior

Fish markets are complicated affairs, organized in different ways and containing an intricate network of interacting relationships. It is therefore not at all clear that the behavior one observes in the aggregate in such markets corresponds to some enlarged version of the behavior of the individual in the classical competitive environment. Yet, in economics, aggregate behavior is often tested to see whether it meets restrictions that can be derived directly from individual maximizing behavior. Thus, it is common practice to treat data arising from aggregate purchases of some commodity over time as if these were the expression of the competitive demand of some representative individual. This approach involves a number of implicit assumptions, in particular that the underlying micro data observed can be thought of as corresponding to individual Walrasian demand, and furthermore that aggregation considerations do not invalidate the use of restrictions derived from individual behavior.

In this section of the chapter, I explain, following Härdle and Kirman (1995), that empirically, for the particular market we study, certain standard properties can be shown to hold at the aggregate level, in spite of the complexity of its organization. In particular, the property that might be thought of as "downward-sloping demand curves" for individual fish holds at the aggregate level, although it does not hold at the individual level. Thus, in a certain sense, the "regularity" of the aggregate behavior is stronger than that of individuals. It might, however, be argued that this market should be modeled not as a competitive one but rather as a full-blown game, and that in this case one could derive the monotonically declining price-quantity relation. However, there is no theoretical reason to expect any such simple aggregate relation. In neither the competitive nor the strategic case is there any simple passage from individual to aggregate behavior. Such a conclusion is directly in the line of work by Gary Becker (1962), who showed that downward-sloping demand curves at the market level could be derived from random individual choice behavior subject only to a budget constraint.[4] He concluded that "households may be irrational and yet markets quite rational," but a better summary of the results here would be that "sophisticated and complicated individual behavior may lead to simple aggregate properties."

I am specifically concerned with the properties of the purchases of the particularly perishable goods—different types of fish—for which we have data at the individual level from the Marseille fish market. Although, as I have mentioned, fish markets have been widely analyzed in the economic literature as competitive markets, it should become clear that it is inappropriate to think of purchases on such markets as corresponding to Walrasian demand, nor is it appropriate to think of prices as equating aggregate supply and demand.

The important point here is that it is the organization of the market for the product in question that prevents it from being competitive in the standard sense. Although it has often been argued that in markets of this sort the presence of a sufficient number of buyers and sellers is sufficient to make the price competitive, this may well not be the case, and casual empiricism suggests that considerable price dispersion may persist. In this case, the notion of a single "market price" loses its significance. This problem arises in the other types of market arrangements used for the sale of fish. If different lots of the same type of fish are auctioned off successively, for example, the average price does not necessarily correspond to the price that would have solved the Walrasian problem for that market.[5] Yet, with rare exceptions, such as Laffont and Vuong (1993, 1995), the standard approach in the empirical literature has been to treat even auction data as if they were generated by competitive behavior. The problem here is that techniques for the econometric analysis of data arising from differently organized markets, such as auctions, have been little developed, and there is always a temptation to return to standard and sophisticated techniques, even if these should not be applied to the type of market in question.

Two justifications are commonly used to suggest that the competitive outcome is a reasonable prediction more or less independent of the type of organization. One is that used by those who perform experiments with, for example, "double auctions." They argue that despite the fact that in the markets they examine individuals set prices and propose quantities, the result is the same as it would have been if obtained through the competitive mechanism. This argument reinforces my basic point. The fact that we observe an aggregate result that conforms to the predictions of a particular model does not justify the conclusion that individuals are behaving as they are assumed to behave in that model.

A different justification is offered by Anton Barten and Leon Bettendorf (1989), who are well aware of the basic difficulty. They suggest that the aggregate behavior in the fish market can be reduced to that of a Walrasian mechanism by looking at an inverse demand system. They reason that:

> Price taking producers and price taking consumers are linked by traders who select a price which they expect clears the market. In practice, this means that at the auction the wholesale traders offer prices for the fixed quantities which, after being augmented with a suitable margin, are suitably low to induce consumers to buy the available quantities. The traders set the prices as a function of the quantities. The causality goes from quantity to price.

Although Barten and Bettendorf are only making explicit what is commonly done, it is clear that one should *prove* that, even if the auction price is well defined, it is indeed related to prices charged to consumers through a simple markup. Necessarily, if different purchasers pay different prices and the markup principle does apply, then a distribution of prices is observed on the retail market.

This brings us back to an important point. Since our market does not function as a standard auction, and individual traders strike bargains among themselves and are well aware of each others' identities, different prices can be charged to different purchasers for the same product, and indeed they are. Thus, discrimination is a major factor in generating the distribution of prices, which, as I have already mentioned, is an important feature of the market. There are significant variations in the average prices paid by different buyers (see Kirman and McCarthy 1990), and a similar phenomenon has been observed by Graddy (1995) for the Fulton fish market in New York. Thus, reducing prices to averages may well lose a significant feature of the data. Furthermore, the average price cannot be regarded as a reasonable sufficient statistic, and other properties of the price distribution must be taken into account. This reduces the plausibility of the argument advanced by Barten and Bettendorf 1989.

As I have mentioned, an alternative approach would be to suggest that the fish market can be modeled as a situation of strategic interaction and then to define the appropriate game-theoretic equilibrium price notion. If there is such an equilibrium—given the heterogeneity of the actors on the market, the fact that they meet pairwise, and the fact that there is imperfect information—it surely corresponds to

Figure 4.1 Distribution of Prices of Whiting for Each Day of a Week

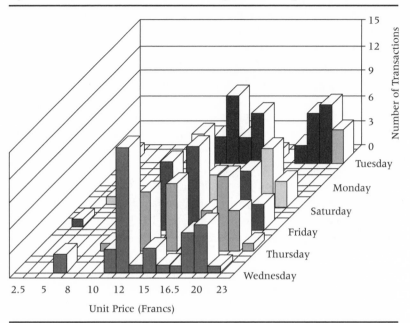

Number of Transactions

15

12

9

6

3

0

Tuesday

Monday

Saturday

Friday

Thursday

Wednesday

2.5   5   8   10   12   15   16.5   20   23

Unit Price (Francs)

Source: Kirman and Vignes (1991).

a nondegenerate price distribution (see Diamond 1987; Butters 1977) rather than to a single "competitive" price for each type of fish.

A first simple test, therefore, of whether this market can be thought of as a good approximation of a competitive one is to look for any significant price dispersion. If this is indeed the case, some sort of model in which the interaction between agents is considered—and there are many—would be more appropriate. Such evidence is overwhelming, as is pointed out in Härdle and Kirman (1995) and Kirman and Vignes (1991). Successive prices charged for the same type of fish to different buyers may differ by as much as 30 percent. Figure 4.1 illustrates the distribution for the prices for whiting over a week.

This raises a second question. Given that there is significant dispersion of prices, does this situation correspond to some sort of equilibrium? All of the models mentioned that predicate a distribution of prices argue that there is an *equilibrium distribution*. This is also what one might expect from simple game-theoretic analysis. Yet, observing this sort of variance and the difference in mean prices from day to day, one might well ask whether there is any sort of coherence of market behavior over time. Perhaps the way in which this market is organized simply precludes any sort of intertemporal stability.

To see whether there is any aggregate stability over time one might ask whether the distribution of prices remains unchanged from period to period. If this is the case, an equilibrium or steady state might be an appropriate concept. It is important to understand what is meant here by distribution. What is examined is the total number of kilos transacted in each price interval. The alternative would be to count the *number of transactions* at each price level, but in effect, we consider each kilo as a separate transaction. This distinction is usually avoided in the literature on price dispersion where individuals demand one unit of an invisible good (see, for example, Rothschild 1973; and Diamond 1987). Thus, the distribution h of prices is given by

$$h(p_j) = \frac{\sum \text{quantities sold at prices in the jth interval}}{\text{Total quantities sold}} \qquad (4.1)$$

Given the fluctuations in daily activity and the varying presence of different traders, it seems unlikely that there would be any constancy from day to day, for example, and this is clear from figure 4.1, which shows the distribution of prices of whiting over a week.

However, if the market is, in a certain sense, repeating itself, one might hope to find some sort of regularity for longer periods. Recall that this is an empirical question; I have not produced any theoretical reason to explain whether such time consistency might occur, nor, if it should, do I have any reason to choose any particular length of period. In Härdle and Kirman (1995), we tested for the constancy of the price distribution of each of four fish—trout, whiting, sardines, and cod—from month to month. The results were striking, as can be seen in figures 4.2 and 4.3. (The results for the other two fish were very similar.)

On the horizontal axis are the transaction prices, and each figure is a nonparametric smoothing of the histogram defined in equation 4.1. Although the visual evidence is convincing, we also tested formally for the intertemporal stability of the price distributions for these fish.

Figure 4.2 Trout, Months 7 Through 9, 1987

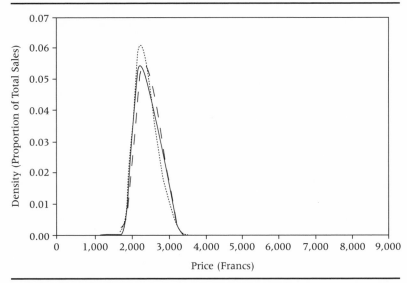

Source: Härdle and Kirman (1995).

One proceeds by fitting a function to each of the distributions, and then measuring the variations in the distance of each of these functions from the others. Figures 4.2 and 4.3 show the results for each of three months for sardines and trout.

Full details of the tests for the stability of the distribution are given in Härdle and Kirman (1995). We could not reject the hypothesis that the distributions were constant over time. That is, when we considered the following hypotheses,

$$H_0: f_i = f_j \quad i \neq j$$
$$H_1: f_i \neq f_j \quad i \neq j$$

(where f_i is the distribution for month i)

for each of four fish over the three months in question, in none of the cases could we reject H_0.

There are, of course, a number of technical problems, which I will not enter into here. Just as an example, although the evidence from

Figure 4.3 Sardines, Months 7 Through 9, 1987

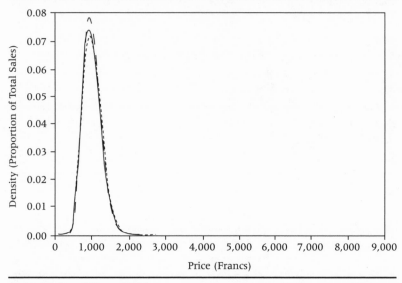

Source: Härdle and Kirman (1995).

the fitted densities seems to be clear, for the *statistical* tests for stability to be valid the observations should be independently and identically distributed. This cannot be strictly true, since, for example, certain buyers pay higher prices. Although these buyers are probably of particular types, such as restaurants, they are identified only by code. There is therefore no prior information on which to condition and which allows one to treat them as belonging to different categories.[6]

Nevertheless, there is overwhelming evidence that the distribution of the prices of each fish are remarkably stable over time. This in turn leads me to suggest that the market has organized itself into a rather stable state even though a great deal of rather complicated interaction may be going on at the individual level.

Price Quantity Relations

The previous discussion shows that although the market has a certain sort of aggregate stability, it cannot be characterized as competitive. However, one might then ask whether it satisfies any of the standard aggregate properties that one would have expected from a competitive market. If such properties can be established, then, given the complicated nature of this particular market, they may well be "emergent" rather than the simple sum of well-behaved autonomous individuals. A classical property is that of a monotonically declining price quantity relation for each of the fish chosen. Härdle and Kirman (1995) use nonparametric methods to fit two different aggregate price quantity relations and find that these relations, in contrast to those at the individual level, do indeed exhibit monotonicity. Economists faced with this evidence might be tempted to say that what we are looking at is aggregate demand and that in this market it obeys the "law of demand." However, as the earlier remarks suggest, the first obvious question is: Does what we are looking at correspond to what we normally define as demand?

Until Marshall, there was considerable discussion as to the correct definition of demand for a single commodity. However, in the more formal literature there was convergence on the rather abstract Walrasian notion that demand simply represents the quantity that an individual wishes to purchase at given prices that he is unable to influence. The subsequent theoretical literature concentrated largely on the extension of the analysis to interdependent markets and the problem of demand systems rather than on single demand equations that still maintained the abstract Walrasian approach. Until recently, the idea that demand should be treated in this way has not been significantly challenged in either the economic or econometric literature. In taking this step, the profession abandoned the idea that market structure might be of importance in determining the outcome of the market.

Once the twentieth-century literature had converged on this precise theoretical definition, econometricians used it as their justification for concentrating on more sophisticated techniques for the estimation and identification of demand systems. They retained the agreed definition of competitive demand: the quantities of goods an individual would buy at given prices were he constrained only by his income. In Elmer Working's (1927) paper, the conceptual nature of demand and supply is not questioned. The only real problem for Working was determining which of the two was fluctuating over time. However, for many markets—and this is the object of the exercise here—this conceptual framework is not satisfactory. For example, in the whole-sale fish market in Marseille all transactions are bilateral and no prices are posted. When we look at the relation between the prices charged and the quantities purchased on this sort of market, we must ask a number of the same questions that were very present in the earlier debate as to the appropriate notion of "demand."

What are the implicit assumptions underlying the usual empirical analysis based on Walrasian demand theory? Are they appropriate here?

The first question that arises is whether the purchaser of a good is in fact the final consumer. If this is not the case, then one would have to show that the properties of individual demand carry over to the properties of the quantities purchased by an intermediary at different prices. If one considers the simple case of a purchaser who is a retailer and has a monopoly locally of the product that he buys and resells, then it is easy to construct examples in which this will not be the case. This question was raised by Working (1927) and mentioned again in the classical studies by Henry Schultz (1938), who used individual properties of demand but made his estimations using data for farm prices, not shop prices. More recently, in the specific study of the Belgian fish market already mentioned, Barten and Bettendorf (1989) refer to this question.

The second problem arises even if one accepts that the final consumers are present on the market in question and that it does function "competitively." This problem is the one of identification—in this case, separating out supply changes from demand changes. In a truly Walrasian—or Arrow-Debreu—world, such a distinction could, of course, not be made, since all transactions over time represent one supply and one demand decision taken in some initial period. However, this problem is usually circumvented in the empirical literature by making an implicit assumption of stationarity and separability, that is, assuming that the market is somehow repeated over time and that decisions are taken in the same way at each point in time. This assumption should, of course, be tested, but meanwhile one can talk of successive observations. The evidence I have given of the stability of price distributions over time does support the idea that there is some sort of intertemporal stability of this market. However, in this case the appropriate theory is the one referred to as temporary general equilibrium theory. The problem with this theory is that, without full knowledge of future prices, expectations have to be taken into account. Without unreasonable assumptions about these expectations, short-run demand loses many of the properties of its Walrasian counterpart. It does not satisfy homogeneity or the Weak Axiom of Revealed Preference, for example (see, for example, Grandmont 1983). Trying to fit a demand system based on the usual theoretical restrictions thus makes little sense.

However, assume for a moment that we are prepared to accept the idea that changes in the prices of fish do not result in a large amount of intertemporal substitution, that is, fishmongers are relatively myopic. In that case, thinking of a sequence of equilibria in a market that repeats itself is more acceptable. Once again this explains why, when considering particular markets, fish has been so widely used as an example (by Marshall, Pareto, Hicks, for example), since with no stocks, successive markets can be thought of as independent. In our case, when fitting our price-quantity relations, we are implicitly treating price changes as the result of random shocks to the supply of fish, although the amount available is, at least in part, a result of strategic choice.

The main problem here, however, is that of aggregation. If we fit a demand system in the usual way, we are assuming that market behavior corresponds to that of an individual. Examination of individual data reveals none of the properties that one would expect from standard individual demand. To see this, look at figures 4.4 and 4.5, where quantities of fish of a particular type, sole, purchased by two different buyers are plotted against the price at which those quantities were purchased.

It would take an extremely optimistic econometrician to argue that the relationship between prices and quantities in these cases is best fitted by monotonically declining relations.[7] Thus, even if such properties are found at the aggregate level, they cannot be attributed to individual behavior.

This is one side of the problem of aggregation. The other is that even if individuals did happen to satisfy certain properties, it is by no means necessary that these properties carry over to the aggregate

Figure 4.4 Sole—Buyer 1

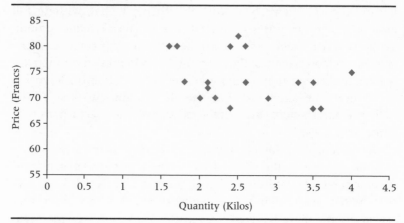

Source: Author.

Figure 4.5 Sole—Buyer 2

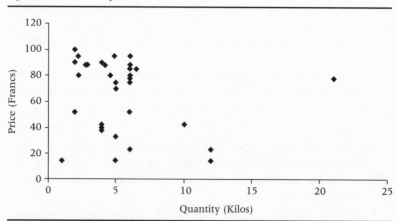

Source: Author.

level (see, for example, Sonnenschein 1972, and Debreu 1974). When the two are taken together, there is no direct connection between micro and macro behavior. Some economists have recently insisted on this basic difficulty in the testing of aggregate models (see Kirman 1992; Summers 1991; Lewbel 1989) when discussing representative individual macro models. As Lewbel observes, however, this difficulty has not stopped the profession—nor is it likely to—from testing individually derived hypotheses at the aggregate level. Hence, although some empirical properties of the aggregate relationships between prices charged and quantities purchased can be established, I would suggest that these should be viewed as independent of standard maximizing individual behavior.

However, determining whether the data do satisfy certain properties that would feature in a standard model is of interest in itself. If the market exhibits such features and one claims that they do not correspond to classical individual maximizing behavior, then one must explain how the market organizes itself so that this comes about. A particular characteristic that one does observe in our case is that over the day markets do more or less clear in the sense that the surplus left unsold never exceeds 4 percent. Furthermore, since sellers become aware, from the reactions of buyers to their offers, of the amount available on the market, and vice versa, it would not be unreasonable to expect average prices to be lower on those days when the quantity is higher. However, the situation is not simple. For example, some buyers transact early, before such information becomes available, and others make only one transaction for a given fish on a given day. Thus, to deduce such a property formally would require very strong and unrealistic assumptions.

To establish whether a property such as that of a monotone and negative relation between quantities purchased and prices will hold, one must empirically examine the behavior of the market. The proposition to test when considering the four fish taken as examples is whether the quantities purchased at each price $D(p)$ for those fish display the monotonicity property, that is, for $p \neq p$ and $p > 0$ p in R_+^4,

$$\big(D(p) - D(p')\big) \cdot \big(p - p'\big) \leq 0$$

In particular, such a property, if D(p) is interpreted as a standard demand system, is described as the Law of Demand by Hildenbrand (1983), following Hicks. It implies that each partial "own demand curve" for the fish should be downward-sloping.[8] Since there is no a priori reason to impose any sort of functional form on the system, the simplest approach is to make a nonparametric fit of the price-quantity relations to establish a weaker property—that for each individual fish they are negatively sloped. Such an approach is open to the criticism that it does not take into account substitution effects between fish. There are three responses to this. First, many buyers, such as restaurant owners, have a predetermined vector of fish quantities, which they do not change very much in response to relative price changes. Second, there are other buyers who buy only one type of fish and therefore do not substitute. Finally, some of the exogenous factors influencing the amount of fish available, such as weather, are common to many fish, thus limiting the amount of substitution possible. For all of these reasons, each of the four fish is analyzed separately.

Undertaking an analysis of the "demand" for each fish amounts to eliciting some of the basic characteristics of the data. Basically, the idea is to take the data for a given fish and aggregate them by taking the quantity of that fish sold on a particular day and the weighted average price for that day.[9] The problem with this approach is how to separate strategies. Not only are there variations in the supply of fish owing to factors like the weather, but more fish is landed on active market days by choice. The variations over the week are due in part to obvious institutional factors (fish shops are closed on Sundays), but also to more indirect ones. As Robbins (1932) observed before his discussion of the market for herring in England: "The influence of the Reformation made no change in the forces of gravity. But it certainly must have changed the demand for fish on Fridays."

The resulting data are fitted by nonparametric smoothing methods (for a full account, see Härdle 1990). Nonparametric methods are used since they enable one to pick up any lack of monotonicity of the fitted curve over some particular price range. Nevertheless, in all four cases the fitted curves are indeed monotone decreasing over a large part of their range. An example is given in figure 4.6.

Figure 4.6 Sardines

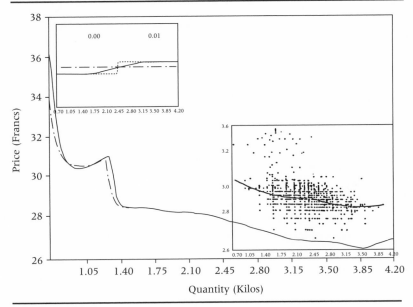

Source: Härdle and Kirman (1995).

Of course, simple inspection of a graph is not sufficient, but formal evidence is given in Härdle and Kirman (1995) that the monotonicity property of the price-quantity relation is robust. Furthermore, aggregation across all fish produces even more striking results, as can be seen from figure 4.7.

The important point to reemphasize here is that the "nice" monotonicity property of the aggregate price-quantity curves does *not* reflect, and is *not* derived from, the corresponding characteristics of individual behavior. Nor indeed, given the previous discussion, should we expect it to be.

A Simple Model

At this point, one might argue that for complicated markets so much is going on at the micro level that it is not worth trying to build a formal model of such a situation. One should be content to

Figure 4.7 All Fish

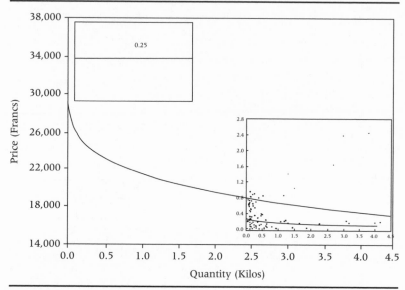

Source: Härdle and Kirman (1995).

have found regularity at the aggregate level. This conclusion seems to me to be throwing in the sponge a little too quickly. It is surely worth at least reflecting on the nature of the model involved. What sort of formal model would be appropriate for fish markets?

Here I sketch a simple model of the sort of market typified by Marseille and restrict myself, for simplicity, to the case of one type of fish. Consider the market for one perishable product with m sellers and n buyers.[10] The market evolves in a fixed number T of rounds. Each seller i has strategies that at each round t specify a vector $X_{it} \in R^n_+$ of the prices he will charge to each of the buyers. A strategy for each buyer j specifies at each round t a demand function $q_{jt}(p):R_+ \rightarrow R_+$. Both the choice of the prices set and the demand functions depend on two things: first, on the strategies of the other players, and second, on who has met whom in the market. The model is then completed by specifying a matching process that, in keeping with the literature, is assumed to be random. Thus, a matching at time t, a realization of the random variable, is a mapping g from the integers $J = \{1, \ldots n\}$ to the integers l = {1,. . . m}. A probability distribution must then be specified over the outcomes of the matching process for every time t. One might think, as an example, of each buyer as choosing a seller with uniform probability 1/m, independently at each time t. However, many other matching processes could be considered, including those in which some particular buyers and sellers are always matched together. A best strategy for a buyer i, then, for each realization of the matching process and for the associated price vectors of each seller j and demand functions of the other buyers h ≠ i, is a demand function for each period t. Similarly for a seller, it consists of specifying the best price vectors for each matching and each period.

The market described by this simple model can be envisaged as follows:

Period 0: Initial stocks become available.

Period 1: Sellers specify prices. Buyers specify demands. Matching takes place. Transactions occur.

Period 2: Given their information about what happened in period 1, sellers respecify prices and buyers respecify demands. Matching occurs. Exchanges follow.

Period T: Last specifications by sellers and buyers occur, as well as last matching and exchanges.

As it stands, I have done no more than give a framework that enables me to define the concept of an equilibrium. To characterize precisely the nature of an equilibrium requires that the strategies chosen in response to the strategies of others be derived from maximizing behavior. For example, a buyer might maximize his expected utility at each round t, given the known strategies of the other players and the matching up until t. The technical difficulties here in proving the existence of an equilibrium are illustrated by Roger Kormendi (1979) and Roland Benabou (1988). Nevertheless, even if we make the appropriate assumptions to obtain an equilibrium, we have made little progress, since what really interests us are the characteristics of the outcomes in the market.

As it stands, there is not much to be said in terms of observable and testable behavior, at either the aggregate or individual level. For example, whether or not we give a complete specification of the maximizing behavior of the individuals, the sort of model I have sketched could not rule out extensive price dispersion (particularly with price discrimination being possible since each seller knows the buyers' characteristics). Furthermore, there is no necessary tendency for prices to decline during the day, as is commonly supposed, and as I have mentioned, there is no a priori reason to assume that individual buyers will or will not search.

One important point to emphasize is that any strategy must be such that if the information set up to time τ is the same in two realizations, the next component of the strategy at time $\tau + 1$ should be the same. Thus, it is important to specify what is known at each time. If, for instance, the individuals know only their own initial stocks and observe only their own transaction outcomes, they are much more limited than if they observe everything that has occurred. Furthermore, individuals may well choose to condition strategies on a limited part of the information they have available.

Having given an outline of the structure of the sort of process involved in the market, it is not surprising that the outcomes do not necessarily satisfy standard competitive properties at the individual or aggregate level, since observed transactions are the results of the interaction between buyers' and sellers' strategies. The observed purchases reflect the demand of agents given what they have observed and given the strategies of the other players. If there is an equilibrium, it should be the case that the market clears at the end of the day. The difference from day to day on the market is the amount of fish available, owing in part to exogenous factors such as weather, but also owing to the choice of sellers when anticipating demand changes. This latter factor should be incorporated into a complete model, but doing so makes things more complicated, since the market days are no longer independent.

All of this suggests that there is not a great deal to be gained by attempting a full-blown optimizing approach to modeling the sort of market that we are dealing with here, not because we cannot prove the existence of an equilibrium, but because we cannot obtain any simple, testable characteristics of that equilibrium.

A Model with Less Rationality: Trading Relationships Within the Market

Although the equilibrium in a fully optimizing context may be difficult to characterize, it is possible that agents use simple rules to make
their choices, in which case the "equilibrium" outcome depends on
the rules chosen. It may be that a simpler approach based on more
rudimentary behavior is more effective in reproducing the sort of
phenomena we observe on real fish markets.

To illustrate this point, just let me remark that we observe in markets like Marseille rather specific patterns of trading relationships.
These must be responsible, at least in part, for the sort of price dispersion that is observed. In addition, although these networks may play
an important role in determining market outcomes, nothing is said in
the sort of model discussed earlier about their impact or their evolution. They could be included as restricting the information available to
the individuals, but this would merely make the analysis less tractable.

What is the nature of the trading relationships? On the one hand,
there are those buyers who regularly buy from the same seller and are
extremely loyal, and on the other hand, there are people who shift
between sellers all the time. This lack of allegiance of itself seems to
be a feature that one should try to explain. Returning to a full game-
theoretic model becomes extremely complicated because one now
has to develop a dynamic game in which the experience of playing
with each seller is taken into account. Alternatively, one has to think
of a situation in which people have strategies that are so complicated
that they can take into account all the possible prices they might face
from each of the different sellers.

What I would like to suggest here is that we develop a much simpler theoretical model in which people simply learn from their previous experience and in consequence change their probability of visiting
different sellers as a result of their experience. I argue that models of
this sort, which attribute very little computational ability or general
reasoning capacity to individuals, may be capable of generating specific features of real markets. This sort of "bounded rationality" approach has received a lot of attention but is often dismissed for its lack
of rigor. In fact, the analysis of the evolution of the "state" of the market in the model can be perfectly rigorous given the specific choice of

rules for the agents. However, we have come to accept that the restrictions we impose on the preferences of individuals, unlike other behavioral rules, are not ad hoc. Therefore, if we replace those assumptions, which by their very nature cannot be empirically tested, with other rules, we are subject to the criticism that we lose the rigor of "proper micro foundations." Let me simply suggest that maximization is not necessarily a reasonable assumption when both the criterion to be maximized and the set of alternatives are highly complicated, and that something is to be gained from simplifying our account of individuals' behavior in complicated situations.

As an example, consider a model that my colleagues and I (Weisbuch, Kirman, and Herreiner 2000) developed as a simplified version of the Marseille fish market. We considered a situation in which buyers do not anticipate the value of choosing sellers but rather develop relationships with sellers on the basis of their previous experience. To be more precise, they update their probability of visiting sellers on the basis of the profit they obtained in the past from them. If we denote by $J_{ij}(t)$ the cumulated profit, up to period t, that buyer i has obtained from trading with seller j, then the probability $P_{ij}(t)$ that i will visit j in that period is given by

$$P_{ij}(t) = \frac{\exp(\beta\, J_{ij}(t))}{\sum_j \exp(\beta\, J_{ij}(t))}$$

where β is a reinforcement parameter that describes how sensitive the individual is to past profits. This nonlinear updating rule will be familiar from many different disciplines and is a special form of reinforcement learning. The latter is based on two simple principles: agents make probabilistic choices between actions, and actions that have generated better outcomes in the past are more likely to be used in the future. Such a learning process has long been adopted and modeled by psychologists (see, for example, Bush and Mosteller 1955) and has recently been used widely in evolutionary and experimental game theory (see Roth and Erev 1995). This approach has the great advantage that it requires no specific attribution of rationality to the agents other than that they are more likely to do what has proved to be successful in the past. The particular form chosen here is widely used. It is found

in the model developed by Larry Blume (1993), for example, to analyze the evolution of the use of strategies in games. Also known as the
logit decision, or the quantal response rule, it is widely used in statistical physics as well.

Consider as an example the case in which there are three sellers in
the market. At any point, each buyer has a probability of visiting each
of the sellers. Thus, he is represented by a point in the three simplex
or triangle, as illustrated in figure 4.8. Each buyer is represented by
such a point in the simplex, and the nature of the relationships is illustrated by a cloud of points. A buyer who shops around—that is,
who is equally likely to visit each of the three sellers—is represented
as a point in the center of the triangle. If, on the other hand, he visits
one of the sellers with probability one, then he is shown as a point at
one of the apexes of the triangle.

Thus, at any point in time, the market is described by a cloud of
points in the triangle, and the question is: How will this cloud evolve?
If buyers all become loyal to particular sellers, then the result will be
that all the points corresponding to the buyers will be at the apexes
of the triangle, as in the right-hand triangle in figure 4.8. This might
be thought of as a situation in which the market is "ordered." On the
other hand, if buyers learn to search randomly among the sellers, then
the result will be a cluster of points at the center, as in the left-hand
triangle in figure 4.8. What Weisbuch, Kirman, and Herreiner (2000)
show is that the situation that develops depends crucially on the parameters β, the discount rate, and the profit per transaction. The stronger
the reinforcement, the more slowly the individual forgets, and the
higher the profit, the more likely it is that order will emerge.

It might be asked whether the features of the actual market in
Marseille reflect the sort of behavior predicted by this admittedly
primitive model. What the model suggests is that the transition from
disorder to order, as β changes, is very sharp. The change depends on
a critical value of β. This is different for each seller and depends on the
frequency of his visits to the market and his profit.

The important conclusion is that one should not expect to find individuals who shop around to some extent but are somewhat more
loyal to some sellers than to others. This is precisely what the data
shows. The behavior of buyers is highly bimodal. Consider the case

Figure 4.8 Buyers' Probabilities of Visiting Sellers

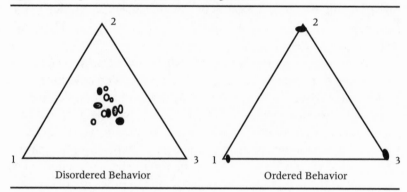

Disordered Behavior   Ordered Behavior

Source: Weisbuch, Kirman, and Herreiner (2000).

of cod. The figure 4.9 histogram shows the number of buyers visiting different numbers of sellers. There is a concentration of buyers who visit only one seller and then a distribution of individuals who visit several sellers, with a median of four per month.

The extent of the loyalty of customers for certain types of fish can be observed from the fact that, for example, 48 percent of all buyers bought more than 95 percent of their cod from one seller—the seller, of course, not being the same for all of these buyers. Thirty-three percent of buyers bought more than 95 percent of their sole, and 24 percent bought more than 95 percent of their whiting, from one seller. In both the whiting and sole markets, more than half of the buyers buy more than 80 percent of their fish from one seller. Furthermore, as the theory predicts, those sellers with the highest sales and those who come to the market most frequently are those who are most loyal. This recalls an earlier model (Whittle 1986) in which there are two sorts of activities, farming and trading, and under certain conditions, markets may emerge, with individuals practicing each of these activities where previously there had been only itinerant traders.

The model proposed by Weisbuch, Kirman, and Herreiner (2000) derives this sort of "phase transition" in a particularly simple model of stochastic choice. We use the "mean field" approach, which is open to the objection that random variables are replaced by their means and, in consequence, the process derived is only an approximation.

Figure 4.9 The Distribution of Loyalty of Buyers of Cod

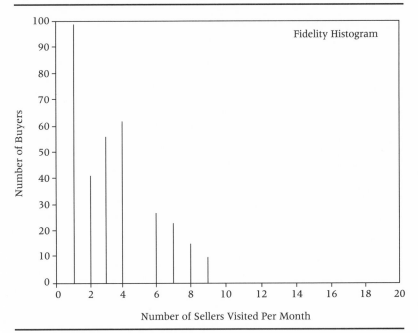

Source: Weisbuch, Kirman and Herreiner (2000).

The alternative is to consider the full stochastic process, but this is often not tractable. To study the stochastic model itself and to envisage several trading opportunities during the day, one must resort to simulations to see whether the theoretical results from the approximation are retained in more complex situations.[11] As it happens, they are. Indeed, quite elaborate versions of the model—in which individuals are faced with several periods and sellers modify their prices and quantities supplied in the light of past experience—still reproduce the "stylized facts" of the simple theoretical model, which are consistent with empirical observations.

An Even Simpler Modeling Approach

As is clear from the previous sections, the problem of modeling even such simple examples as fish markets is that if one tries to incorporate some of the realistic features of the microscopic interaction between the actors, the model rapidly becomes analytically intractable. One answer to this problem is provided by the so-called multi-agent modeling approach (see, for example, Arthur et al. 1997), in which agents are endowed with simple rules that govern their reaction to their economic circumstances. As time goes on, they place more weight on those rules that turn out to be more profitable. In one sense, the previous model is a special case of this, since the rules can be thought of as determining the choice of seller. However, once the rules are extended to cover a variety of choices, the behavior of the model quickly becomes too complicated to model formally. This suggests, by a sort of Occam's razor approach, that we should use a model with as simple an updating procedure as possible. In such a model one hopes to find, as emergent features, some of the salient aspects of the real empirical markets that interest us. In Kirman and Vriend (2000), we developed a simple model that reproduces two of the features of the Marseille fish market: a division between loyalty and shopping behavior on the part of buyers, and price dispersion. Furthermore, sellers learned to handle their clients in a way that corresponds to what happens in reality. In the theoretical model developed by Weisbuch, Kirman, and Herreiner (2001), the problem of handling several periods in the day was already sufficient to oblige us to resort to simulations. By adding the extra complication of pricing behavior and the handling of clients, there is little hope of producing a comprehensive theoretical model that reproduces all of the characteristics of the real market.

In the simple simulated model developed in Kirman and Vriend (2001), ten initially identical sellers and one hundred initially identical buyers met in the market hall for five thousand days for morning and afternoon sessions. They traded single individual units of a perishable commodity. On each day the sequence of events was as follows.

In the morning before the market opened, the sellers purchased their supply outside the market for a given price that was identical for all sellers and constant through time. The market opened, and the buyers entered the market hall. Each buyer required one unit of fish per day. All buyers simultaneously chose the line of a particular seller. The sellers then handled these lines during the morning session. Once the sellers had supplied all the buyers who were willing to purchase from them, the morning session ended. All unsatisfied buyers chose the line of a seller in the afternoon. After sellers sold to those buyers who were willing to purchase from them, the afternoon session came to an end. All unsold stocks perished. Those buyers who did purchase fish resold that fish outside the market at a given price that was identical for all buyers and constant through time.

Each buyer could visit at most one seller in the morning and one seller in the afternoon. What decisions did these actors face? Buyers had to choose a seller for the morning session. They then had to decide which prices to accept or reject during the morning session. If necessary, they also had to decide on a seller for the afternoon. Finally, they had to decide which prices to accept or reject during the afternoon session. Sellers had four decisions to make. They had to decide what quantity to supply, how to handle the line of buyers with which they were faced, what prices to set during the morning session, and what prices to set during the afternoon session.

In the model described, each agent used a classifier system for each decision; thus, each agent had four such systems "in his head." Each classifier system consists of a set of rules. Each rule consists of a condition "if . . ." and an action "then . . .," and in addition, each rule is assigned a certain strength. The classifier system decides which of the rules will be the active rule at a given point in time. It checks the conditional part of the rule and decides which rule, among all the rules for which the condition is satisfied, to choose. This is done by a simple auction procedure. Each rule makes a "bid" to be the current rule; this bid equals current strength + ε, where ε is white noise. The rule with the highest bid in this auction becomes the active rule. The white noise means that there was always some experimenting going on, and always some probability that a rule, however bad, would be chosen. The classifier system updates the strength s of a rule that has been active and has generated a reward at time $t - 1$ as follows.

$$s_t = s_{t-1} - c \cdot s_{t-1} + c \cdot reward_{t-1}$$

where $0 < c < 1$. Hence, as long as the reward generated by the rule on day $t - 1$ is greater than its strength at $t - 1$, the strength will increase. The strength of each rule converges to the weighted average of the rewards generated by that rule. What the reward is depends on the rule in question. Suppose that in our market example the rule for the buyer is of the form: *If the price proposed by the seller for one unit of fish in the morning is eleven francs, then accept.* The reward for using this rule would then be the profit generated by using it. In this case, the reward would be the price at which the unit of fish is sold on the retail market minus the price paid (eleven francs). When the model is started, the strengths of all rules are equal.

What the agents in this model are doing is learning by an even simpler version of reinforcement learning than that encountered previously. Details of the particular rules in the simulation model of the Marseille fish market can be found in Kirman and Vriend (2000).

Although such an approach seems to be innocent of theoretical presuppositions, it should be noted that the very choice of rules among which the agent chooses conditions the outcomes. Ideally, one would like to start with agents who are totally ignorant. However, this implies that they would somehow generate a set of rules with which they experimented. This pushes the analysis back many stages to a very fundamental level. What is done here is in line with standard practice, which is to provide the agents with a set of rules and simply note that this particular set of rules conditions, to some extent, the outcomes of the process. As an example, consider the fact that we would like agents to learn how to handle the lines with which they are faced. In an ideal world, we would like the agents to realize that their handling of the lines is important and to work out how to handle them. As it is, by giving different rules explaining how to handle lines, the modeler is already biasing the behavior of the seller by suggesting to him what is important in generating his profit. However, what is not biased is the choice among the rules presented. Thus, the rule chosen will be the best available for handling lines among those presented, given the agent's experience, but he might well himself have focused on some other aspect of the market. With these reservations, it is still worth examining the results of the simulations to see to what extent they reflect reality.

One might ask whether some of the features of the market could not be modeled in a more theoretical way. For example, in the afternoon session it seems as if buyers and sellers are faced with a version of the ultimatum game (see, for example, Güth and Tietz 1990). Since, in the model, sellers propose a price that buyers either accept or refuse, it would seem that the sensible price to propose is just slightly less than the price at which the fish could be sold on the outside market; this indeed is the subgame perfect outcome of the ultimatum game. However, it has long been noted that this is not what one observes in experimental outcomes or in reality. One obvious reason is that we are observing a repeated game in the market. Thus, a refusal today has implications for behavior tomorrow, even if agents are not aware of this. Buyers learn to accept or reject prices on the basis of the profitability of doing so, while sellers learn in a similar way which prices to ask. What is crucial here, as noted by John Gale, Ken Binmore, and Larry Samuelson (1995) and by Al Roth and Erev (1995), is that the relative speed of learning on each side of the market governs which outcomes occur. The importance of this becomes clear as soon as we look at the results of the simulations.

Let us first look at the prices asked and accepted in the morning session, as shown in figure 4.10.

There is first of all a lengthy period during which learning takes place, and then prices settle at ten francs, an amount that is one franc greater than the price at which fish is bought by sellers outside the market, and one greater than the perfectly competitive price. What is interesting is that during the learning period—which governs the final outcome—two things are going on. Sellers are learning to ask prices close to the ultimatum price, fourteen francs, which is one less than the price at which fish can be sold on the outside market. However, buyers are not learning as quickly to accept such prices. Where does this difference come from? The answer is that initially some buyers accept high prices because they have not learned to do otherwise. This encourages sellers to charge such prices. However, buyers start to find out that they can obtain higher profits by refusing high prices and accepting lower ones. There are always some such prices to be found. As sellers learn that buyers are not accepting their prices, they start to decrease the prices they ask, and simultaneously buyers, as they observe that the prices being asked are descending, start to decrease their acceptance levels. Once again, sellers' learning "leads" that of buyers, and as a result, the prices converge. Two separate learning processes

Figure 4.10 Time Series of Average Prices Asked and Accepted During
Morning Sessions

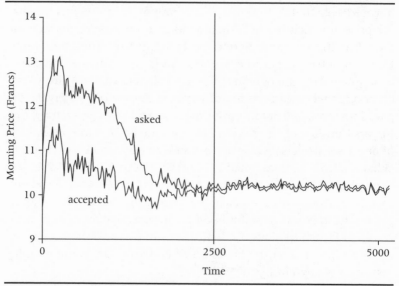

Source: Kirman and Vriend (2001).

are also going on in the afternoon, and once again convergence occurs, but to a higher price (eleven francs) than in the morning. The
evolution of afternoon prices can be seen in figure 4.11.

  This outcome might seem extraordinary, since if buyers become
aware that prices in the afternoon are higher than prices in the morning, they should presumably always buy in the morning. This is not correct. To see this, consider a situation in which the distribution of prices
asked is the same in the morning as in the afternoon. Suppose now that
those buyers who encounter prices in the upper tail of the distribution
reject them in the morning. The result would be that the average price
paid in the morning is lower than the average price paid in the afternoon. In other words, it is not the average price that is rejected. The figures show the average at any point in time. In figure 4.12, the price
distribution over the last 2,500 days is shown, and it can be seen that it
does not become degenerate and concentrated on one price. Thus, a
phenomenon observed on the real market in Marseille, as we saw earlier, emerges in our artificial fish market.

Figure 4.11 Time Series of Average Prices Asked and Accepted During
Afternoon Sessions

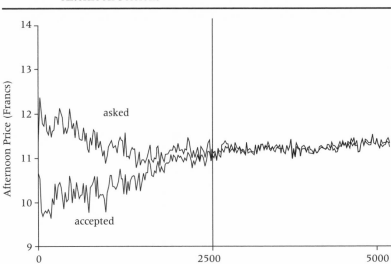

Source: Kirman and Vriend (2001).

A second feature of the real market, as discussed earlier, is loyalty. In the previous model, we simply established the pattern of loyalty but did not suggest any macroeconomic consequences of that feature. To pursue this question, we here construct an index of loyalty with a value equal to 1 if the buyer is perfectly loyal to one seller, and a value equal to 1/n where n is the number of sellers when the buyer systematically visits each seller in turn, that is, when he exhibits the most extreme "shopping around" behavior. More specifically, the loyalty index is given by:

$$L_{ij}(t) = \sum_{x=1}^{t} \frac{r_{ij}(t - x)}{(1 + \alpha)^{t-x}}$$

This is an indicator of how often buyer i visits seller j. It is a global statistic covering the whole period, but there is a discount factor represented by α. Here we took $\alpha = 0{,}25$ and $r_{ij}(t) = 0{,}25$ if buyer i visits seller j at time t, and α and $r_{ij}(t) = 0$ otherwise.

Figure 4.12 Price Distribution During the Last 2500 Periods

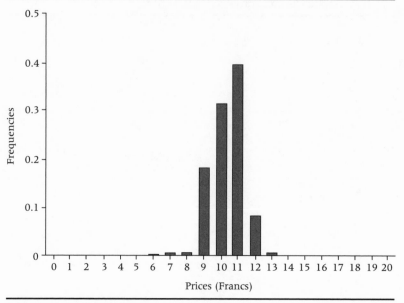

Source: Kirman and Vriend (2001).

Nothing was built into the rules of the sellers to make them favor loyal buyers. The sort of rules they had were of the form: *If loyalty equals a certain value, then choose a certain probability of serving that client,* and, *If loyalty equals a certain value, then charge p.* The probability chosen depends on whether the seller learns to favor loyal customers or not. Which p is charged depends on how successful that choice turns out to be. The time series of average loyalty is shown in figure 4.13.

What happens is that 90 percent of the buyers actually get a higher payoff by being loyal, as can be seen in figure 4.14. What this means is that when basically loyal customers shop stochastically from time to time at another seller, as they do, the profit realized is lower on average than when they buy from their regular supplier.

Furthermore, nine out of ten of the sellers get a higher profit when dealing with loyal buyers, as shown in figure 4.15. In other words, the profit, on average, from a loyal customer is higher than from a chance shopper. Here the difference in revenue represents the frac-

Figure 4.13 Time Series of Average Loyalty During Morning Sessions

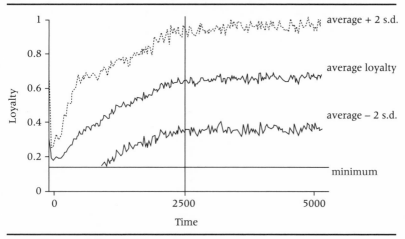

Source: Kirman and Vriend (2001).

Figure 4.14 Average Payoff Advantage for Buyers of Returning to Same Seller Versus Switching Sellers

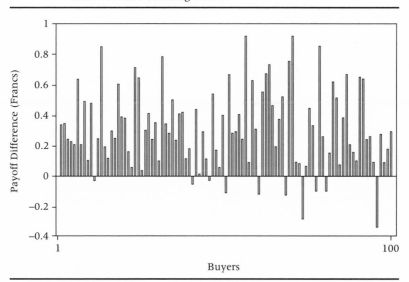

Source: Kirman and Vriend (2001).

Figure 4.15 Average Payoff Advantage for Sellers of Dealing with Repeat
Customers Versus Customers Who Switch

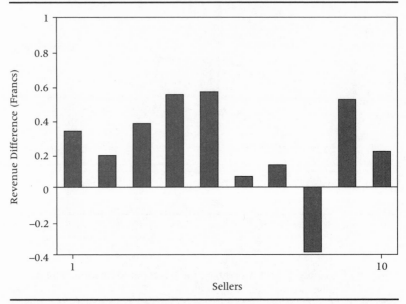

Source: Kirman and Vriend (2001).

tion of the average revenue from loyal customers above or below the
average profit realized from transactions with casual buyers.

This is a reflection of the fact that what is happening here is not a
zero-sum game. Only when a transaction takes place do buyers and
sellers realize a profit. Thus, payoffs are highly conditioned on acceptance and rejection and on the prices asked. The question then
becomes: How do loyal buyers tend to be handled by sellers? In all
but one of the cases, sellers learn to give priority in service to loyal
buyers, but to charge them higher prices than shoppers. Buyers learn
that when they become loyal, their profit is higher, since they are
more likely to be served even though they pay higher prices. Thus,
loyalty is profitable both to buyers and sellers.

What about the one seller who did not find loyal customers more
profitable than shoppers? This seller learned to charge low prices to
loyal customers but to give them low priority in the line. One might
ask why he did not learn to adopt the more profitable strategy learned

by the other sellers. The answer is that, with the sort of local learning that is going on, a move toward better service and higher prices for loyal customers can never develop. To make such a move would imply increasing prices and improving service. Buyers would immediately observe the higher prices, but not necessarily the better service in terms of priority in the line. They would thus be less likely to visit this seller. As this seller observed that his customers were drifting away, he would go back to his former behavior and therefore never learn the more profitable strategy.

It is interesting to note that on average in the Marseille fish market, loyal buyers pay higher prices than shoppers. Those buyers who buy more than 50 percent of their fish per year from one seller pay on average 5 percent more than the other buyers, even though almost all the large buyers are loyal. We thus have here a clear organizational feature with a very specific macroeconomic consequence.

What is interesting is that this very simple rudimentary artificial fish market generates some of the features that we observe on the real fish market. Such a model has the advantage that it can always be extended to examine other aspects of the real market, whereas constructing a theoretical model that incorporates all of these features is a more than ambitious task.

Conclusion

The message of this chapter is rather simple. Markets are an important feature of all economies. Each market is characterized by an organization and structure that have an impact on the outcomes observed. Fish markets, as markets for particularly perishable goods, are especially suitable for economic analysis and have frequently been so used. However, even standard models of fish markets do not seem well adapted to shedding light on the nature of the economic outcomes that one might expect. Curiously enough, the particular example I study, the fish market in Marseille, does exhibit rather a lot of regularity at the aggregate level. Nevertheless, this regularity is not due to individuals behaving in isolation in a regular way, as in the standard competitive model. The complicated organization of this sort of model breaks any simple link between individual and aggregate behavior. A number of the special features of this market, such as the special trading relationships that have developed, are difficult to account for in the standard framework. I have suggested a simple theoretical approach that does capture the formation of such trading relations. Furthermore, it seems that multi-agent simulation, an even simpler approach based on very simple rules for learning from past experience, is rather successful in reproducing some of the features of the real fish market and shows the link between organizational features and aggregate outcomes.

Notes

1. In fact, it is not quite true that all fish is perishable, since some species can be sold again the next day. However, buyers are perfectly aware of which fish have already been placed on the market; therefore, there are no inventories of fresh fish. It was this feature that led Pareto and Marshall to use it as an example. John Hicks (1989) pointed out that Marshall himself actually talked about the corn market, whereas his successors used the fish market to avoid the problems posed by the carrying over of inventories.

2. Unfortunately for the author, who visited it at these times, the market is now open during the day rather than at night.

3. In fact, some fourteen hundred buyers appear in the records, but many were hardly present.

4. This idea has been developed recently by Dhananjay Gode and Shyam Sunder (1993).

5. It should be noted here that Robert Wilson (1977) and Paul Milgrom (1981) have argued that in this framework too the price converges to the "true value" when enough objects are auctioned among enough buyers. Thus, here again, economists could argue that prices aggregate all the information that might be circulating in a market.

6. In treating our observations as drawn from the same population in this way, we are following theorists like Henri Theil (1971), who in his "convergence" approach thought of N consumers as independent elements of an infinite consumer population, and the parameters of their utility functions as identically distributed.

7. The examples shown here are not at all exceptional. We examined hundreds of such individual relations, and for almost none of them was there any significant evidence of a monotone declining relationship.

8. Of course, to take observed quantities purchased as representing a marginal curve is not correct, since the ceteris paribus condition is violated. However, this makes the resultant monotonicity more rather than less convincing.

9. An alternative approach that yields similar results (see Härdle and Kirman 1995) is to take the total quantities of fish sold at each individual price over the whole period.

10. In Kirman and Vignes (1991), we considered a continuum of buyers and sellers, but only to facilitate the solution of the technical problem of establishing the continuity of strategies.

11. A detailed discussion of this sort of problem is given by Masanao Aoki (1996), who thinks of the buyers in the markets as being partitioned between the sellers and each buyer as having a probability of transiting from one seller to another. He looks at the limit distributions of such a process.

References

Aoki, Masanao. 1996. *A New Approach to Macroeconomic Modeling.* New York: Cambridge University Press.

Arthur, W. Brian, et al. 1997. "Asset Pricing Under Endogenous Expectations in an Artificial Stock Market." In *The Economy as an Evolving Complex System II,* edited by W. B. Arthur, S. N. Durlauf, and D. Lane. Reading, Mass.: Addison-Wesley.

Barten, Anton P., and Leon J. Bettendorf. 1989. "Price Formation of Fish: An Application of an Inverse Demand System." *European Economic Review* 33: 1509–25.

Becker, Gary S. 1962. "Irrational Behavior and Economic Theory." *Journal of Political Economy* 70: 1–13.

Benabou, Roland. 1988. "Search, Price Setting, and Inflation." *Review of Economic Studies* 55(3): 353–76.

Blume, Lawrence. 1993. "The Statistical Mechanics of Strategic Interaction." *Games and Economic Behavior* 5: 387–424.

Bush, R. R., and F. Mosteller. 1955. *Stochastic Models for Learning.* New York: Wiley.

Butters, G. R. 1977. "Price Distribution of Sales and Advertising Prices." *Review of Economic Studies* 44: 465–91.

Debreu, G. 1974. "Excess Demand Functions." *Journal of Mathematical Economics* 1: 15–23

De Ruyt, Claire. 1983. "Macellum Marché Alimentaire de Romains." *Publications d'Histoire et d'Archéologie* 35. Université Catholique de Louvain, Louvain-la-Neuve.

Diamond, P. 1987. "Consumer Differences and Prices in a Search Model." *Quarterly Journal of Economics* 102: 429–36.

Ekelund, R. B., Jr., and S. Thommesen. 1989. "Disequilibrium Theory and Thornton's Assault on the Laws of Supply and Demand." *History of Political Economy* 21: 567–92.

Gale John, Ken Binmore, and Larry Samuelson. 1995. "Learning to Be Imperfect: The Ultimatum Game." *Games and Economic Behavior* 8: 56–90.

Gode, Dhananjay K., and Shyam Sunder. 1993. "Allocative Efficiency of Markets with Zero-Intelligence Traders: Markets as a Partial Substitute for Individual Rationality." *Journal of Political Economy* 101: 119–37.

Gorman, W. M. 1959. "The Demand for Fish: An Application of Factor Analysis." Research paper 6, series A. Birmingham, Eng.: Faculty of Commerce and Social Science, University of Birmingham. Abstract in *Econometrica* 28: 649–50.

Graddy, K. 1995. "Testing for Imperfect Competition at the Fulton Fish Market." *Rand Journal of Economics* 26: 75–92.

Grandmont, J. M. 1983. *Money and Value: Econometric Society Monographs in Pure Theory.* Cambridge and Paris: Cambridge University Press and Editions de la Maison des Sciences de l'Homme.

Güth, W., and R. Tietz. 1990. "Ultimatum Bargaining Behavior: A Survey and Comparison of Experimental Results." *Journal of Economic Psychology* 11: 417–40.

Härdle, Wolfgang. 1990. *Applied Nonparametric Regression.* Cambridge: Cambridge University Press.

Härdle, Wolfgang, and Alan Kirman. 1995. "Nonclassical Demand: A Model-free Examination of Price Quantity Relations in the Marseille Fish Market." *Journal of Econometrics* 67: 527–57.

Hicks, J. 1989. *Market Theory of Money.* Oxford: Oxford University Press.

Hildenbrand, W. 1983. "On the Law of Demand." *Econometrica* 5: 997–1019.

Kirman, Alan P. 1992. "Whom or What Does the Representative Individual Represent?" *Journal of Economic Perspectives* 6(2): 117–36.

Kirman, Alan P., and M. McCarthy. 1990. *Equilibrium Prices and Market Structure: The Marseille Fish Market.* Unpublished paper. GREQAM, Marseille.

Kirman, Alan P., and A. P. Vignes. 1991. "Price Dispersion: Theoretical Considerations and Empirical Evidence from the Marseille Fish Market." In *Issues in Contemporary Economics*, edited by Kenneth G. Arrow. London: Macmillan.

Kirman, Alan P., and Nicholas Vriend. 2001. "Evolving Market Structure: An ACE Model of Price Dispersion and Loyalty." *Journal of Economic Dynamics and Control* 25(3–4): 459–502.

Kormendi, Roger C. 1979. "Dispersed Transactions Prices in a Model of Decentralized Pure Exchange." In *Studies in the Economics of Search*, edited by Steven A. Lippman and John J. McCall. Amsterdam: North Holland Publishing Company.

Laffont, Jean Jacques, Hervé Ossard, and Quan Vuong. 1995. "Econometrics of First Price Auctions." *Econometrica* 63(6): 953–80.

Laffont, Jean Jacques, and Quan Vuong. 1993. "Structural Econometric Analysis of Descending Price Auctions." *European Economic Review* 37: 329–41.

Lewbel, A. 1989. "Exact Aggregation and a Representative Consumer." *Quarterly Journal of Economics* 104 (August): 622–33.

Milgrom, Paul R. 1981. "Rational Expectations, Information Acquisition, and Competitive Bidding." *Econometrica* 49: 921–43.

Mill, John Stuart. 1967 [1869]. "Thornton on Labor and Its Claims." In *Collected Works: Essays on Economics and Society.* Toronto: Toronto University Press.

Negishi, Takashi. 1986. "Thornton's Criticism of Equilibrium Theory and Mill." *History of Political Economy* 18: 567–77.

———. 1989. "On Equilibrium and Disequilibrium: A Reply to Ekelund and Thommesen." *History of Political Economy* 21: 593–600.

Robbins, Lionel. 1932. *An Essay on the Nature and Significance of Economic Science.* London: Macmillan.

Roth, A. E., and Ido Erev. 1995. "Learning from Extensive-Form Games: Experimental Data and Simple Dynamic Models in the Intermediate Term." *Games and Economic Behavior* 8: 164–212.

Rothschild, M. 1973. "Models of Market Organization with Imperfect Information: A Survey." *Journal of Political Economy* 81: 1283–1301.

Schultz, H. 1938. *The Theory and Measurement of Demand.* Chicago: University of Chicago Press.

Sonnenschein, H. 1972. "Market Excess Demand Functions." *Econometrica* 40: 549–63.

Summers, Larry H. 1991. "The Scientific Illusion of Empirical Macro-economics." *Scandinavian Journal of Economics* 93(2): 129–48.

Theil, Henri. 1971. *Principles of Econometrics.* New York: Wiley.

Thornton, W. T. 1870. *On Labour: Its Wrongful Claims and Rightful Dues, Its Actual Present and Possible Future.* 2nd ed. London: Macmillan and Co.

Weisbuch, Gerard, Alan Kirman, and Dorothea Herreiner. 2000. "Market Organization and Trading Relationships." *Economic Journal* 110: 411–36.

Whittle, P. 1986. *Systems in Stochastic Equilibrium.* New York: Wiley.

Wilson, Robert. 1977. "A Bidding Model of Perfect Competition." *Review of Economic Studies* 44: 511–18.

Working, E. J. 1927. "What Do Statistical 'Demand Curves" Show?" *Quarterly Journal of Economics* 41: 212–35.

Discussion

Comments and Further Thoughts on "Market Organization and Individual Behavior"

Alessandra Casella

At a very broad level, Alan Kirman's chapter reminds us that aggregating individual behaviors into a macro economy is a complicated matter. Far from confirming the comforts of models in which all individuals are assumed identical and thus each is representative of the whole economy, the Marseille fish market (of all places!) demonstrates empirically that the link between individual behavior and aggregate outcomes is so little understood that it still strikes us as unpredictable. Stated in these terms, the message is important and too often neglected, but well known.

In fact, the research summarized in this chapter belongs in a literature that challenges the foundations of contemporary economics in a more radical manner: not only does the aggregate market behavior not mirror the characteristics of the individual transactions, but it presents the standard regularities that are the cornerstones of economic theory, although these same regularities are absent at the individual level. In particular, the aggregate demand curve is downward-sloping, as we are all taught it should be, even while quantities and prices are not negatively correlated for individual buyers. Economic theory is often criticized, not least by sociologists, for the unrealistic demands it makes on individual rationality and for the equally unrealistic requirements of its paradigm, the perfectly competitive model. But there seems to be another possibility. Suppose that individual agents in fact are not fully rational, or that the market structure is indeed much more complex and decentralized than the ideal world of perfect competition. Could the market outcome still approach the one theorized by mainstream economists? The results in the first part of Kirman's chapter suggest that the answer could well be yes. In Gary Becker's (1962) striking sentence: "Households may be irrational, and yet markets quite rational."

Becker (1962) developed a theoretical model in which agents make random choices subject only to their budget constraints—sellers cannot offer to sell a good, or buyers to pay a price, beyond what they have on hand—while a central auctioneer quotes prices following a traditional Walrasian tâtonnement process: raising prices if there is excess demand and lowering them if there is excess supply. His result was that the mechanism still generated a downward-sloping market demand curve and an upward-sloping market supply. Thus, Becker's contribution was a theoretical model in which a competitive market organization, combined with random individual actions, yielded aggregate competitive outcomes.

More recently, Becker's idea has received new attention following the experimental work on double auctions. The double auction (often oral, and increasingly computerized) is the trading mechanism followed by most organized exchanges around the world; it governs transactions of stocks, bonds, metals, commodities, and derivative securities. Double auctions are called *double* auctions because not only multiple buyers but also multiple sellers compete for trade. During a double auction, both bids and asks are permitted, and exchange can happen at any time during the trading period; thus, there is dispersion in realized prices, and net trades are the result of many bilateral transactions. Because of their practical importance, their intuitive resemblance to the abstract idea of "the market," and the extreme difficulty of characterizing their properties theoretically, double auctions have been the object of a large volume of experimental work. By far the most important and most common result from these experiments is that double auctions appear to be very efficient market mechanisms, independently of both their specific details—which can vary widely—and, remarkably, the number of players. Three or four buyers and three or four sellers are sufficient to induce prices and allocations that closely approximate the competitive equilibrium (see, for example, the discussions in Smith 1982, and Friedman and Ostroy 1995). This remains true even when one side of the market is allowed to communicate and agree on "conspiracies" before the market is open. The conclusion is so robust that it has led to the hypothesis that something in the rules of the exchange is powerful enough to overcome both limits in players' rationality and opportunities for monopoly profits. The puzzle is compounded by theory's inability to characterize formally the equilibrium of a double auction or to rationalize the tendency toward competitive outcomes. A continuous double auction is a very complex game of incomplete information in which not only all price quotes but their specific sequence and their time, relative to the end of the period, transmit information and must be chosen and interpreted strategically. When the strategic interactions are studied explicitly (as in Wilson 1987), the problem is so difficult that it seems implausible that real-world individuals would be solving it routinely.

To explore this remarkable efficiency, Dhananjay Gode and Shyam Sunder (1993) have speculated that if the competitive outcome is somehow imposed by the rules of the game, then it should be observable even with "zero-intelligence agents," that is, agents making random choices subject only to a budget constraint, as in Becker (1962). The results support their intuition. Computer simulations show that prices quickly converge to their competitive values, and agents extract close to 100 percent of the maximum possible surplus (which corresponds to the sum of producers' and consumers' surplus in the efficient competitive equilibrium). Thus, Gode and Sunder's (1993) contribution is to extend Becker's (1962) intuition to a different, common, and complex form of market organization, the double auction, and to show through numerical simulations that individual rationality is not required for efficiency.

It is with this literature in mind that the research summarized in Kirman's chapter should be read. The Marseille fish market is not a double auction, because buyers and sellers are not immediately informed of all bids and asks available on the market. It is a more decentralized trading mechanism in which acquiring information on the transactions conducted by different sellers involves delays and costs. Given this added complication and what we know about double auctions, Kirman's statement that the market organization in Marseille is too complex to be modeled analytically seems very plausible. Nor do we know much about individual strategies, although, in line with the complexity of the market, some form of bounded rationality again appears realistic. The lack of a downward-sloping demand curve at the individual level and the dispersion in realized prices cannot be used as a strong argument for limited rationality— we have not specified the environment, and we do not know what optimal strategies may look like—but it indicates that individual behavior does not approach the competitive benchmark. Taking these three considerations into account—decentralized market exchange, individual bounded rationality, and noncompetitive realizations at the individual level—it is indeed remarkable that the actual data generated at the market level appear ordered in a well-behaved, downward-sloping demand curve. Once again, the market seems to obey the standard prescriptions of economic theory, even while the individuals do not, and the rules of the game depart from those of simple centralized markets.

If Becker's (1962) result was theoretical and Gode and Sunder's (1993) conclusion was established through computer simulations, Kirman and Vignes's (1991) and Härdle and Kirman's (1995) findings are empirical, based on the analysis of realized market prices and quantities. From this perspective, the research approaches the studies testing the efficiency of financial markets (see the survey in LeRoy 1989). However, these studies typically impose a stricter theoretical structure and posit rational and forward-looking individual behavior. As stressed by Kirman, an important advantage provided by the specific case of fish markets is that the good is perishable and the intertemporal considerations at the heart of asset markets can be bypassed. In addition, at least to a first approximation, supply can be considered the realization of a random process, dependent on the weather and the vagaries of different types of fish: realized traded quantities can indeed be mapped against prices and interpreted as tracing a demand curve, without the complications of an endogenous supply. The implication is that the interpretation of the market data is less ambitious than in financial markets but simpler and less subject to ambiguities: there is no joint testing of a specific theoretical model, no claim of overall efficiency, and less room for disagreement on the meaning of the results.

Disregarding for a moment what Becker (1962), Gode and Sunder (1993), and to a much lesser extent Kirman conclude in support of aggregate efficiency, notice what this line of work teaches us about aggregation. When the problem of aggregation is taken seriously, typically we are led to recognize that even very simple rules of behavior at the individual level can result in complex aggregate behavior (see, for example, Durlauf 1993; Blume 1993; and Kirman 1993). But the opposite is quite possible too: rules of individual behavior that we do not quite understand, and that may be complicated or conceivably random, can result in simple and predictable aggregate order. The conclusion has been obtained in other contexts (see, for example, Caplin and Spulber 1987)[1] but is important and worth repeating.

The fundamental question posed by Kirman's chapter is then whether we should care at all about the underlying structure of individual interactions. If the market follows the simple, "rational" regularities that economists have been positing all along, maybe traditional macroeconomists were right: there is a macroeconomy whose behavior is predictable and whose rules cannot be derived analytically from individual strategies. In fact, insisting on rigorous micro foundations may be sterile and misleading. And other social scientists, criticizing what they see as economists' extreme reliance on rationality, self-interest, and competition, may be ignoring that none of these characteristics need be very pronounced at the individual level. Kirman tells us that many buyers tend to remain faithful to one or a few sellers, suggesting that long-term personal relationships explain individuals' willingness to tolerate fluctuations and dispersion in prices. It is quite possible that the underlying micro relationships have more in common with personalized networks than with anonymous market behavior. Social connections, including those formed over time on the market itself, appear to dominate strict considerations of economic gain. But does it matter? If it does not matter for explaining market-level behavior, could it matter for policy?

The question can be divided into two parts. First of all, does the micro structure affect the macro performance? Even if markets are somehow able to "organize" the sum of all individual strategies, it does not follow that all features of the aggregate outcome, and especially the path toward a stationary equilibrium, are independent of individual actions. Gode and Sunder (1993) compare the market outcome of their computerized "zero-intelligence traders" with an identical experiment run with graduate business students. Human traders converged to the equilibrium price faster and with less volatility. (By construction, zero-intelligence traders do not learn, although they do eventually converge to the equilibrium price because of the discipline imposed by the budget constraint.) As for efficiency, human markets showed lower efficiency in the first period, but again, quick learning and thus higher and sustained efficiency in later periods. Although in this experiment the average efficiency across all periods was effectively indistinguishable between zero-intelligence agents and human traders, the pattern was different with the two types of traders, suggesting that one or the other may perform better in different environments.

Second, and equally important, policy may be concerned not only with aggregate outcomes but also with distribution. How do different individual rules affect the distribution of the market surplus? In the Gode and Sunder experiment, surprisingly enough, the dispersion in profits was much higher for zero-intelligence agents than for human traders.

It is clear then that to begin addressing these questions in the case of the Marseille fish market, more must be said about individual rules of behavior. And this is the scope of the second part of Kirman's chapter. The difficulty of the problem imposes limits on what can be asked: here the question becomes whether the observed regularity of matchings, together with the dispersion in realized prices, can be generated by plausible rules of thumb. Kirman discusses two alternative mechanisms, both of which can give rise to an "ordered" market in which buyers are "loyal" to particular sellers, even when confronted with fluctuations in prices and quantities. The first mechanism (proposed and studied in Weisbuch, Kirman, and Herreiner 2000) allows a buyer to choose whether to remain faithful to a particular seller, based on the cumulative history of returns from their bilateral relationship relative to the returns experienced by other market participants. Thus, the only decision is the choice of trading partner, but the available information is very rich and covers the whole market. The second mechanism (Kirman and Vriend 1998) studies a larger set of decisions (pricing to individual buyers and order of service, for the sellers; choice of seller and quantity demanded, for the buyers) but allows only local learning: each pair of traders knows only their own common history. The common conclusion is that microstructure "networks" (as opposed to anonymous market behavior) can indeed be the endogenous result of reasonable behavior.

The weakness of bounded rationality models is that the posited rules, and the set of allowed choices, always appear arbitrary. In this specific case, the observed empirical behavior of the Marseille fish market could provide very useful and strong tests. Kirman discusses (too briefly!) data supporting the observed correlation between high prices and privileged service for loyal customers. But more could be done by exploiting the aggregate regularities of the fish market. Do the bilateral relationships that emerge in the model aggregate into a downward-sloping market demand curve? Only the second of the models discussed in the chapter generates endogenous price series, but the criterion could be used both to test that specific model and, in the future, to compare it to other plausible mechanisms.

In general, more could be learned by linking the microstructure of transactions to the aggregate market outcome. At this point, we do not have the answer to the question raised earlier: What is the effect of repeated and personalized bilateral matchings on aggregate surplus? We know that loyal buyers and sellers do better than itinerant ones in simulations of the model in which average loyalty is high. But how does aggregate surplus vary with parameters of the model that encourage or discourage loyalty? Without this information, we cannot make the link to policy that is one of our concerns.

I have called the repeated pairing of buyers and sellers a "network" to emphasize the personal element of the relationship: the terms of the transaction differ depending on the identities of the buyer and the seller. This is not the anonymous world of competitive market exchanges. There is a somewhat different meaning, however, that economists give to the word "networks," and it does not apply to the bilateral matching discussed here. In this alternative definition, a network is a group of agents who share a public good, that is, a good that cannot be bought efficiently in the market. The two more common and more important examples are information and enforcement of contracts. It is true, of course, that in the models discussed in the chapter a buyer and a seller both know the history of their relationship, but this does not require any sharing of information and is consistent with each agent simply remembering his own past experiences. An information network in these models could be designed naturally by defining a subset of agents whose experiences are common knowledge to all other members of the subset. This would amount to the availability of an intermediate volume of information, relatively to the knowledge of all market transactions in the first model and to the strictly local learning of the second.

In some recent work with James Rauch and alone, I have explored the effect of networks for sharing public goods on the aggregate performance of the market, in terms of both aggregate efficiency and the distribution of surplus. In particular, these works address the problems posed by insufficient information and unreliable contract enforcement for international trade, and the possibility that a network of personal ties may arise in response. Cohesive ethnic groups dispersed among many countries have historically been particularly successful at identifying and securing business opportunities across national borders. Be it overseas Chinese in East Asia, Indian and Pakistani traders in East Africa, Greek shipping families in nineteenth-century European ports, or other historical examples out of many, the members of these groups usually share a close geographical origin, a language, often a religion, and a preference for personal and informal agreements. A fundamental reason for their success appears to be the ability to exploit their close personal ties to transmit reliable information and ensure compliance with past promises—a clear sign of the weaknesses of the anonymous market in international transactions.

With few exceptions, economists have neglected the obstacles to introducing a new product in a foreign market. Businesspeople, on the other hand, know how hard it is to enter a new environment: the difficulty is not only convincing customers of the quality of their product (as studied, for example, by Grossman and Horn 1988; Bagwell and Staiger 1989; Bagwell 1991), but also finding the right market niche, the right distributors, and the right angle for dealing with bureaucracy or with advertisement. It is here that a direct connection to someone who knows the country well is particularly valuable.

Rauch and I (Casella and Rauch 1998; Rauch and Casella 1998) have studied a model in which a successful trade venture requires a productive match between two partners (for example, a producer and a distributor). In domestic markets, everybody knows each other's type—and hence how good a match would be—but in international markets, traders discover their compatibility only after the match has been concluded. As expected, the information barrier reduces the volume of trade and the ability to exploit efficiently differences in countries' endowments and costs. As a result, international trade and world GDP fall. Suppose now that a group of traders united by some common tie has members located in different countries. If a member of the group decides to use his ties and trade through the group, then he acquires, and reveals, all the relevant information. Alternatively, he can always enter the anonymous market. From an aggregate point of view, the existence of the information-sharing group is an increase in the amount of information available to traders, and the outcome indeed is a higher volume of international trade, a realignment of international prices, and an improvement in world GDP. The presence of the network raises aggregate efficiency.

However, these preferential ties are available only to a subset of all traders, and the gains are not shared equally by all. In fact, even if there is no systematic difference ex ante in the quality of the matches that members of the group as a whole would provide—relative to the remainder of the traders—the preferential ties are particularly valuable to those among them who, if well matched, are the most productive.

These are the traders who choose to exploit the ties. The process of self-selection removes from the market some of its most desirable participants. As noted by a Hong Kong–based merchant banker, referring to one of the dominant figures of the Hong Kong economy: "Li Ka-shing calls the boys before he calls the brokers" (Sender 1991, 31). Even in the presence of aggregate gains, the worsened composition of the market can hurt individuals who are excluded from the group. The distribution of income becomes more unequal.

As mentioned earlier, a second and related obstacle to international trade that personal ties can help overcome is the difficulty of enforcement. Even among industrialized countries of similar cultures and economic development, national laws differ, and courts have been less than consistent in enforcing judicial awards rendered abroad. Businesspeople needing predictability of the law must face the uncertainty that surrounds the resolution of international disputes. International conventions have tried to overcome the problem.[2] The unanimous opinion among legal scholars, however, is that they have been remarkably ineffective: "There is a strong possibility that a judgement given by the courts of a given state should be unenforceable outside the territory of the state" (David 1985, 17).

A cohesive group can solve this difficulty because it can provide enforcement without recourse to the courts by excluding the cheating party from the flow of regular transactions. But in the absence of pre-existing ties, can a group emerge endogenously, providing the public good that the group's market exchanges need?

The experience of international commercial arbitration provides a fascinating example of the issues involved. Arbitration is the most frequent mechanism for the settlement of private disputes in international trade and is estimated to be invoked in more than 80 percent of private international contracts (see the sources in Casella 1996). The legal literature agrees that "international arbitration is regarded by the international business community as the normal means of settling disputes arising from international transactions" (Schmitthof, in Schultz and van der Berg 1982, 287), and that the recourse to arbitration is rising exponentially: "There is a clear evidence of something of a world movement [toward international arbitration]." (Kerr, Lord

Justice of England, preface to Craig, Park, and Paulsson 1990, xii). The growing acceptance of international arbitration parallels the growth of trade flows.

Arbitration in the modern world is neither a search for conciliation nor a system of private enforcement. It finally relies on the enforcement power of the courts, and the story of its increased popularity is the story of the courts and the legislatures' recent willingness to recognize the legitimacy of arbitration awards and lend their authority in supporting these awards. In particular, it is the story of the disproportionate recognition of foreign arbitral awards, relative to foreign courts' decisions. In many countries, the legal status of arbitration has undergone great changes in recent years, moving toward reduced court interference and simpler and stricter rules for enforcement, particularly with regard to international arbitration. England passed the Arbitration Act in 1979, France issued two decrees on arbitration in 1980 and 1981, Italy passed a new law in 1983, the Netherlands and Portugal in 1986, Switzerland in 1987, and Spain in 1988.

Why is international arbitration favored over courts' decisions? And why is it granted more latitude than domestic arbitration? The answer appears to be that international arbitration is understood to apply to a particular group of individuals sophisticated enough to be allowed to waive some of the courts' basic protections (for example, the right of appeal);[3] specialized enough to require judgments from tribunals that are up-to-date on the usages of the trade; and involved in deals of sufficient size to justify the high fees that these tribunals collect. "International arbitration is the jurisdiction of the business circles engaged in international trade" (Jakubowski, in Schultz and van der Berg 1982, 178). The largest international arbitration centers have begun to publish a selection of arbitral awards. These awards are acquiring the role of precedents, invoked in successive decisions and giving concrete content to the abstract concept of lex mercatoria, an evolving body of legally binding resolutions not founded on any national law.

If correct, this description is extraordinary: a subset of private individuals ("the business circles involved in international trade") have organized themselves in a jurisdiction providing to its members a specialized and binding code of laws that does not emanate directly from national laws. They have taken over one of the defining characteristics of the state, but they have done so in a specific realm where the crossing of national borders makes the reference to state powers difficult to enforce. Thus, this "private" and international jurisdiction has been granted the support of the traditional "public" jurisdictions (the legislatures and the courts) in explicit acknowledgment of its indispensable role in modern international economies.

Although the establishment of international arbitration has favored the growth of international trade, it has also prevented an increasing share of disputes, and in fact those posing some of the most complex and novel questions of law, from finding their way to the courts, and thus it has not contributed to the development of the regular jurisprudence. As in the case of preferential transmission of information among members of a group, the development of a parallel channel devoted to the needs of a subset of all traders may have positive aggregate effects but at the same time worsen the functioning of the common institution freely available to all (Casella 1996).

The combination of aggregate benefits with redistribution in favor of the members of the network, and thus declining performance of the alternative, anonymous channel open to all—be it impersonal exchanges in the market or access to a nondiscriminatory public good—is a direct consequence of addressing problems of information or enforcement through personal connections. Self-selection in the use of the network isolates agents or projects that have more to gain from revealing their true types and from guaranteeing that contracts are unambiguous and binding. The loss of these transactions lowers the average quality of the remaining trades, creating a "lemon" effect that harms individuals who do not interact through the network (for an elegant application to labor markets, see Montgomery 1991).

Whether these same effects operate in the models described by Kirman and in the Marseille fish market is hard to tell. The bounded rationality models from which the microstructure of the market emerges make it difficult to understand exactly why the networks come into being, and what the weaknesses of the market would be in their absence. But in the end, these questions deserve asking because it is the influence of the networks both on aggregate efficiency and on the distribution of welfare that constitutes, in my opinion, the central challenge for policy.

Notes

1. Andrew Caplin and Daniel Spulber (1987) study the effect of monetary policy in a world where price-setting firms are faced with a fixed cost of changing their nominal prices. Individual firms choose to keep their nominal price constant as long as their real price falls within an acceptable band. It would seem that an increase in money supply could affect real activity: if the resulting inflation and the corresponding decline in its real price are not too large, a firm would not adjust its nominal price. The result would be a change in real profits. However, inflation is generated endogenously from firms' pricing decisions, and the only steady-state outcome requires that firms be distributed uniformly along the acceptable band of real prices. The implication is that any increase in money supply must be mirrored by an identical burst of inflation: most firms do not readjust prices, but a discrete mass does, and moves all the way to the nominal price's upper bound. Average real prices are unchanged, and monetary policy has no impact on real activity, exactly as in the simplest model in which costs of changing nominal prices do not exist.

2. The most important of these agreements is the 1968 Brussels Convention on Jurisdiction and the Enforcement of Judgments in Civil and Commercial Matters, among the countries of the European Union.

3. British law, for instance, recognizes the right of parties to waive future appeals against arbitral awards only in the case of international disputes.

References

Bagwell, Kyle. 1991. "Optimal Export Policy for a New Product Monopoly." *American Economic Review* 81: 1156–69.

Bagwell, Kyle, and Robert Staiger. 1989. "The Role of Export Subsidies When Product Quality Is Unknown." *Journal of International Economics* 27: 69–89.

Becker, Gary. 1962. "Irrational Behavior and Economic Theory." *Journal of Political Economy* 70: 1–13.

Blume, Lawrence. 1993. "The Statistical Mechanics of Strategic Interactions." *Games and Economic Behavior* 5: 387–424.

Caplin, Andrew, and Daniel Spulber. 1987. "Menu Costs and the Neutrality of Money." *Quarterly Journal of Economics* (November): 703–25.

Casella, Alessandra. 1996. "On Market Integration and the Development of Institutions: The Case of International Commercial Arbitration." *European Economic Review* 40: 155–86.

Casella, Alessandra, and James Rauch. 1998. "Anonymous Market and Group Ties in International Trade." Working paper 133. New York: Russell Sage Foundation (June).

Craig, Lawrence, William Park, and Jan Paulsson. 1990. *International Chamber of Commerce Arbitration*. New York: Oceana Publications.

David, René. 1985. *Arbitration in International Trade*. Deventer, Netherlands: Kluwer.

Durlauf, Steve, 1993. "Neighborhood Feedbacks, Endogenous Stratification, and Income Inequality." In *Dynamic Disequilibrium Modeling: Proceedings of the Ninth International Symposium on Economic Theory and Econometrics*, edited by William Barnett, Giancarlo Gandolfo, and Claude Hillinger. Cambridge: Cambridge University Press.

Friedman, Daniel, and Joseph Ostroy. 1995. "Competitivity in Auction Markets: An Experimental and Theoretical Investigation." *Economic Journal* 105: 22–53.

Gode, Dhananjay, and Shyam Sunder. 1993. "Allocative Efficiency of Markets with Zero-Intelligence Traders: Market as Partial Substitute for Individual Rationality." *Journal of Political Economy* 101: 119–37.

Grossman, Gene, and Henrik Horn. 1988. "Infant-Industry Protection Reconsidered: The Case of Informational Barriers to Entry." *Quarterly Journal of Economics* 103: 767–87.

Härdle, Wolfgang, and Alan Kirman. 1995. "Nonclassical Demand: A Model-Free Examination of Price Quantity Relations in the Marseille Fish Market." *Journal of Econometrics* 67: 227–57.

Kirman, Alan. 1993. "Ants, Rationality, and Recruitment." *Quarterly Journal of Economics* 108: 137–56.

Kirman, Alan, and Annick P. Vignes. 1991. "Price Dispersion: Theoretical Considerations and Empirical Evidence from the Marseille Fish Market." In *Issues in Contemporary Economics*, edited by Kenneth G. Arrow. London: Macmillan.

Kirman, Alan, and Nick Vriend. 1998. "Evolving Market Structure: A Model of Price Dispersion and Loyalty." Unpublished paper. Department of Economics, Virginia Polytechnic Institute and State University, Blacksburg.

LeRoy, Steve. 1989. "Efficient Capital Markets and Martingales." *Journal of Economic Literature* 27: 1583–1621.

Montgomery, James. 1991. "Social Networks and Labor Market Outcomes: Toward an Economic Analysis." *American Economic Review* 81: 1408–18.

Rauch, James, and Alessandra Casella. 1998. "Overcoming Informational Barriers to International Resource Allocation: Prices and Group Ties." Working paper 134. New York: Russell Sage Foundation (June).

Schultz, Jan, and Albert van der Berg. 1982. *The Art of Arbitration, Liber Amicorum Sanders*. Deventer, Netherlands: Kluwer.

Sender, Henry. 1991. "Inside the Overseas Chinese Network." *Institutional Investor* (August): 29–43.

Smith, Vernon L. 1982. "Microeconomic Systems as an Experimental Science." *American Economic Review* 72: 923–55.

Weisbuch, Gerard, Alan Kirman, and Dorothea Herreiner. 2000. "Market Organization and Trading Relationships." *Economic Journal* 110: 411–36.

Wilson, Robert. 1987. "Equilibrium in Bid-Ask Markets." In *Arrow and the Ascent of Economic Theory: Essays in Honor of Kenneth J. Arrow*, edited by George Feiwel. London: Macmillan.

Chapter 5

Organizational Genesis, Identity, and Control: The Transformation of Banking in Renaissance Florence

John F. Padgett

Current organization theories explain organizational form essentially through selection. That is, instead of focusing on the dynamics of emergence, the field as a whole adopts as its epistemology consequentialism, which emphasizes the relative performances, and hence death rates, of different forms in different environments. The hope of the field is that the performance relationship between form and environment is sufficiently invariant that equilibrium fixed points will be reached, independent of dynamic path.

This shared epistemological stance hardly implies that theoretical consensus has been reached. Strong debates flourish over which selection environment is the most powerful (markets versus states versus professions); over what is the proper unit of selection (standard operating procedures versus contracts versus legitimation principles versus structural phenotypes); and over what role strategic choice plays in macroselection (constitutive versus epiphenomenal). All these debates reveal that "performance," the criterion for selection, is far more difficult to define, much less measure, than it may at first appear. Such operational difficulties aside, the field's epistemological convergence on consequentialism has had the virtue of permitting debates to be tight and well focused.

But this consensus has been purchased at a cost. It is no accident that hardly anyone since Arthur Stinchcombe's (1965) hoary but path-breaking classic has broached the topic of the genesis of organizational form, including within that topic, as Stinchcombe did, the systematic relationship between processes of organizational birth and the surrounding social contexts out of which organizations are constructed. This challenging issue currently is pushed under our collective rug through a variety of simplifying assumptions.[1] Biology-inspired organization theories use randomization (sometimes supplemented with diffusion) to sidestep the question; economics-inspired organization theories posit that good ideas are available to everyone (perhaps through costly search); and culture-inspired organization theories rely on ideational templates (themselves not explained). Each of these approaches can deal with reproduction, or choice within given alternatives; none can deal with the genesis of the alternatives themselves.

The lacunae these fixes hide are revealed most obviously in comparative or historical research, which regardless of time or place tends to discover a cornucopia of organizational forms, well beyond the range of our usual Americanist vision. Arguably, all these forms are "adapted" to a local "environment" that has "selected" them on some criteria of "performance." But the sheer diversity of ways in which these analytic terms must be operationalized to fit various historical cases threatens to make the entire metaphor vacuous.

The essential theoretical problem, well understood in Stinchcombe's original article, is causal feedback between organizational forms and environments. In no time or place have organizations faced a fixed topology or landscape of environmental resources over which they must maximize. Not unlike species in the Amazonian jungle, organizations have faced instead a plethora of other interconnected organizations and social networks into which they must fit, the dynamics of which they themselves affect. Path-dependent histories of coevolving organizational forms can walk—and have walked themselves—into all sorts of self-sustaining corners of abstract possibility, including many beyond our experience.[2]

Beyond simply waving our hands at the glorious indeterminacy of human (and natural selection) agency, the question, of course, is how to construct a framework for analyzing systemic interactions and feedback in such a way as to (post-hoc) explain the emergence of new organizational forms. Here I use my empirical work on Renaissance Florentine banking—arguably the "birthplace" (along with Genoa and a few other Italian city-states) of financial capitalism—as a platform both for more closely structuring the analytic problem of organizational genesis and for speculating about empirically plausible theoretical solutions. Perhaps understanding the mechanisms that generated the history-shaping sequence of innovative organizational forms in this one creative epoch will suggest mechanisms underlying organizational genesis more generally.

The Florentine discussion is founded on years of original primary research, many of the findings of which are summarized here for the first time. Because of this, some of what I state below is not yet known in the history profession. Here though, because of the theoretical purpose of this volume, I have intentionally suppressed evidentiary detail (to be published elsewhere) and have used the case simply as a springboard to more general thinking about organizational genesis. Let no one mistake the inductive sequence, however: I am inferring general theory from unpacking a particular case. The generality of the conclusions here can be established only through careful comparison with analogous cases.[3]

Structuring the Problem of Organizational Genesis

Viewed from the very proximate perspective of the founder, the birth of an organization can be understood in quasi-biological terms. In both biological and social systems, birth is rooted in a logic of recombination: unlike what our models sometimes imply, spontaneous generation never occurs. It is the absence of a theory of recombination that inhibits social-science understanding of genesis: we need to take more seriously than we do the fact that nothing exists without a history.

The analogue to DNA in social organization is the set of ideas, practices, and social relations of the founder. For shorthand, I call this set the "logic-of-identity" of the founder. At the genotypic level of analysis, it is the recombinatorial history of these ideas, practices, and social relations, controlled through social interactions between persons, that social science most needs to understand. To take an example central to this chapter, who an individual is as a banker is deeply affected by who that individual is as a person (modified, of course, by what he has learned in his role). And who the individual is as a person, in turn, is the product of the "mating system" of the population, concatenated to generate historically intertwined lineages of practices and persons.

Understanding organizational genesis at the level of genotype, therefore, cannot be divorced from understanding the social production of careers and biographies—namely, from understanding the careers of ideas, of practices, and of social relations as they interleave through the biographies of their person carriers.

An analytic focus on genotype in no way implies that organization is just one individual's blueprint. How logics-of-identity unfold into organization is hardly a matter of automatic template and design.[4] Actual living organizations, social or biological, are the developmental products of these founder logics, interacting with the inherent properties of the social or biological raw materials being assembled.[5] In economic organization, these raw materials in large part are the social networks of business interaction partners, selected into (and selecting) the organization through trading and personnel flows. Out of this soup of founding logics of identity and cross-cutting social networks, an autonomous organization emerges and sustains itself through time if an autocatalytic "metabolic chemistry" of technology and work routines crystallizes out of this ideational-social mixture (Fontana and Buss 1994; Padgett 1997).[6]

This micro, organic view of organization is crucial prelude, both because it defines the terms of analysis—namely, logics-of-identity, social network materials, and energic resource flows—and because it defines a developmental research agenda: how to understand their dynamic interactive unfolding through time. In the Florentine case, I am concerned with economic partnership—that is, not with all aspects of the banking firm (employees, trading, and so on) but with the capital-formation nucleus of the firm. In this context, "logics-of-identity" refer to the historically variable rules for capital formation and pooling in Florentine society, and "social networks" refer to the socially structured channels (family, neighborhood, social class, patronage) through which potential bankers with capital found each other to form, and re-form, firms.[7]

This firm-level, developmental perspective on organizational genesis, while invaluable for clarifying the terms of analysis, in the end proves incomplete for understanding invention. Viewed from the macro perspective of a "market" or a "profession," the birth or reconstitution of a new firm is just one instance in a larger flow of capital and people through the society's respective market and profession systems.[8] Firm morphology at the level of partnership was and is shaped by the layering of two flows: liquidities of different types of capital, and careers of different types of bankers.[9] Overlooking the patterned layering of these macro flows prevents us from even approaching the most interesting historical question: How are completely new (albeit path-dependent) and possibly epoch-shaping innovations in organizational form produced? Biologists label this question "speciation."

To make progress at the difficult speciation level of analysis requires unfamiliar thought, I argue, about *multiple* logics-of-identity, about *multiple* social networks, and about their concatenation.[10] The lives of all people, in all eras, participate in one way or another in economic, political, and kinship activities.[11] Societies differ in how they put these domains together. The autocatalytically stabilized logic of recombination in any one sector is regulated by the personnel and resource flows produced by other sectors. This I take to be the operational meaning of "socially embedded" (Granovetter 1985). More than that, however, occasionally perturbations in one recombinant domain dynamically reverberate in, or spill over explosively into, another domain to tip that other domain's own autocatalytic regime.

Descriptively, this is "refunctionality": the use of one social or biological organizational form for a completely different purpose (see Skocpol 1976; Sewell 1980; Stark and Bruszt 1998). In my observation, such cross-domain rewirings—often produced in the heat of Florentine political crisis—were the catalysts that ultimately generated the most important, epoch-shaping organizational innovations in Florentine economic history. Such economically innovative consequences of political revolt, observed in the Florentine case, were hardly either immediate or inevitable. They occurred only when and if these sometimes violent rewirings became institutionalized into new mating systems, which moved Florentines across domains in new ways, reliably reproducing new types of biographies and careers.

Thus, I agree with Jacob Burckhardt ([1860] 1954), and implicitly with Richard Goldthwaite (1968), that Florentine invention ultimately is to be explained as the social construction of a new type of person. Where I part company with these distinguished and deeply informed judgments is their occasional suggestion that the nature of this new Renaissance person was either modern or individualist.[12] The economic history I observe in the undeniably innovative Florentine banking industry is, at the industrial level of analysis, neither unidirectional, teleological, nor intentional.

Four Phases in the Development of Florentine Domestic Banking

To operationalize the discussion, let me now outline concretely the morphological changes, at the level of partnership, that Renaissance Florentine banking created, from 1300 to 1500, to produce the famous "birth of financial capitalism."

It helps entrée into this topic to simplify, indeed to oversimplify, the periodization of Florentine domestic banking into four distinct phases of development: the pre–Black Death era of family banking (before 1348), the pre–Ciompi revolt era of guild banking (1349 to 1378), the post-Ciompi era of popolani social-class banking (1380 to 1433), and the Medici era of patronage banking (1434 to 1494). Although this timing is defined primarily on political lines, economically based domestic banking partnerships had very distinct organizational profiles in each of these political eras. It is an oversimplification to interpret the relationship between these periods as phase-transitions—namely, as sharp breaks during which one mode of organization completely superseded and transcended prior modes. The path-dependent biological metaphors of sedimentation and induction, according to which new organizing modes arise on the shoulders of older historical "residues" in order to remobilize and recast them, is closer to the actual truth. Nevertheless, simply to introduce the distinctive Florentine developmental trajectory, I map out here a succession of ideal types. These four idealizations all have distinctive organizational, market-structure, cultural-meaning, and social-embedding components, which together point the way to how economic banking markets were rooted in their broader, changing social context.

From the dawn of Florentine international banking in the Commercial Revolution of the 1200s (Lopez 1976) to the political, economic, and demographic crises of the 1340s, the organization of Florentine domestic banking was dominated by the family. In the early 1300s, when my guild registration observations begin, fully 80 percent of Arte del Cambio (that is, banking guild) partnership dyads were among members of the same family.[13] Guilds existed and were politically active, but at the level of internal bank organization they had not yet displaced family as the social logic of partnership.

Partly because patrilineage itself in this late-medieval period was often large and solidary, banks in this era grew to larger sizes (measured either in capital or in number of partners) than did any banks subsequently. Banking was just one of many activities in the diversified portfolios of patrilineages.[14] Because of this, economic "capital" (revealingly called "corpo") assumed the cultural meaning of the social raw material out of which banks were constructed: it was considered "patrimony," to husband, to nurture, and to pass down through the generations, like land. Career mobility between banks was essentially zero, with the result that banks simply were born, grew, and died, with no mergers, recombinations, or splintering (until the death of the father).

Market "competition" had a Darwinian feel: sometimes harsh death-rate selection pressure prevailed within various customer niches, but there was little cost-cutting or explicit coordination between banks.[15] Exchange relations between banks, to the extent that they could not be avoided altogether, were managed through notarized contracts, because families deeply distrusted each other. Relative to subsequent phases, banks preferred to operate autonomously, developing corporate organizations with vertical integration (linking trade, bills of exchange, and diplomacy) if possible.

In virtually every economic aspect above the lowest level of pawnbrokers and mere money changers,[16] in other words, the logic of Florentine banking organization was colored by the logic of patrilineage during this late-medieval period.

Through a political process described later in the chapter, patrilineage throughout Florence weakened, for reasons having little specifically to do with banking.[17] The guild moved from the background of regulatory control to the foreground of socially constituting partnerships. Not only lower-level employees but also partners themselves formed and re-formed themselves according to a logic of master-apprentice, displacing the earlier logic of father-son. This implied internal hierarchy: large experience and corpo differentials between nonfamily partners, often socially anchored in cross-class neighborhood relations.[18] But it also implied social mobility: the goal of the apprentice was artisanal autonomy, with the consequence that firms constantly splintered. Apprentices spun off to become either solo operators or masters of new apprentices.

The market-structure consequences of this newer guild-based firm-formation logic are straightforward. Owing to constant fissure, firm-size distributions were deconcentrated in the extreme. In the guild era of 1348 to 1376, having one to three partners in Arte del Cambio banks was practically universal; in contrast, the presence of seven to twenty partners was not unusual in the preceding patrilineage era. Owing again to constant fissure, career mobility ties among firms were dense; one's competitor could be one's ex-apprentice. In this context, deconcentration was a reflection of community solidarity more than a sign of neoclassical perfect competition.[19] "Capital" is best conceived in this regime as a personal-career "stake": the goal of the artisan was to carve out a good life for himself, not necessarily to maximize profits.[20] Within ranges, wool-firm production levels were chosen not individually by firms but collectively by masters in their guilds (Najemy 1981). Account books, typically not double-entry, displaced contracts and notaries as the medium for interbank exchange, since now bankers could trust each other enough simply to walk across the piazza (either in Florence or in another city) jointly to clear their books.

After the 1378 revolt of the Ciompi wool workers, guilds effectively were crushed, owing to their role in this political crisis (Brucker, 1968). The popolani as a social class moved in to dominate partnerships in all major Florentine industries, in a way quite analogous to their republican domination of politics in this same era.[21] The consequences for partnership formation of this embedding of banking into social class were the following. Within domestic banking itself, class endogamy became the soil out of which sprang a hybrid family-nonfamily partnership form, with a nucleus of brothers or cousins surrounded by a periphery of same-class partners, into whose family the brothers or cousins often married. Even absent formal marriage, amicizia, or friendship relations were central. "Family" therefore reemerged in banking partnerships, but in the looser horizontal parentado sense of marriage in-laws (and close friends), not in the vertical patrilineage sense of father-son. In capital accumulation, dowry and credit grew in importance, relative to inheritance.

Perhaps even more profound were the cross-industry consequences of popolani dominance. In the guild regime, intra-industry career mobility was high, but cross-industry career mobility was low. In contrast, the post-Ciompi period witnessed an efflorescence of cross-industry organizational "systems," of which the diversified conglomerates of Francesco Datini (the merchant of Prato) and the Medici are the most famous.[22] In particular, there was an explosion of partnership links between overseas merchant-banking firms and their domestic bank counterparts, although wool and silk manufacturing firms were included in these organizational systems as well. Perhaps for the first time it is legitimate to think of "capital" in the modernist sense of "investment," albeit investment among closely linked companies.[23]

Even more extensively knitting together firms than partnership systems were the open-ended credit relations that developed within the core of the Florentine banking industry at this time. Standing cross-accounts and the standardized protocol of double-entry bookkeeping were now the technical mechanisms facilitating this explosion of unsecured credit, backed "only" (but all-importantly) by trust and reputation.[24]

It is no doubt an exaggeration to impute the goal of "domination of the market" to individual entrepreneurs of this era, if only because this was still far beyond their organizational capacity. But clearly there was a "visible hand" managerialist logic of coordination and control across multiple markets and firms not present in earlier phases. And the power-drenched reality of "domination of the market"—institutionalized politically in republican baliè and in near-monopoly by the popolani of guild-consul and Mercanzia offices—was in fact achieved at the level of social class, if not at the level of individuals.

Banks and banking during the popolani oligarchic era were constructed on the social infrastructure of politically inspired elite-construction mechanisms—intermarriage, amicizia, and emergent clientage.[25] Such organizational innovations generated economywide, not just industrywide, financial elites.

Although organizational developments in economics certainly cannot create ideas, this third popolani phase is the economic-cum-political backdrop to the famous ideological construction of civic humanism during this same period (Baron 1966). Civic humanism imparted to the new economywide elite a deep self-consciousness about its own importance in Western history (see Emirbayer and Goodwin 1994).

In the post-1434 Medici era, developments in domestic banking are only imperfectly revealed because of an unfortunate gap in the Arte del Cambio records. One major clue, however, is unequivocal: the social-class composition of domestic bankers, as well as of partners in other industries, shifted dramatically from overwhelming popolani domination to an equal distribution between popolani and "new new men" (a parvenu class of families defined by their entrance into the Signoria after the 1378 Ciompi revolt). In the case of domestic banking, this compositional shift was neither gradual (it occurred immediately upon the accession of Cosimo de' Medici) nor accidental: new matriculation data reveal virtually an affirmative action policy of equal rates of admission into the guild. In short, all signs point to an implementation of exactly the same Medicean political control strategy for banking that Nicholas Eckstein (1995) has uncovered for neighborhood gonfaloni during this same period. I have already analyzed the emergence and effectiveness of this "class-balancing" Medicean control technique in the pre-1434 period (Padgett and Ansell 1993).

It is an inferential leap from this clear evidence of social-class composition to an interpretation of domestic banking under the Medici as "extreme patronage" in logic.[26] Nevertheless, a series of collateral data make this interpretation plausible at least as a working hypothesis: (1) Louis Marks (1960) has demonstrated the emergence of a Medicean "financial oligarchy" in the domain of state finance, with extremely personal and highly politicized linkages between high-level financiers and the emergent Medici court.[27] (2) The Medici demonstrated unequivocal patronage behavior toward lower-level Jewish pawnbrokers (Fubbini 1996), whom the Medici brought into Florence soon after their accession, and who were evicted from the city by Savonarola immediately upon their 1494 fall. (3) The functional segregation between domestic banking and the government bond market broke down under the Medici, as an explosion of Monte commune and dowry-fund prestanze (forced loans) unleashed a secondary market of speculative trading in discounted bonds (Molho 1994), in which domestic bankers participated heavily (Goldthwaite 1985). (4) The Medici mobilized domestic bankers into their extra-constitutional financial advisory committees, to reform taxes, the mint, the Jews, and other pressing financial matters (Marks 1960; Brown 1992). All these pieces of evidence, while external, not internal, in character, show the same progressive Medicean entanglement of banking in state fiscal administration.

If this extreme-patronage interpretation of domestic banking under the Medici proves correct, then we should witness, on the economic front, a progressive separation of finance from entrepreneurship. Instead of inter-industry organizational systems, in which managerialist elites control multiple markets, high-level financiers withdraw into the state, reaching out to remaining entrepreneurs through short-term, more speculative loans. Even domestic bankers themselves can become "clients" in this dynamic. In actual historical fact, domestic banking under the Medici became far more stratified than before. A few highly successful and long-lived banking firms, sitting on Medici advisory committees, were offset in ratio within the Arte del Cambio records by many more small, purely local, impoverished firms with relatively poor economic prospects outside of bond-market speculation.

Thus, in the paradigmatic case of Renaissance Florence, it appears to be the centralizing court, not liberal laissez-faire, that spawned the emergence of highly specialized classes of financiers (both wealthy and impoverished) who were differentiated from production and trading and related to business primarily through immediate, short-term gains.[28] Although further research into this question is required, it appears that only in the Medici period did finance become segregated into organizations different from those for business and trading. Before this period, "merchant-banker" is a more accurate term than just "banker."

Partnerships and Careers

In this "birth of financial capitalism" narrative, the most glaringly obvious empirical fact is the temporal covariance of political and economic transformation. It is the inner logic of this covariance that most needs analysis. To proceed, I follow the biologically inspired framework sketched earlier and break the organizational genesis problem down into three levels of analysis: first, a micro "genotypic" level of analysis, in which the central issue is how organizational sequences are produced through the interweaving of careers; second, a mezzo "developmental" level of analysis, in which partnership mating is regulated through social and political network-embedding; and third, a macro "speciation" level of analysis, in which the central issue is how social-network rekeying of logics-of-identity is accomplished, across political-cum-market regimes. This section focuses on genotypic mating, the next section on developmental regulation, and the last section on speciation.

Each of the four phases of Florentine domestic banking history rested on a distinct institutionalized conception of partnership—that is, its modal "logic-of-identity." Banking organizations (at least their partnership cores) were the unfolding and concatenation of these building-block elements through time.

In figures 5.1 through 5.6, I represent prominent examples of these partnership conceptions graphically. These figures summarize schematically modal patterns of career structures that I have discovered empirically. Bankers in these figures are represented as vectors of two components: economic capital (corpo) and human capital (years of banking experience). In both cases, the notation "+" means "large amount of capital possessed," "$\frac{1}{2}$" means "small amount of capital possessed," and "0" means "no capital possessed." Partnership relations are represented as different matching profiles, or capital complementarities, between the two bankers' vectors. Which match between capital vectors is "complementary" depends on social embedding—that is, on the underlying social relation that spawned the partnership. Economic viability constraints are built into the representation through the requirement that the sum of economic capital and the sum of human capital each equals at least 1 (or "+").[29]

Family Firms

In the family regime, the distinct logic-of-identity was father-son; hence, the network of partnership recruitment was patrilineage. In figure 5.1, father-son is represented as a match between the two capital profiles: father's C/E = (+/+) and son's C/E = (0/0). Their personal feelings aside, father-son formally is an altruistic relationship in which someone who has everything sponsors (or "makes") someone else who has nothing.

Figure 5.1 shows how, in a patrilineage regime, such father-son relationships typically unfolded and concatenated through time to generate the life history of a patrilineage bank. Such banks developmentally were produced through simple agglomeration: father-son firms started small and kept growing larger by adding more and more extended family members, until sooner or later disaster caused bankruptcy and massive collapse.[30] Authority within the firm, among the partners, was hierarchical, not equalitarian. Career advancement was generational: sons had to wait for their fathers' death and their inheritance. Interfirm employment transfer, to another family, was virtually unthinkable; hence, the economic fate of the banker was tied to his firm.[31]

Figure 5.2 shows the analogous logic for brothers, one that is more appropriate for nuclear than for patrilineal families. Empirically, brother-brother firms existed throughout Florentine banking history, unlike the father-son firms, which were mostly contained to the patrilineal period. Brothers would often split up and divide their inheritance, including the bank, upon the death of their father, whether or not the father was active in the firm (Kent 1977; Goldthwaite 1983). I label as "strong brotherhood" the variant in which brother partnerships lasted beyond the death of the father, and as "weak brotherhood" the variant in which it did not.[32]

Note that figures 5.1 through 5.5 can all be read in two ways: as bankers coming together under different partnership logics to produce life histories of firms, and as life histories of firms developing bankers' careers. This double reading is an example of the network-analysis concept of duality (Breiger 1974; White and Jorion 1992). Duality is the network architecture through which markets socially construct persons.

Figure 5.1 Typical Life Course for Family Firms: Father-Son Mode

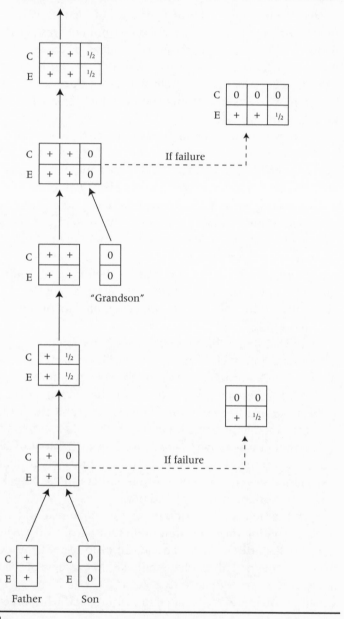

Figure 5.2 Typical Life Course for Family Firms: Brother-Brother Mode

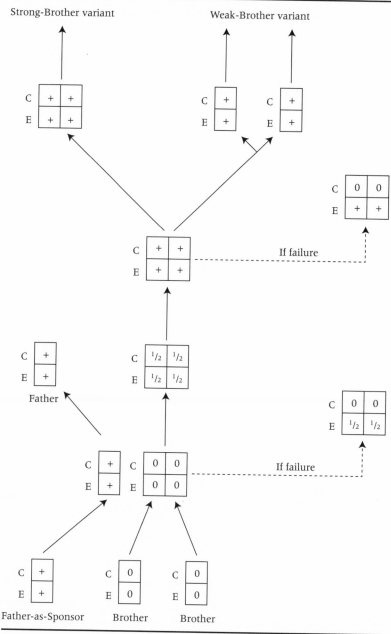

Source: Author.

Guild Firms

In the guild regime, the distinct logic-of-identity was master-apprentice; the social network of recruitment was primarily the neighborhood, typically cross-class. A master differed from a father in that he required his apprentice to gain some experience (usually, though not necessarily, under himself) before promoting him to partner. Also, the expected duration of the partnership was shorter: instead of waiting "until death do us part," an apprentice typically wanted to become an independent master as soon as he was capable of sustaining an economically viable firm. Other than that, masters and fathers were similar: both had hierarchical authority, grounded in their superiority on both the corpo and experience fronts.

Figure 5.3 illustrates graphically the consequences of concatenating this social logic through the life history of a firm. The developmental sequence of guild banks was repeated schism, as "apprentice" partners built up enough wealth and experience to declare independence by starting their own firms. Empirically, I have observed that popolani and magnati bankers behaved differently in their later-life stage as fully autonomous masters: experienced masters of popolani and magnati social-class backgrounds continued to sponsor young lower-class apprentices as partners, while experienced masters of lower-class backgrounds (new men, new new men, and no-date) preferred to become solo operators. The net result was a loose pecking order among guild masters: Cambio masters of popolani and magnati background disproportionately reproduced bankers of all social classes.[33]

Loose pecking orders notwithstanding, relations among banks were personal and solidaristic. Not only was this market structure grounded socially in the daily practice of bankers sitting around the same piazze every day, as mentioned earlier, but the same career logic that generated guild banks also produced biographies of dense ex-partnership ties among competitors (who as a result were not all that competitive).[34]

Popolani Firms

In the popolani regime, the distinct logic-of-identity was social class; hence, the network of partnership recruitment was intermarriage and elite amicizia (friendship). Figures 5.4 and 5.5 illustrate the capital-complementarity consequences for partnership.

Figure 5.3 Typical Life Course for Guild Firms

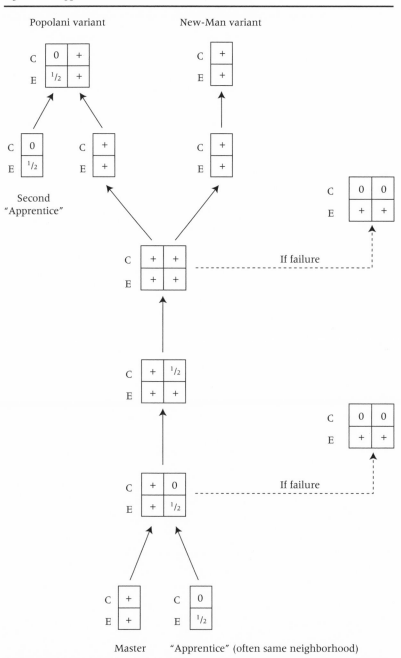

Figure 5.4 Typical Life Course for Popolani Firms: Intermarriage Mode

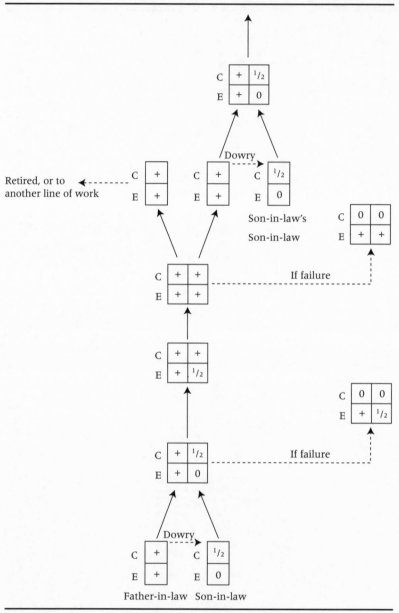

Figure 5.5 Typical Life Course for Popolani Firms: Amicizia Mode

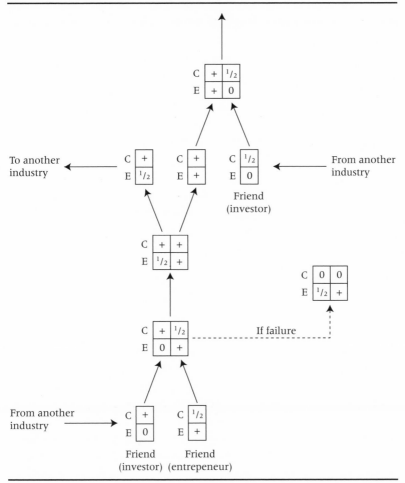

The intermarriage variant of social-class logic is presented in figure 5.4: the father-in-law gives a dowry to his son-in-law, who uses that as corpo in a partnership either with the father-in-law himself, if the father-in-law is in the same industry, or with a friend of the father-in-law if he is not. Sons-in-law had more corpo actually in hand than did sons, who relied instead on future inheritance.[35] Even though this greater wealth gave to sons-in-law more clout in the partnership than sons or apprentices had, they remained subordinate.

As shown in figure 5.5, the amicizia variant of social-class logic produces, for the first time, an asymmetry in capital complementarity: the partner superior in corpo is not necessarily also superior in experience. The logic of "friends" is to help each other out in need, in the sense of giving to the other what the other lacks. Applied to partnership, this logic implies the exchange of corpo for experience. Applied to loans, this logic implies a heavy reliance on unsecured credit and loose repayment schedules—although only among friends with solid reputations.[36]

In-law and amicizia relations vary in duration: a father-in-law relation lasts until the death of the wife, whereas a friendship relation varies widely in duration. Likewise, the degree of equality in corpo can vary. One tends to assume that sons-in-law are less wealthy than fathers-in-law, but dowries in the Florentine elite sometimes reached uncomfortably high levels from the perspective of the father-in-law. Similarly, one tends to assume that friends are roughly equal in wealth, but Florentine friendship readily bridged wealth differences, perhaps because of the extreme wealth disparities both within a social class and within a family itself. The point is that building partnership on the social-class foundations of intermarriage or friendship automatically introduces more flexibility in duration and in relative authority than can exist in the patrilineage or guild context.

A second, historically crucial consequence of a shift of economic partnerships onto social-class foundations is the automatic opening of the door to cross-industry ownership connections. Given Florentine fathers' bias in passing down their occupation to their sons, in-laws and friends were more likely to be in different industries than were relatives (and by definition, fellow guildmen were in the same industry). Both parentado and amicizia naturally generated cross-industry partnerships once they became mobilized into economic activities.

Medici Firms

I will not sketch the Medici period in the same detail here because of the gap in Arte del Cambio records mentioned earlier.[37] In the overall summary figure 5.6, however, I illustrate the capital-complementarity meaning of extreme patronage: patron's C/E = (+/0) coupled with client's C/E = (0/+). This is extreme asymmetry in partners' corpo and experience: a wealthy financier with no knowledge sponsoring a poor entrepreneur with no wealth.

Gene Brucker (1969, 1977) is the historian who most persuasively has emphasized both the pervasiveness and the flexibility of the Florentine concept of patronage—extensible from the relatively equalitarian overtones of amicizia in the republican period to the sharply hierarchical emphasis of magnificenza in the Medicean period. Sharp economic and political organizational changes were probably built, in other words, on a social ground of cultural and linguistic continuity.

As mentioned earlier, empirically domestic banks in the Medici period were characterized by stratification into two tiers: an upper tier of politically connected firms, with "patrons" sometimes serving in the economic role of functional "silent partners," and a lower tier of impoverished, atomized firms, often active in the secondary market of government bonds. "Extreme patronage" refers to banks in the first tier.

Organizational Identity and Control[38]

In each of these phases, role was framed by identity (Goffman 1974, 293–300). That is, Florentine bankers' understanding of what it meant to be a partner was affected, in each of these periods, by their conception of themselves as persons, outside of the bank. Social embeddedness, however, is not mere social determinism, because who bankers were outside of the bank was distinctly non-obvious. It is not as if bankers in all four periods were not simultaneously fathers, neighbors, friends, and patrons.[39] They were all of these things all of the time. Multiple, overlapping social networks shaped banking because they defined the generative context, or raw material, out of which banks emerged. But for an even deeper explanation of organizational genesis, we need a yet-to-be-specified identity-construction

Figure 5.6 Summary of Alternative Vertical Partnership Relations (C & E Profiles at Beginning of Relation)

$$\begin{array}{c|c|c} C & + & 0 \\ \hline E & 0 & + \end{array}$$

Extreme patronage
(Medici period)

$$\begin{array}{c|c|c} C & + & {}^{1}/_{2} \\ \hline E & 0 & + \end{array}$$

Popolani amicizia
(Popolani "system")

$$\begin{array}{c|c|c} C & + & 0 \\ \hline E & {}^{1}/_{2} & + \end{array}$$

New-man amicizia
(Datini "system")

$$\begin{array}{c|c|c} C & + & + \\ \hline E & + & 0 \end{array}$$

Kindred/parentado
(Same generation)

$$\begin{array}{c|c|c} C & + & 0 \\ \hline E & + & + \end{array}$$

Guild master-master

$$\begin{array}{c|c|c} C & + & {}^{1}/_{2} \\ \hline E & + & 0 \end{array}$$

Kindred/parentado
(Cross-generation)

$$\begin{array}{c|c|c} C & + & 0 \\ \hline E & + & {}^{1}/_{2} \end{array}$$

Guild master-apprentice

$$\begin{array}{c|c|c} C & + & 0 \\ \hline E & + & 0 \end{array}$$

Father-son

Source: Author.
Note: Each of these modes has variants in how they unfold, depending on how long the relation is expected to last.

mechanism that leverages banking into one or another aspect of its surrounding social context.

From the Florentine evidence, this mechanism appears to be political in character. Most authors discuss "identity" and "framing" in cultural or linguistic terms, and there is in fact a linguistic aspect to the Florentine story. In my opinion, however, more fundamental than language for banking was how Florentine political institutions shaped actual (not just interpreted) biographies. Biographies are different from careers in that the concept of careers refers to life sequences within a single domain of activity (economic, political, family), whereas the concept of biography refers to life sequences across multiple domains (interleaving economic, political, and family). When constructing his own biography (as opposed to career), the smart Florentine banker needed to attend to how other Florentines rewarded or punished moves in one domain in the currency of other domains. For example, a move in economics shaped family options; a move in family shaped political options; a move in politics shaped economic options; and vice versa around the causal loop. In Florence, clear distinctions between domains were blurred precisely because of the strength of such interaction effects.

No activity inherently took priority in Florentine consciousness: attaining wealth, status, and power were all important pursuits. It is especially important in a paper on banking to note that banking was not necessarily a lifelong activity: the average length of a career in domestic banking during the guild and popolani periods (1348 to 1399) was 8.21 years, according to Arte del Cambio records.[40] But of course, analogous statements could be made about politics and even family. Rather than arguing which was more important, the main point is to emphasize the multiplicity of Florentine activities and concerns.[41]

In this multivalent context, which aspects of their external lives did bankers select as identities to be relevant for the attainment and maintenance of their position as a banker? The answer to this question has two parts: First, since partnerships are dyads, not single individuals, the identity of one party to a relation is as much the selection of the alter as it is of the ego: identity is negotiated, not chosen (see Leifer 1988).[42] As such, identities are rooted in matching processes. And second, the micro terms of dyadic negotiations are not usually idiosyncratic;

they are grounded in public discourse by institutionalized rules of access, which shape the normal terms of translation between multiple domains.

Recruitment systems reproduce regimes of identity, once they are already in place. New bankers are recruited or sponsored by existing bankers, through the same networks that existing bankers experienced as the reasons for their own success. An industry thereby selects those aspects, or identities, of the multifaceted persons of entrants that it deems relevant to the types of banks it makes. Viewed microscopically: who you become as the person behind your banking role is which of your pasts the industry has made into the reason for your coming to occupy that role. Compositionally, this does not imply social homogeneity, as many filtering arguments suppose, because recruitment networks are not necessarily closed. But it does imply industry convergence on some dimensions of classification of heterogeneous personnel rather than others.[43]

Recruitment systems typically are anchored in elites. Even if new entrants to an industry are heterogeneous, the very process of moving them up into the core of that industry transforms multifaceted human material into the classifications of the core.[44] Clear, univocal personal identities thus are the consequence of tight social control.[45]

Elites themselves experienced their own incorporation numerous years in the past. In stable regimes, therefore, elite-policed personnel matching systems reproduce the control patterns laid down in the past. In unstable regimes, conversely, either political conflicts or interruptions of economic mobility can disrupt the smooth operation of organizational reproduction and set the stage for morphological rekeying. Either way, the memory of past historical fractures becomes layered into the current network structure.

This internalist reproduction mechanism applies equally well, with different social network content, to each of the four phases of Florentine banking development. As such, social matching-recruitment systems alone cannot explain differences among them. Besides path-dependent reproductive matching at the level of careers, however, the second answer to the identity-construction question is translation at the level of biography. "Rules of translation" and "protocols" are concepts that apply not only to language and to software. How people are moved across different activity domains is "translation" in social structure. As in linguistics (see Duranti and Goodwin 1992), where a person or text is coming from, and where it is going to, are crucial for the indexical interpretation of the current multivocal person or text.

For biography, translation means access. In the short-term time frame of making public policy decisions, bankers may need to translate their problems into terms that can compute in the public arena. In the longer time frame of a biography, bankers may need actually to enter the political arena.

In the late-medieval era, patrilineage (aggregated into fluid factions) was the core recruitment network into Florentine political office. Guild succeeded patrilineage during the so-called guild-corporatist regimes of the early Florentine republic. The popolani logic of state service undergirded the Albizzi "consensus" republicanism of 1378 to 1434, so celebrated in civic humanism. And loyalty to the Medici party determined political access after 1434, institutional appearances notwithstanding.[46] By "political access" I mean the actual (albeit changing) legal rules for eligibility to fill and to vote for offices in the Florentine republic. Repeated struggle over these inclusion rules, between new and old cohorts, was what domestic politics in the Florentine Renaissance was largely about (Brucker 1962, 1977).

Patrilineage, guild, social class, extreme patronage—viewed from the perspectives of politics and economics simultaneously, these identities were protocols through which politics and economics communicated. John Najemy (1991) has made the perceptive observation that Florentine political institutions are better understood as dialogues of power between contending groups than as instruments of domination by any one group. Here I extend the point to individuals: personal identities are micro institutions that enable economic, political, and family roles to communicate. Communication occurs, moreover, in two senses: by permitting actions in one domain to be interpreted in another, and by allowing human beings to move readily across domains.

When does all this matter for actual bankers? The answer is—in a pinch. Quite apart from the reality of multiplicity of goals, firms faced with bankruptcy often needed to reach into their bankers' political and familial networks to stave off disaster. Concretely, this meant that in the patrilineage regime, bankers had to become Bardi (or whatever their family name was) in order for politics effectively to understand their plea for help. But in the guild-corporatist political regime, bankers had to become Cambio guildmen to be effective. And similarly, they had to become popolani or Mediceans for effective translation of their economic requirements into the politics of those regimes. Bankers, of course, were free not to play this game, but not participating greatly diminished their chances for economic survival, especially during times of crisis.

One implication of this "selection under crisis" dynamic was that banking morphologies had to be robust. On the one hand, firms had to be structured in a way that allowed them to "compute" with other firms in the industry, through capital and personnel flows. On the other hand, firms had to be structured in a way that allowed them to "compute" with other potential allies in politics. Once created under conditions of stress, moreover, organizational form reproduced through career recruitment, long after the founding crisis had passed.

Paradoxically, this does not imply that bankers needed to reason self-consciously as politicians. Quite the opposite: to the degree that bankers' understanding of their own identities converged with institutional definitions, they were free to behave "naturally" (that is, without profound self-reflection) in political arenas and "naturally" in economic domains, leaving their politics at their bank-office door. Cross-domain translation, embodied in person-role framings, is performed for the most part institutionally by recruitment and access systems; "mind control" over each and every individual certainly is not required for system reproduction of individual identities.

In each of the four Florentine banking regimes, the "person" behind the banking role became whichever political identity was necessary to maintain the banker's occupancy of that role. As a consequence, as the elite access rules linking markets and politics changed, so did the logics-of-identity framing of elite banking roles.

The recruitment and translation mechanisms for the construction of identity operate similarly in the sense that both are institutionalized methods of control that select the features of the person relevant to entering and maintaining his or her position. As such, to the extent that people learn the reality of how they are treated, I argue that a person's cognitive understanding of his or her own identity is less an infinitely flexible interpretation than it is a socially constructed fact.[47]

The Coevolution of State and Market

Now to the hard question of speciation: what were the dynamics of transition between banking regimes—from family banks to guild banks to popolani systems to extreme-patronage finance? This question is so challenging that I cannot pretend fully to answer it here. But we shall at least begin, with discussions of the family-to-guild transition during the first years of the republic, and the guild-to-popolani transition during the Ciompi revolt. The political side of the popolani-to-Medici transition has been discussed at length in Padgett and Ansell (1993) and so receives more cursory treatment here. These discussions concentrate on the changing roles and identities of merchant-bankers and do not attempt in this brief compass to focus equally on all groups.

The central features of my interpretation of these fundamental Florentine transitions are as follows:

1. During the early years of the republic, merchant-bankers reacted to threatening magnates (themselves organized as patrilineages) by reaching out politically to prosperous immigrants through guild corporatism. Over time, this originally instrumental move transformed their own identities from patrilineages into Cambio (and other arti maggiori) guildmen.

2. During the Ciompi revolt, merchant-bankers reacted to the threatening Ciompi (themselves organized by guild aspirations) by reaching out politically to other economic elites through civic republicanism. Over time, this originally instrumental action by merchant-bankers transformed themselves from guildsmen into popolani.

3. During the Milan and Lucca wars of 1425 to 1430, the Medici merchant-bankers reacted to threatening oligarchy (defined as popolani) by reaching out politically to new-new men through San Giovanni patronage, thereby transforming themselves into a Medicean political party.

In all three cases of regime speciation, the transition rhythm was roughly similar:

(a) a constant background of new (and exiled) persons demanding political and economic inclusion;

(b) war and/or economic shock;

(c) polarization of the political system along lines of cleavage inscribed into the previous institutional order;

(d) spillover of polarization, if intense enough, into a few cross-cutting odd bedfellows;

(e) conservative reaction by merchant-bankers to the threat posed to their business, through reaching out politically from within the fractured elite to groups defined in complement to the threat;

(f) victory, purge of losers, then reconsolidation of a new regime, which was characterized legally by transformed identities layered on top of the old ones[48];

(g) after a generation or so, the repetition of some version of the sequence.

In political science, this process of changing political-identity dimensions is called realignment.

The net effect of these transformations in Renaissance Florence was the preservation of most, but not all, merchant-bankers in a position of power.[49] They adaptively shifted their alliances and modes of access in political dialogue with varying others, in a defensive effort to preserve who they were. An unintended consequence, however, was that "who they were" itself changed, with all the attendant consequences for the organization of banks that implied.

Each of these transition sequences was initiated by a war or economic shock:

The 1282 to 1293 founding of the republic, on the basis of guild corporatist ideology, was initiated by defeat of the Florentine Ghibellines in a civil war, coupled with a boom, not a crisis, in the Florentine economy. This boom came from international trading through the Guelf alliance (Schevill 1961). Florence was larger and more prosperous in this turn-of-the-century patrilineage era than at any time subsequently (Villani 1350/1844).[50]

Wars between England, France, and Flanders, however, caused sharp retrenchment in the banking industries all over northern Italy during the subsequent 1300 to 1343 period (LaSorsa 1904; Sapori 1926; Kaeuper 1973; Housley 1982; English 1988). Internationally oriented bankers took advantage of their newly ensconced Arte del Cambio and Mercanzia political positions to crack down economically on purely domestic money changers and bankers, through strict enforcement of guild regulation (Najemy 1972; Astorri 1998).[51] Hierarchy was established within guilds, and the raw numbers of Florentine bankers shrank as free entry to the industry was abolished. Bankers' strictly instrumental political behavior from 1283 to 1292 as guildmen gradually became infused, by 1343, into their own economic-cum-political identities, through this crackdown process.

The 1378 Ciompi revolt was immediately preceded by the 1375 to 1378 War of the Eight Saints with the pope and by a sharp decline in the wool industry—perhaps caused by papal interdict, perhaps not (Trexler 1974; Hoshino 1980; Franceshi 1993a). The War of the Eight Saints was itself the product of a bitter domestic struggle between magnates and new men; centered on political persecutions by the Parte Guelfa (Brucker 1962), it destroyed forever the pro-papal Guelf alliance.

Environmental shocks, however, while central to the explanation of timing, do not explain the form into which a system reconfigures itself. As paleontologists and others realize, environmental shocks are a dime a dozen: some of them have transforming consequences, many of them do not.[52] Metaphorically speaking, how a crystal responds to the blow of a hammer depends not only on the direction and force of the blow but also the fault lines within the crystal itself.

In the patrilineage-to-guild transition, the organizational response of the banking industry to the events just described depended crucially on the political history of the family in Florence. It was no accident that patrilineage—and in particular the father-son bond—declined in partnership importance during the period of 1283 to 1343. The Florentine republic was engaged in a legal, and even physical, war against it.

This political assault on patrilineage played out in numerous ways. Large numbers of violent, feudally oriented families were legally declared magnati in 1392 by the guild-corporatist republic (Lansing

1991); as such, they were prohibited en bloc from holding major political office.[53] In the aftermath of the early 1300s feuds between Black and White Guelfs (made famous by the participation and subsequent exile of Dante), the family towers (urban castles) of the losing White Guelfs were knocked down and their urban family estates were expropriated, thus repeating the fate of the Ghibellines a few decades before. The passage of laws of so-called emancipation gave fathers and sons for the first time the right voluntarily to appear before the Mercanzia court to declare economic divorce (Kuehn 1982): fathers could choose publicly to renounce (before the fact) legal obligation for the debts of their sons, and vice versa. It does not appear that this emancipation option was exercised frequently (Kuehn 1982). Nonetheless, the option itself was a direct assault on the inner legal logic of family banks.

This multifaceted assault on patrilineage is paradoxical from the perspective of popolani families. Over time, the assault did achieve its titular objective of harming the family-organizational foundation of the magnates, those bitterly sworn enemies of guild corporatism. But popolani and magnati were identical in family organization.[54] Hence, the popolani assault on patrilineage also hurt the organizational foundation of themselves.

The resolution of the paradox is that the popolani, unlike the magnati, had guilds as alternative organizational bases of political power. Hence, their control over the state could be preserved as long as popolani families effectively shifted from patrilineage to guilds as the organizational foundation for their control. Strengthening the patrilineage side of themselves, conversely, would have mobilized, not demobilized, their opponents. I hypothesize, but have not yet proven, that this instrumental reasoning about political design was self-conscious on the part of the popolani.

This is strictly an analysis of politics. How was this politically based patrilineage-to-guild organizational shift transposed into the domain of economics?

The answer is the early 1300s financial crisis, discussed earlier. In response to this crisis, with the short-term goal of calling in outstanding credits to help them weather the Europe-wide economic storm (English 1988), Florentine international merchant-bankers used the newly politicized guild framework to strengthen their control over the domestic economy of Florence. This increased economic control had at least two facets. First, in 1308 the Mercanzia commercial court was established, with the twin economic-cum-political objectives of collecting "delinquent" debts and of coordinating internationalist control over the five major domestic guilds (Astorri 1998). Second, the Arte del Cambio banking guild itself was used to squeeze lower-level "free-entry" money changers out of the industry (Najemy 1972). Partly owing to economic bankruptcies, and partly owing to this political squeeze, the number of active Arte del Cambio bankers dropped off drastically from 313 "bankers" in 1300 to 117 bankers in 1340, even before the well-known (but more temporary in its effects) Bardi bank crisis of 1342.

Through this thirty-year sequence, political expediency became transformed into economic identity: popolani merchant-bankers shed their social identity as fathers and became guild masters, in both their economic and political organizations.[55]

Organizationally speaking, the core issue in the 1378 Ciompi transition, I would argue, was how the term popolani became transformed from the mere attributional category it was in the guild-corporatist regime into the generative logic it became in the Albizzi civic-republican regime. On the political side, this transformation led to the replacement of a collectivist ideology of corporate rights with an individualizing ideology of state service (Najemy 1982). On the economic side, partnerships were now constructed into systems on the logics of parentado (intermarriage) and amicizia (friendship).

These linked transformations are one of the major steps, if not the most important one, along the broader road from medieval to Renaissance Florence. Radically innovative as they were, however, I argue that they can be understood as the path-dependent reworking of the guild-corporatist republic by the Ciompi revolt. I alluded earlier to the "exogenous" triggering events of this revolt. We can obtain a deeper understanding of the reworking, however, from unpacking the political process through which guild corporatism exploded.

It is by now established that the Ciompi revolt of the workers was not, in ideology at least, a Marxist economic-class revolt, as an earlier generation of scholars held. Rather, it was, in inspiration at least, a moderate demand by sottoposti wool workers to create their own guilds (Brucker 1968). Economic conditions in the wool industry imparted an urgency to their request, but the request itself was for citizenship, not wages.

Wool industry conditions notwithstanding, the workers' revolt did not come out of the blue. Parte Guelfa persecutions of new men, themselves fueled by festering magnate exclusions of the past, had polarized the minor guilds into radicalized defense of the guild-corporatist order. In an escalating spiral, reactionary persecution of new men as "Ghibellines" begat radical proscription of conservatives as "magnates" (Brucker 1962). The governing major guilds were shredded by this cross-pressure, since the economic and marriage interests of elite guildmen conflicted. In such volatile circumstances, elite demagogues or heroes (depending on your point of view), like Salvestro d'Alamanno de' Medici, arose to fight for the popolo minuto and against the Guelf pope. Interlinked foreign and civil wars became at some point unstoppable.

The Ciompi wool workers themselves did not exactly come into this picture at the behest of the minor-guild alliance. But the times were extremely propitious for the expression of citizenship rights for "little people" (popolo minuto), who could help tip the volatile balance. (It certainly helped also that many of these muscular wool workers were ex-soldiers.) Wool workers poured into the streets and defeated magnati and popolani supporters of the Parte Guelfa in pitched battles and started to burn many of their houses.[56] What started as a corporatist demand for guild citizenship escalated behaviorally into a true economic-class (that is, workers') revolt, even without the self-identification of sottoposti and popolo minuto as "workers." Large numbers of the economic elite fled the city, in fear for their lives, to their country villas or to their overseas merchant-banking establishments. The teetering wool industry went from decline to collapse; essentially there were no employers left in the city.

The organizational consequences, for the conservatives, of crushing this revolt become obvious once one understands the nature of the challenge. Conservatives were remolded into an economic-cum-social class in complement to the economic-cum-class challenge of the Ciompi from below. Old magnati-popolani distinctions were somewhat effaced, although never again through the mechanism of Guelfism. The gap between major and minor guilds, already present in the previous regime, intensified.

More important than either of these two reworkings of old categories were the profound transforming effects on the identities of major-guild members. Guild distinctions between various types of elite merchants were virtually eradicated: in the short run through their bonding experience of flight and countercoup, and in the longer run through their joint agreement, expressed through baliè, to emasculate the guilds. Victorious elites, understanding that the guilds had opened the door to class warfare, vowed never to let that happen again. So they eliminated guilds as the foundation to the Florentine constitution, taking over the appointment of guild consular leadership and demoting guilds to little more than social clubs.[57]

Cross-guild political cooperation in electoral reform, through class-based elite networks of parentado and amicizia, thus preceded (but only by a few years) the analogous cross-industry cooperation of different economic elites in partnership systems. This coevolution between states and markets is not surprising once one realizes that these two organizational systems were constructed essentially by the same people, as they mobilized their parentado and amicizia networks in different domains.[58] It is this wending of biography across sectors, as I argued earlier, that not only establishes protocols of communication in systems but also frames the "identity behind the role" in individuals.

Conclusion

What is life? In biological chemistry, life is a tangled web of self-regulating loops of chemical reactions that reproduce themselves through time (Eigen 1992; Buss 1987; Fontana and Buss 1994; Padgett 1997; Jain and Krishna 1998). The history of life is thus a path-dependent series of bifurcating networks, each step of which must lock in to stabilize itself before it can take the next step (Goodwin 1994). Neutral drift at the level of individual molecules is consistent with discontinuous tipping at the level of autocatalytic chemical networks (Fontana and Schuster 1998). Viewed from a distance, evolution is a growing bush of coadaptations, refunctionalities, and dead ends, with selective pruning but no inherent teleology (Gould 1980, 1989).

The contribution of the line of research in this chapter to this evolutionary theory is to emphasize the multiple-network character of these bifurcations. Human beings, just like chemical molecules, participate in multiple loops of self-regulating activity. As such, perturbations in one loop may rebound, for good or ill, into other loops. In addition to this point about developmental regulation, I argue that the possible trajectories of evolution of one social network (such as economic partnerships) are shaped by the structure of the surrounding social networks in which that network is embedded. Burgeoning pressures in one network, moreover, may urge other networks down one trajectory of possibility or another.

Because of such network interaction effects, the abstract history of financial capitalism should not be reified away from the concrete particulars of Florentine or any other history. Naturally, diffusion across settings also occurs. But explaining diffusion is different from explaining invention. In the social sciences, we have plenty of models for the former, but precious few for the latter.

In this chapter, I have used my empirical research on Florentine banking as a platform from which to sketch a more general theory or interpretation of the genesis of organizational morphology. At the level of organizational genetics, this theory involves career matching. At the level of organizational development, it involves bankers' logics-of-identity, which are regulated by the biographical political access of elites and which unfold through bankers' social networks to spawn banks. At the level of organizational speciation, this theory involves the realignment of cross-domain bankers' identities, which function at the system level as dialogues or protocols through which politics and markets communicate with each other.

Whether such a framework is exactly what Stinchcombe had in mind in his 1965 inspiration is hard to say. But this article is one attempt to follow the markers of the fading trail he blazed.

This paper was originally prepared for presentation to the seminar series on social and institutional change at the Robert Woods Johnson Foundation, Princeton, New Jersey, organized by Paul DiMaggio. I appreciate the insightful comments of Art Stinchcombe on the earlier draft.

Notes

1. This topic is challenging in biology as well. Many authors have pointed out that the impressive advances of the "modern synthesis" of Mendel and Darwin into population genetics have been purchased at the cost of "abolishing the organism," that is, of ignoring the complex interactive ways in which genotype, coupled with molecular environments through feedback networks of chemical reactions, aggregates up into phenotype during the process of development. Phenotype is assumed, but not explained, in current natural selection theory (see Buss 1987; Fontana and Buss 1994; Kauffman 1993; Goodwin 1994; and Newman 1994).

2. Coevolution, rather than evolution, is the term biologists use to discuss these species interaction effects. Arguably, however, the problem goes deeper than the population dynamics models, based on food webs, typically used to operationalize this concept (for a premier example, see May 1973). Such models do not address where species themselves come from, only their relative population sizes.

3. The Santa Fe Institute has created a new research program, entitled "The Coevolution of States and Markets," under my direction, which is currently pursuing exactly this agenda. Ongoing participants in this program include Walter Powell, David Stark, and Douglas White.

4. Likewise, the notion of gene as "blueprint," automatically producing organisms independently of the chemical reaction environment through which it operates (and which regulates it), is discredited in biology.

5. In organization theory, institutionalists (for example, Meyer and Scott 1983; Powell and DiMaggio 1991) put more emphasis on the first ideational half of this interaction; social embeddedness theorists (for example, Granovetter 1985; Padgett and Ansell 1993) emphasize the second "raw material" half. In biology, Goodwin (1994) and Newman (1994) are especially strong on the second side, emphasizing the channeling impact of organic raw materials on development.

6. I do not emphasize the point, but in addition, a far-from-energy-equilibrium metabolic chemistry, be it molecular or human, needs to be fed with environmentally available resources that it can process (Prigogine and Stengers 1984). Were I to focus empirically on trading (food) more than on partnership (DNA), this point would assume more prominence.

7. Because of the focus here on partnership, not trading, the otherwise important role of energic resource flows (apart from capital itself, of course) recedes into the background.

8. I place these presentist terms in quote marks here to remind us that the way Florentines organized "markets" and "professions" bears only some resemblance to what twentieth-century Americans understand by these terms.

9. By "different types of capital" I mean the sources of capital. In Florentine society, the options were inheritance, dowry, internal past profit, external investment by economically passive investors (aristocrats, churchmen, and so on), and external investment by other Florentine firms. Stock markets did not yet exist, even though government bond markets did. The patterns of flow of these different types of capital through Florentine society varied radically, both cross-sectionally and across time.

10. In this chapter, I am generalizing from the one particular, highly centralized pattern of concatenation of multiple networks with multiple attributions that was analyzed in Padgett and Ansell (1993).

11. This, of course, does not imply that all people are thinking simultaneously about all things at every moment.

12. But see Goldthwaite (1983, 1987) for a modification of his earlier (1968) position.

13. Operationally, "family" here means either same surname (indicating lineage, not nuclear family) or, if no surname existed (for example, "Giovanni son of Paolo"), same father.

14. Other activities included land, church, political competition, and physical violence.

15. Albeit, about a later period, Goldthwaite (1987, 23) perceptively has observed: "[Florentine] merchant bankers undoubtedly competed with one another for the sale of their goods and the attraction of clients— but not to the extent that they devised techniques for product variation and cost-cutting in their home industry and for underselling and market domination abroad."

16. Pawnbrokers and money changers were too small to require any partners at all.

17. Among Arte del Cambio banks, the percentage of family-based partnership dyads dropped from 80 percent to about 40 percent during the period 1300 to 1340. (Note that this decrease long preceded the 1342 banking crisis so discussed in the literature; see Sapori 1926.) These numbers may help to adjudicate the debate about family in Florentine historiography between Goldthwaite (1968) and Kent (1977). The existence of decline supports Goldthwaite's position, although the timing is earlier

than the period he analyzed. But 40 percent is still a large number. This fact thus supports Kent's point about the continued importance of Florentine family throughout the Renaissance. Looking closer at the Arte del Cambio numbers reveals that the decline of 1300 to 1340 was disproportionately due to the virtual disappearance of father-son partnerships. Partnerships between brothers, and to a lesser extent between cousins, remained common throughout the period from 1300 to 1500.

18.   As in "take on your lower-class neighbor's son" first as apprentice, and then, if that works, as partner. The terms of the partnership contract often compensated the subordinate partner for his extra labor with a share of profits greater than the share of capital contributed.

19.   See McLean and Padgett (1997) for formal statistical tests of the neoclassical perfect-competition model for Florence, using primary data on thousands of transactions collected from the 1427 catasto. These tests in particular reject the neoclassical hypothesis of impersonality in exchange. Of course, some economists, including those in this volume, have recently moved beyond the textbook neoclassical assumption that the only things that matter in exchange are price and quality of goods.

20.   Indeed, without double-entry bookkeeping (invented by the time of, but not used much in, the guild period), the concept of "profit" was hard to measure precisely, at least on an ongoing basis. Even modern historians as distinguished as Armando Sapori (1926) and Raymond de Roover can differ widely in their calculation of fourteenth-century "profit rates," using the account books of the period (de Roover 1958). When partnerships dissolved, there was an accounting of profits in order to split proceeds and settle debts. But before partnership dissolution, while the bank legally operated, overall accountings were not regularly performed. This is not to say that during the guild period partners had no informed, rough-and-ready sense of how things were going in general. But theirs was a detailed knowledge of specific transactions ("tacit knowledge"), which is highly dependent on the personal expertise of the partner. Guild-style bankers certainly cared about making money, but there was no social need in such a highly personalized context for the measurement of relative performance as objectified "profit."

21.   Social classes in Renaissance Florence were defined in terms of the political age of the family. In particular, the date at which one's ancestors first were selected to serve on the governing city council (the Signoria) was a publicly known fact and measured one's family's prestige. Like the Boston Brahmin descendants of the *Mayflower*, the popolani were the most prestigious social class in Florence; their ancestors had controlled

the Republic from its founding in 1282 until the ascension of Walter Brienne, the Duke of Athens, in 1343. Thus, the term "social class," as I use it, refers to status, not to wealth or occupation.

22. Federigo Melis (1962) is responsible for the somewhat vague term "systems." De Roover (1966) calls these cross-industry organizational systems "holding companies," but in fact they were networks of overlapping but legally separate partnership contracts, coordinated by centrally placed partners in each of these contracts.

23. There was no such thing as a stock market, which was invented later by the Dutch and the British, largely for political reasons (Carruthers 1996).

24. Melis (1962) in particular heavily emphasizes the role of fiducia in the banking of this period. See also Goldthwaite (1987).

25. Brucker (1969, chapter 3; 1977, chapter 5) in particular has emphasized the explosion of amicizia and clientage during this republican period.

26. I distinguish extreme patronage from patronage by the social (and wealth) distance between the parties. Patronage in the popolani period linked near equals; hence, it was cognitively and linguistically very close to amicizia (McLean 1996). Patronage in the Medici period, in contrast, linked people of vastly different social statuses, more akin to magnificenza (Jenkins 1970).

27. For a sharp challenge to Mark's conclusion, see Goldthwaite (1996).

28. A second historical factor, not accounted for within this extreme-patronage interpretation, is the fact that many republican merchant bankers and their families were politically exiled, although their overseas business firms were not necessarily destroyed as a consequence. (I thank Richard Goldthwaite for this observation.) The Strozzi family (Gregory 1997) is one well known example of how overseas business thrived in spite of political exile. (The Alberti family [Baxendale 1991], however, is a counterexample.) Political exile is a dramatic and obvious blow to "system" partnership ties linking foreign and domestic branches. Given the unprecedented magnitude of Cosimo's exile policy, it is even possible that this political policy negatively affected the economic integration of the Florentine domestic economy into at least some sectors of European international trade.

29. In a more formal representation, both these capitals, of course, would be made continuous.

30. Of course, extension in this way is dependent on underlying family structure: popolani and magnati extended clans were inherently capable

of growing larger firms in this manner than were the more nucleated families of the new men.

31. The prevailing legal doctrine of unlimited liability, of course, made much sense in this social context.

32. I suspect, but have not yet confirmed to my own satisfaction, that the strong brotherhood mode is characteristic of the lower social classes, while the weak brotherhood mode is more characteristic of the upper social classes.

33. Guilds, in other words, while truly motors for social mobility, were also mechanisms for popolani masters' control over the other masters so admitted. The 1378 Ciompi revolt uncovered vulnerabilities in this particular mechanism of control.

34. Industrial districts come to mind as contemporary analogues.

35. I leave aside the complications that Florentine sons-in-law sometimes experienced in collecting their dowries.

36. The concept of "friend" is not so elastic as to imply no repayment at all (pure gift), but it is elastic enough to allow "repayment" in numerous social currencies. The post-1420 Medici were well known for repaying their economic loans in political currency (Molho 1979).

37. I need to find new primary sources before I can fill this gap.

38. The heading refers to Harrison White's *Identity and Control* (1992), in deference to the early training and wealth of ideas I received from White, while I was an assistant professor. This chapter shares with that book a concern with similar themes, although the mechanisms are different.

39. Using the diaries of the Niccolini family as source material, Christiane Klapisch-Zuber (1985, chapter 4) paints a marvelous portrait of the multiplicity of such relations for this family in Renaissance Florence. My only quibble with her insightful analysis would be to draw a sharper distinction than she does between friend and godparent, the latter to me being more like a patron. Indeed, Klapisch-Zuber admits that the Florentines themselves did not equate these two categories (89). Friend was typically intra-class, whereas patron was typically cross-class, but of course, as I too emphasized earlier, these blended into one another.

40. This figure does not correct for truncation effects. The 1348 Black Death makes left-hand truncation largely irrelevant. But right-hand truncation, post-1399, probably makes approximately nine years a more accurate statistic.

41. This is a central argument in Padgett and Ansell (1993); see also Weissman (1989). For the contrasting presumption that medieval Italian state formation was driven primarily by an economic logic, see Greif (1994).

42. Note that this formulation of the concept of "identity" denies any essentialist connotation: identity is the cognitive person-framing of person-role interactions, not a fixed psychology located deep within people. In the context of economics, for example, the identity of a banker could be "father." But in the context of the dinner table, the identity of a father could be "banker." This relativist interpretation is consistent with White (1992), who in turn takes seriously the decades of research in psychology about the weakness of sustained empirical evidence for anything like a stable core "personality" (Mischel 1990).

43. To paraphrase Mary Douglas (1986), institutions do the thinking, although I would be quick to add, not necessarily only through the culturalist mechanisms that she emphasizes. For a quite different application of this "identity from mobility-as-control" argument in the setting of the U.S. Congress, see Padgett (1990).

44. John Najemy (1982, chapter 8) offers a profound analysis of post-Ciompi Florentine electoral reform along these lines. James C. March and James G. March (1977) give a similar argument, albeit in the completely different terminology of mathematical statistics.

45. From radically divergent normative premises, Harrison White (1992), Morris Janowitz (1991), and Antonio Gramsci (1971) all would agree with this conclusion. The converse of this point—namely, that effective control over others is rooted in multivocality—has been developed in Padgett and Ansell (1993).

46. These enormously simplified summaries can be fleshed out with Najemy (1982) and Rubinstein (1966), which are the definitive histories of electoral reform in Florence.

47. Depending on the details of multiple-network structure, such learning can lead toward sphinx-like multiple identities, as in the case of Cosimo de' Medici (Padgett and Ansell 1993), as well as toward the more clear and univocal identities emphasized here.

48. Old identities were never abolished; they just retreated in salience into the background.

49. Perhaps this is one reason for the remarkable continuity of many famous Florentine families in the face of the economic and political turbulence

of Renaissance Florence. This familial continuity has been most astutely analyzed, from the perspective of marriage, by Anthony Molho (1994).

50. As explained earlier, banks were still overwhelmingly family-based in 1300, in spite of the brand-new guild-corporatist state framework. Bank partnerships themselves absorbed political guild-identity in their economic logic only in reaction to the macro-economic decline of 1300 to 1343.

51. Florence's rigorous self-policing of debts through the state stands in marked contrast to the "bailout" policies of Siena (English 1988). Such policies explain the decline of Sienese bankers, relative to Florentine bankers, in newly emergent international money markets.

52. Indeed, the effect of war on regimes is wildly variable: sometimes the shock of war increases consolidation of the existing regime (for the Florentine case, see Baron 1966; more generally, see Tilly 1975), yet sometimes the shock of war causes regime collapse, even without overt defeat (for the Sienese case, see Caffero 1998; more generally, see Skocpol 1979).

53. Although particular remissions were granted to individual families throughout the period from 1292 to 1434, this legal exclusion lasted as a category until the Medici abolished it in 1434. Over time, one serious consequence of exclusion was the splintering of magnate patrilineages as ambitious branches, more interested in cooperating with the guild and popolani regimes, separated themselves from their parent magnate lines (Klapisch-Zuber 1988). Such splintering eventually had so substantial an impact that by 1434 the remaining magnates hardly represented a threat anymore.

54. Indeed, they were heavily intermarried as well.

55. In this chapter, I am not analyzing what happened to family organization in domains outside of politics and economics. There are complicated things to say on this issue, some of which contradict the "decline of patrilineage" thesis supported here. See, for example, Cohn (1988, 1992), who has found that the percentage of inheritance passing down through family increased, rather than decreased, during the Trecento. One possible resolution of this contradiction is that patrilineage within the old popolani-magnati core declined in practical economic importance, even as "mimicking" of patrilineage by new men increased.

56. Of course, such tactics were part of the repertoire of the popolani themselves. They were unaccustomed, however, to seeing such methods used against them, especially by the likes of the Ciompi.

57. See Rubinstein (1981), Najemy (1982), and Franceschi (1993b) for institutional details. Fortunately for my data, guilds continued to register matriculation and partnerships; however, they did little else. I have discussed the marriage side of this transformation of popolani into oligarchy in Padgett and Ansell (1993).

58. I add the qualifier "essentially" only because of the well-known tendency for brothers to construct their little divisions of labor—one politician, one businessman (Goldthwaite 1968).

References

Astorri, Antonella. 1998. *La Mercanzia a Firenze nella Prima Meta del Trecento.* Florence: Leo. S. Olschki Editore.

Baron, Hans. 1966. *The Crisis of the Early Italian Renaissance.* Princeton, N.J.: Princeton University Press.

Baxendale, Susannah Foster. 1991. "Exile in Practice: The Alberti Family in and out of Florence." *Renaissance Quarterly* 44: 720–56.

Breiger, Ronald L. 1974. "The Duality of Persons and Groups." *Social Forces* 53: 181–90.

Brown, Alison. 1992. "Lorenzo, the Monte, and the Seventeen Reformers." *In The Medici in Florence: The Exercise and Language of Power,* edited by Alison Brown. Florence: Leo. S. Olschki Editore.

Brucker, Gene. 1962. *Florentine Politics and Society, 1343–1378.* Princeton, N.J.: Princeton University Press.

———. 1968. "The Ciompi Revolution." In *Florentine Studies: Politics and Society in Renaissance Florence,* edited by Nicolai Rubinstein. Evanston, Ill.: Northwestern University Press.

———. 1969. *Renaissance Florence.* Berkeley: University of California Press.

———. 1977. *The Civic World of Early Renaissance Florence.* Princeton, N.J.: Princeton University Press.

Burckhardt, Jacob. [1860] 1954. *The Civilization of the Renaissance in Italy.* New York: Modern Library.

Buss, Leo W. 1987. *The Evolution of Individuality.* Princeton, N.J.: Princeton University Press.

Caffero, William. 1998. *Mercenary Companies and the Decline of Siena.* Baltimore: Johns Hopkins University Press.

Carruthers, Bruce G. 1996. *City of Capital: Politics and Markets in the English Financial Revolution.* Princeton, N.J.: Princeton University Press.

Cohn, Samuel K. 1988. *Death and Property in Siena, 1205–1800: Strategies for the Afterlife.* Baltimore: Johns Hopkins University Press.

————. 1992. *The Cult of Remembrance and the Black Death*. Baltimore: Johns Hopkins University Press.

De Roover, Raymond. 1958. "The Story of the Alberti Company of Florence, 1302–1348, as Revealed in Its Account Books." *Business History Review* 32: 14–59.

————. 1966. *The Rise and Decline of the Medici Bank, 1397–1494*. New York: Norton.

Douglas, Mary. 1986. *How Institutions Think*. Syracuse, N.Y.: Syracuse University Press.

Duranti, Alessandro, and Charles Goodwin. 1992. *Rethinking Context: Language as an Interactive Phenomenon*. Cambridge: Cambridge University Press.

Eckstein, Nicholas A. 1995. *The District of the Green Dragon: Neighborhood Life and Social Change in Renaissance Florence*. Florence: Leo. S. Olschki Editore.

Eigen, Manfred. 1992. *Steps Toward Life: A Perspective on Evolution*. Oxford: Oxford University Press.

Emirbayer, Mustafa, and Jeff Goodwin. 1994. "Network Analysis, Culture, and the Problem of Agency." *American Journal of Sociology* 99: 1411–54.

English, Edward D. 1988. *Enterprise and Liability in Sienese Banking, 1230–1350*. Medieval Academy of America.

Fontana, Walter, and Leo W. Buss. 1994. "'The Arrival of the Fittest': Toward a Theory of Biological Organization." *Bulletin of Mathematical Biology* 56: 1–64.

Fontana, Walter, and Peter Schuster. 1998. "Continuity in Evolution: On the Nature of Transitions." *Science* 280: 1451–54.

Franceschi, Franco. 1993a. *Oltre il "Tumulto": I Lavoratori Fiorentini dell'Arte della Lana fra Tre e Quattrocento*. Florence: Leo. S. Olschki Editore.

————. 1993b. "Intervento del Potere e Ruolo delle Arti nel Governo dell' Economia Fiorentina del Trecento e del Primo Quattrocento: Linee Generali." *Archivio Storico Italiano* 151: 863–909.

Fubbini, Riccardo. 1996. "Prestito ebraico e Monte di Pieta a Firenze (1471–1473)." In *Quattrocento Fiorentino: Politica, Diplomazia, Cultura*, edited by Riccardo Fubbini. Pisa: Pacine Editore.

Goffman, Erving. 1974. *Frame Analysis: An Essay on the Organization of Experience*. Boston: Northeastern University Press.

Goldthwaite, Richard A. 1968. *Private Wealth in Renaissance Florence: A Study of Four Families*. Princeton, N.J.: Princeton University Press.

————. 1983. "Organizzazione economica e struttura famigliare." In *I Ceti Dirigenti nella Toscana Tardo Comunale*. Florence: Francesco Papafava Editore.

————. 1985. "Local Banking in Renaissance Florence." *Journal of European Economic History* 14: 5–55.

————. 1987. "The Medici Bank and the World of Florentine Capitalism." *Past and Present* 114: 3–31.

———. 1996. "Lorenzo Morelli, Ufficiale del Monte, 1484–88: Interessi Privati e Cariche Pubbliche nella Firenze Laurenziana." *Archivo Storico Italiano* 154: 605–33.

Goodwin, Brian. 1994. *How the Leopard Changed Its Spots: The Evolution of Complexity.* New York: Simon & Schuster.

Gould, Steven J. 1980. *The Panda's Thumb.* New York: Norton.

———. 1989. *Wonderful Life: The Burgess Shale and the Nature of History.* New York: Norton.

Gramsci, Antonio. 1971. *Selections from the Prison Notebooks,* edited and translated by Quintin Hoare and Geoffrey Nowell Smith. New York: International Publishers.

Granovetter, Mark. 1985. "Economic Action and Social Structure: The Problem of Embeddedness." *American Journal of Sociology* 91: 481–510.

Gregory, Heather. 1997. *Selected Letters of Alessandra Strozzi.* Berkeley: University of California Press.

Greif, Avner. 1994. "On the Political Foundations of the Late Medieval Commercial Revolution: Genoa During the Twelfth and Thirteenth Centuries." *Journal of Economic History* 54: 271–87.

Hoshino, Hidetoshi. 1980. *L'Arte della Lana in Firenze nel Basso Medioevo.* Florence: Leo. S. Olschki Editore.

Housley, Norman. 1982. The Italian Crusades. Oxford: Clarendon Press.

Hutchins, Edwin. 1995. *Cognition in the Wild.* Cambridge, Mass.: MIT Press.

Jain, Sanjay, and S. Krishna. 1998. "Autocatalytic Sets and the Growth of Complexity in an Evolutionary Model." *Physical Review Letters* 81: 5684–87.

Janowitz, Morris. 1991. *On Social Organization and Social Control.* Chicago: University of Chicago Press.

Jenkins, A. D. Fraser. 1970. "Cosimo de Medici's Patronage of Architecture and the Theory of Magnificence." *Journal of the Warburg and Courtauld Institutes* 33: 162–70.

Kaeuper, Richard W. 1973. *Bankers to the Crown: The Ricciardi of Lucca and Edward I.* Princeton, N.J.: Princeton University Press.

Kauffman, Stuart A. 1993. *The Origins of Order.* New York: Oxford University Press.

Kent, F. W. 1977. *Household and Lineage in Renaissance Florence.* Princeton, N.J.: Princeton University Press.

Klapisch-Zuber, Christiane. 1988. "Ruptures de Parente et Changements d'Identité chez les Magnats Florentins du XIVe Siècle." *Annals ESC* 43: 1205–40.

———. 1985. *Women, Family, and Ritual in Renaissance Italy.* Chicago: University of Chicago Press.

Kuehn, Thomas. 1982. *Emancipation in Late Medieval Florence*. New Brunswick, N.J.: Rutgers University Press.

Lansing, Carol. 1991. *The Florentine Magnates: Lineage and Faction in a Medieval Commune*. Princeton, N.J.: Princeton University Press.

LaSorsa, Saverio. 1904. *L'organizzazione dei Cambiatori Fiorentini*. Cerignola: Tip. edit. dello "scienza e diletto."

Leifer, Eric. 1988. "Interaction Preludes to Role Setting: Exploring Local Action." *American Sociological Review* 53: 865–78.

Lopez, Robert S. 1976. *The Commercial Revolution of the Middle Ages, 950–1350*. Cambridge: Cambridge University Press.

March, James C., and James G. March. 1977. "Almost Random Careers: The Wisconsin School Superintendency, 1940–1972." *Administrative Science Quarterly* 22: 377–409.

Marks, Louis F. 1960. "The Financial Oligarchy in Florence Under Lorenzo." In *Italian Renaissance Studies*, edited by E. F. Jacob. London: Faber and Faber.

May, Robert M. 1973. *Stability and Complexity in Model Ecosystems*. Princeton, N.J.: Princeton University Press.

McLean, Paul D. 1996. "Patronage and Political Culture: Strategies of Self-Presentation, Roles, and Identity in Renaissance Florence." Ph.D. diss., Department of Political Science, University of Chicago.

———. 1998. "A Frame Analysis of Favor Seeking in the Renaissance: Agency, Networks, and Political Culture." *American Journal of Sociology* 104: 51–91.

McLean, Paul D., and John F. Padgett. 1997. "Was Florence a Perfectly Competitive Market?: Transactional Evidence from the Renaissance." *Theory and Society* 26: 209–44.

Melis, Federigo. 1962. *Aspetti della Vita Economica Medievale: Studi nell'Archivio Datini di Prato*. Siena: Monte del Paschi di Siena.

Meyer, John, and W. Richard Scott. 1983. *Organizational Environments: Ritual and Rationality*. Beverly Hills, Calif.: Sage Publications.

Mischel, Walter. 1990. "Personality Dispositions Revisited and Revised: A View After Three Decades." In *Handbook of Personality Theory and Research*, edited by Lawrence Pervin. New York: Guilford Press.

Molho, Anthony. 1979. "Cosimo de Medici: Pater Patriae or Padrino?" *Stanford Italian Review* 1: 5–33.

———. 1994. *Marriage Alliance in Late Medieval Florence*. Cambridge, Mass.: Harvard University Press.

Najemy, John M. 1972. "The Guilds in Florentine Politics, 1292–1394." Ph.D. diss., Harvard University.

———. 1981. "'Audiant omnes artes': Corporate Origins of the Ciompi Revolution." In *Il Tumulto dei Ciompi*, edited by Istituto Nationale di Studi sul Rinascimento. Florence: Leo. S. Olschki Editore.

———. 1982. *Corporatism and Consensus in Florentine Electoral Politics, 1280–1400.* Chapel Hill: University of North Carolina Press.

———. 1991. "The Dialogue of Power in Florentine Politics." In *City-States in Classical Antiquity and Medieval Italy,* edited by Anthony Molho, Kurt Raaflaub, and Julia Emlen. Ann Arbor: University of Michigan Press.

Newman, Stuart A. 1994. "Generic Physical Mechanisms of Tissue Morphogenesis: A Common Basis for Development and Evolution." *Journal of Evolutionary Biology* 7: 467–88.

Padgett, John F. 1990. "Mobility as Control: Congressmen Through Committees." In *Social Mobility and Social Structure,* edited by Ronald L. Breiger. Cambridge: Cambridge University Press.

———. 1997. "The Emergence of Simple Ecologies of Skill: A Hypercycle Approach to Economic Organization." In *The Economy as an Evolving Complex System II,* edited by Brian Arthur et al. SFI Studies in the Sciences of Complexity. Reading, Mass.: Addison-Wesley.

Padgett, John F., and Christopher K. Ansell. 1993. "Robust Action and the Rise of the Medici, 1400–1434." *American Journal of Sociology* 98: 1259–1319.

Powell, Walter W., and Paul J. DiMaggio. 1991. *The New Institutionalism in Organizational Analysis.* Chicago: University of Chicago Press.

Prigogine, Ilya, and Isabella Stengers. 1984. *Order out of Chaos.* New York: Bantam.

Rubinstein, Nicolai. 1966. *The Government of Florence Under the Medici, 1434–1494.* Oxford: Oxford University Press.

———. 1981. "Il Regime Politico di Firenze Dopo il Tumulto dei Ciompi." In *Il Tumulto dei Ciompi: Un Momento di Storia Fiorentina ed Europea,* edited by Istituto Nazionale di Studi sul Rinascimento. Florence: Leo. S. Olschki Editore.

Sapori, Armando. 1926. *La Crisi delle Compagnie Mercantili dei Bardi e dei Peruzzi.* Florence: Leo. S. Olschki Editore.

Schevill, Ferdinand. 1961. *History of Florence.* New York: Frederick Ungar.

Sewell, William, Jr. 1980. *Work and Revolution in France: The Language of Labor from the Old Regime to 1848.* Cambridge: Cambridge University Press.

Skocpol, Theda. 1976. "Old Regime Legacies and Communist Revolutions in Russia and China." *Social Forces* 55: 284–315.

———. 1979. *States and Social Revolutions.* Cambridge: Cambridge University Press.

Stark, David, and Laszlo Bruszt. 1998. *Postsocialist Pathways: Transforming Politics and Property in East Central Europe.* Cambridge: Cambridge University Press.

Stinchcombe, Arthur. 1965. "Social Structure and Organizations." In *Handbook of Organizations,* edited by James G. March. New York: Rand McNally.

Tilly, Charles. 1975. *The Formation of National States in Western Europe.* Princeton, N.J.: Princeton University Press.

Trexler, Richard. 1974. *The Spiritual Power: Republican Florence Under Interdict.* Leiden: Brill.

Villani, Giovanni. 1844–45. *Cronica di Giovanni Villani,* edited by F. Dragomanni. Florence:(Originally published in 1350–?)

Weissman, Ronald. 1989. "The Importance of Being Ambiguous: Social Relations, Individualism, and Identity in Renaissance Florence." In *Urban Life in the Renaissance,* edited by Susan Zimmerman and Ronald Weissman. Dover: University of Delaware Press.

White, Doublas R. and P. Jorion. 1992. "Representing and Analyzing Kinship: A Network Approach." *Current Anthropology* 33: 454–62.

White, Harrison C. 1992. *Identity and Control: A Structural Theory of Social Action.* Princeton, N.J.: Princeton University Press.

Discussion

Comments and Further Thoughts on "Organizational Genesis, Identity, and Control: The Transformation of Banking in Renaissance Florence"

Gregory Besharov and Avner Greif

Do new organizational forms spring, fully formed, from the head of their founder? Does the environment forge new forms from old, with ceaseless heating and hammering? Do their constitutive elements change so that existing organizations take new forms in mad pursuit of new opportunities? In "Organizational Genesis, Identity, and Control: The Transformation of Banking in Renaissance Florence," John Padgett develops a general theory of the genesis of organizational forms in which, to some extent, each of these three mechanisms has a role.

In Padgett's theory, there is a founder of an organization who imbues a firm with its organizing conception. The term "logic-of-identity" describes the way in which the "ideas, practices, and social relations of the founder" map to the choice of organizational form. The nature of the firm is not determined entirely by the logic-of-identity but is further influenced by the firm's social environment. "Actual living organizations, social or biological, are the developmental products of these founder logics, interacting with the inherent properties of the social or biological raw materials being assembled." Social networks *select* the organizations by favoring some over others, and they also *are selected into* the organization through recruitment and personnel flows.

These selections occur partly through the mechanism of career access in which members of social networks differentially obtain political patronage. "An autonomous organization emerges and sustains itself through time if an autocatalytic 'metabolic chemistry' of technology and work routines crystallizes out of the ideational-social mixture of founding logics-of-identity and crosscutting social networks." The triad of logic-of-identity, social networks, and energic resource flows composes the terms of analysis, a "framework for analyzing systemic interactions and feedback in such a way as to (post-hoc) explain the emergence of new organizational forms."

Padgett develops this general theory inductively from the study of Renaissance Florentine domestic banking, specifically the investigation of the "capital-formation nucleus of the firm" in the thirteenth and fourteenth centuries. In this context, logics-of-identity are historically variable rules for capital formation, chosen, according to the theory, by the founder at the time of inception. The social networks are socially structured channels (such as family, neighborhood, and social-class patronage) through which potential bankers with capital find each other to form firms. The energic resource flows are not used substantially in the analysis. (That energic resource flows do not have a larger role is somewhat surprising, given that the theory was developed inductively from the historical study.)

In contrast, the economic theory of organizations—and economics more generally—is based on the central principles of optimization and equilibrium. Firm structure is an optimization problem. To maximize the value of her firm, the owner chooses an organizational form either, in some models, according to an understanding of the relationship between structure and profitability or, in other models, by imitation of previously successful organizational forms.[1] In both types of models, the final structure of an industry's organizational forms is in equilibrium such that no agent can do better by adopting an alternate form. A common starting point for the literature is Ronald Coase's (1937) insight that markets and firms are different responses to the problem of transaction governance. Oliver Williamson (1991) has characterized transactions on the basis of their uncertainty, frequency, and various types of asset specificity, and he has hypothesized that as transactions increase along those dimensions (for example, more uncertainty), the optimal organizational form moves from market through hybrid to hierarchy. The notion that changes in relevant transaction costs could lead to changes in organizational form is so much a part of the optimization framework that it is often unstated. Stability in organizational form is the result of stable parameters of the optimization (or, perhaps, changing parameters that result in the same optimum) or accumulated institutional capital of some sort, rather than a fixed component such as logic-of-identity. Large shifts in form can occur in short order in response to changes in the environment. In this context, a new organizational form can be seen as an extreme case of a large shift in form in response to novel transactional environments. We would stress that there are alternative approaches, but they are truly "alternative" in the sense that they are departures from the standard.

It should be clear that the notion of optimization does not exclude path dependence. Unlike some sociological theories, however, standard notions of organization path dependence in economics are not the result of small departures from routine or strategy caused by the bounded rationality of decisionmakers (for example, Hannan and Freeman 1989). In economic models, the past constrains the present through expectations, beliefs, sunk costs, network externalities, and organization-specific capital that make the manager's optimal choice persistent.

In recent years, there has been convergence between economics and sociology. Economists are conceiving of economic systems as part of a broader social system, and sociologists are turning their attention to issues that have been historically confined to the domain of economics. Members of both fields are interested in the social factors that constrain behavior, including such issues as identity construction, preference formation, and the importance of status.[2]

In this comment, we hope to reveal issues that hinder interdisciplinary communication. We are motivated in large part by the difficulties we faced in understanding the style of argument made in Padgett's paper. We think that discussing it from an economic perspective would best support the intention of this volume by informing those outside the field on the craft, creed, and critical approach of modern economics. Though economics may be relatively united in its methodology for a social science, the variation in the beliefs of economists is substantial, so we try to adopt the mind-set of a mainstream economist interested in institutional analysis. The next section describes the structure of economic models. The section following discusses substantiation of economic models. Conclusions follow.

Models and Modeling

At least since Adam Smith or David Ricardo, economists have presented their theories in models. These models may differ in language of argument, some relying heavily on mathematics and others entirely on words, but they share several main characteristics. First, the variables under examination can be categorized as either invariant within the model (exogenous) or influenced by other variables in the model (endogenous). Exogenous factors in economic models often include such things as the preferences of individuals, the technology and objectives of firms, and, in organizational analysis, the characteristics of transactions. Second, models specify causal relations, that is, they specify exactly how the endogenous variables are jointly determined within the system by the exogenous variables. Although few variables may be exogenous in the strict sense when the economic system is considered as a whole, in the partial equilibrium models common to organization theory such an assumption is weaker; regardless, some aspects of the model must be taken as given if any variables are to be determined causally.[3] On both measures, this paper proceeds in a manner to which economists are not accustomed.

Padgett draws heavily from biological theory to create his model. He makes a strong claim about why we do not understand the genesis of organizational forms. "It is the absence of a theory of recombination that inhibits social-science understanding of genesis: we need to take more seriously than we do the fact that nothing exists without a history." In biological models, recombination is a useful description of the genesis of new genotypes because there is in fact a process of recombination that occurs. Is there any such recombination in organizational genesis? Padgett writes that "birth is rooted in a logic of recombination." Yet he provides no support for why this is more useful than, say, a theory rooted in cognitive psychology. The factors that enter into the mind of a potential founder of an organization are many and varied. A cognitive theory would address how an individual processes relevant information to determine the logic-of-identity for her new organization. Such information could well be historical. If the founder does not know precisely the relationship between form and outcome, then she may rely on historical relationships to inform her choice. This is not to say that a model of recombination cannot be useful for understanding organizational genesis. It would be valuable to know why a process that governs DNA is more appropriate than a model that borrows more directly from the study of individual decisionmaking.

The logic-of-identity is the analog of DNA in the model and describes the origin of organizational forms. But without specifying a mechanism for the way in which the logic-of-identity maps to the choice of organization, what do we actually learn about organizational genesis from the exercise? When patrilineage was politically and socially important, firms were patrilineal. When patrilineage became less important, guilds moved to the forefront and became the basis for logics-of-identity. Then guilds were crushed, and the popolani moved in. Padgett argues that speciation of new organization forms was catalyzed by political changes. It is not clear how we know that the changes would not have occurred even in the absence of the political change or how similar political changes at a different time would have had a similar or different effect. If organizational changes began before the political change—as seems to be the case at least in the Ciompi-caused transition—then there may even have been a common factor that caused both. In the absence of an imputed relationship, "logic-of-identity" is merely a name for a direct transmission device from the political environment to firm structure and does not add to the analysis.

This absence of causal specification makes it difficult to evaluate the claim regarding path dependence in the model. If exogenous changes in politics lead to changes in the "field" out of which organizations are created, then the causal relation does not depend on previous organizational forms, but only on political history. For economists, this is a crucial theoretical distinction. The political determination of organizational form would imply an absence of learning from experience. For example, the bankruptcy of the Bardi and Peruzzi on the eve of the Black Death would be posited not to have influenced the structure of subsequent businesses, although there are reasons to believe that it did (Greif 1999). The mere fact that organizational forms drew on preexisting social networks is not to say that the past had any importance.

Other unclear causal relations include the formation of social networks. They are "selected into . . . the organization through trading and personnel flows," but the manner in which they do so is not specified. The statement of an empirical finding naturally raises the question of why it occurred, but no analysis is provided. Another example of an unclear causal relation is the claim that the social-class banking of the post-Ciompi era implied "open-ended credit relations" while the guild-based banking of the pre-Ciompi era did not. The causal link is not given. To state that "class" implies open-ended credit while the cross-class-within-neighborhood does not pushes the question one step down but does not constitute an answer.

Changes in other environmental variables could supplant the role of logic-of-identity in the formation of new organizations. A change in the legal environment appears to be relevant in the shift away from father-son partnerships in Renaissance Florence. The paper notes that in early 1300 the passage of emancipation laws "gave fathers and sons for the first time the right voluntarily to . . . declare economic divorce . . . fathers could choose publicly to renounce . . . legal obligation for the debts of their sons, and vice versa." The change in liability, independent of contemporary logics-of-identity, could have caused the shift in organizational forms. If so, the logics-of-identity would not have been necessary for organizational change. Nor is it clear that changes in logic-of-identity are sufficient. Can one account for the observed organizational changes based only on political factors while excluding lines of causation other than those entailed by the logic-of-identity shift?

One last reason for the importance of specifying causality is that doing so implies the degree of relevance of various factors. Models are exercises in selective blindness. Many things may matter, but as one examines more endogenous variables and more dimensions, one can make finer distinctions between observations. At some point, the fineness of the distinction is not worth the additional complexity. For example, it is not clear that we should care about father-son versus brother-cousin partnerships unless they cause substantial differences in outcomes.

Substantiation

The discussion of causality leads naturally into substantiation. In economic analyses, lines of causality are often substantiated by showing that changes in the variables considered exogenous resulted in changes in the endogenous variables as predicted by the model. Since the modeler had past data to use in constructing the theory, the ability of a model to determine the correct relations for data unknown to the modeler when making the model is considered evidentiary support.

The most severe deficiency in the way the paper elaborates on its claims, from an economist's point of view, is that it does not clearly delineate the lines dividing "facts" from "conjectures." This, in turn, makes it difficult to understand which conjectures the paper needs to substantiate and how it does so. Consider the statement that in each banking phase "role was framed by identity." It is not clear what could be done to support the statement, or whether we are supposed to take it as given. Another claim that would be difficult to substantiate is that "Florentine bankers' understanding of what it meant to be a partner was affected, in each of these periods, by their conception of themselves as persons, outside of the bank." How would one determine their conception of who they were as people outside of the bank? Part of the substantiation problem is that claims are being made regarding things that cannot be assayed.

Similar difficulties arise in the description of the various historical eras: we are informed that in the pre–Black Death era of family banking, partnerships were between fathers and sons, they were relatively large, and there was no interbank career mobility. Although the paper, owing to space limitation, does not provide historical evidence to support these claims, it is rather clear what the evidence is that could be brought to bear. These claims can be considered as facts in the sense that there is evidence that can directly refute or support them. But the description of the banking partnerships goes beyond providing such facts; it also provides other characteristics of the era. For example, we are informed that capital "assumed the cultural meaning of the social raw material out of which banks were constructed." How do we support objectively such a claim? Is it part of the facts or part of the interpretation? Similarly, we are told that in the following guild era partners "formed and re-formed themselves . . . [thereby] displacing the earlier logic of father-son . . . [with] guild-based firm-formation logic." As discussed previously, logic-of-identity is not something that is directly reflected in the historical evidence, so how can it be part of the description?

The issue of substantiating claims regarding logics-of-identity is indicative of a larger issue of nonmeasurability. Imbuing an organization with its logic-of-identity is an inherently intentional action in the sense of Merton's (1936) "The Unanticipated Consequences of Purposive Social Action." Given an organization with an observed form, the logic-of-identity is not extricable because of interactions with social networks. It is difficult to know how one could ever verify an intentional construct to an economist's satisfaction. First, there may be strategic misrepresentation by individuals of their stated intentionality. Second, even if there were no such misrepresentations, economists do not require that individuals be fully aware of the reasons for their decisionmaking, only that the decisionmaking be optimal given their information. Even if the exogenous and endogenous variables were presented distinctly and the causal relations were clear, substantiation cannot even conceivably occur if the relevant variables are not measurable. A model could describe perfectly some relation, but if one of the aspects of the relation is not measurable, then it would not be possible to test it as specified. If by their nature logics-of-identity are unobservable and their effects may be confounded with those of social networks, then it is impossible to determine whether they operate in the manner specified.

The substantiation to which we refer is not only whether the posited theory can account for the relevant observations, but also whether there are other theories that can do so. We do not attempt to provide a full alternative explanation, but we would like to raise the issue of whether the observed history can be explained without invoking a "logic-of-identity." Consider the notion that different social networks link the banking and political spheres in different periods. This does not necessitate that "a person's cognitive understanding of his or her own identity" would change between the periods. Indeed, the paper itself asserts that "Florentine political institutions shaped actual (not just interpreted) biographies. . . . Which aspects of their external lives did bankers select as identities to be relevant for the attainment and maintenance of their position as a banker?" This statement implies that there is a "banker's identity" that is fixed over time. It could be the case that what has changed is the means to achieve an end, not the end itself, which would call into question the independent explanatory force attributed to the concept of logic-of-identity.

The last notion of substantiation involves the implications regarding certain changes in endogenous variables as a result of changes in exogenous variables. Referred to as comparative statics, these relations are a major component of economic analysis in that they make predictions that can be empirically tested. In this case, it would be important to know that political changes that did not result in new organizational forms were not predicted by theory to do so. Since the hypothesized relations should hold for the data that generated the model, a true test requires confirmation that the hypothesized relations hold for data that were not used in formulating the model in the first place.

Conclusion

Perhaps the greatest motivation of interdisciplinary borrowing is the presence of a phenomenon that is anomalous in one discipline and explained in another.[4] For example, economists may model the underlying or initial conditions of two situations as identical yet observe conflicting outcomes. Sociologists may have objects of analysis or causal relations that differentiate the situations and explain the inequivalent results. If firm behavior were to depend on logics-of-identity, for example, then some pattern of observed results could be inexplicable for an economist and understood by an analyst familiar with the theories developed in this paper.

The importance of anomalous behavior for interdisciplinary borrowing follows from consistency in substantiation. Phenomena for which one field's theories are consistent with observations present no need to look to other fields at all. The structure of reward in a profession is likely to motivate its members to expand the frontiers of that field's knowledge rather than explore alternatives to conventional wisdom, unless these alternatives can account for phenomena that existing theories cannot. Economic theory provides an explanation for the genesis of organizational forms, and it is not clear that other theories are necessary to explain the observed history.

Among the topics in sociology that have been relatively unexplored within economics is that of identity—largely, in our opinion, because it has not been clear in the past how the concept aids economic analysis. Whether a banker be popolani, magnati, or peasant is of relatively little concern to economists unless the banker's status has "real" consequences (that is, those associated with efficiency or distribution), such as the allocation of capital through banks, the talent and skills of bankers in so doing, and the distribution of income that results. If economists do not consider roles and identity an important organizational concept, then the differences in organizations that the paper discusses may not be, for them, different organizations at all. We expect that such issues as the number of partners, the capitalization of firms, self-conceptions, and so on, can be of only personal, as opposed to professional, interest to economists unless these issues further their understanding of "real" consequences. The variation we have been told about in the paper involves the social identities of bankers, the method of advancement, the number of partners, and the capitalization of their firms. It is not clear whether there were differences in the types of loans by industry or amount, in the separation between capital provision and management of the firm, or in other issues that economists would consider real. Yet previous work shows that variation in social aspects can have real consequences. The conditionality of business relationships, for example, on one social identity rather than another can have important consequences. Indeed, it has been shown to be important in the context of premodern trade (see, for example, Greif 1994). This paper, however, does not develop such links.

The issues regarding endogenous and exogenous variables, causation, and substantiation raised in this comment imply that it is very difficult for economists to understand the details of the argument and how to evaluate it. An economist's specification of the problem would start by presenting facts such as who the partners were, how large the partnerships were, whether employees were drawn from the partners' families, and what we know about the prices that prevailed. Then it would proceed to present the argument: detailing the causal relationships between these variables in each period of time and explaining how the factors led to change from one period to another. Next, it would offer substantiation by showing that the hypothesized changes in endogenous variables from changes in exogenous variables actually occurred. Finally, it would examine whether an alternative theory could better describe the observed relations or whether, following Occam's razor, a simpler theory would perform as well.

A final barrier to interdisciplinary exchange is that the borrowed explanation must be consistent with the existing concepts of the borrowing field. That is, it may be that one field's explanation violates a fundamental supposition of the other field's theory in a way that cannot be reconciled or, more weakly, is not useful. The notion of "intentionality" may be one such case in that it may be irreconcilable with the economic paradigm of purposive optimization. If the genesis of organizational form lies in such matters, economists may be reluctant to adopt the explanation even if morphological genesis is anomalous within economic models.

These barriers may seem substantial, and indeed we think they are. Nonetheless, economists have learned to communicate with, and borrow from, psychologists, historians, and political scientists. The subject of this paper, the genesis of organizational morphology in the context of banking, is of interest to economists. Various other sociological issues are also of interest, such as identity construction, preference formation, and the importance of status. Sociologists know much about these subjects, but for economists to benefit from that knowledge, we need communicate across methodological barriers. As economists, we tend to think that gains from trade will occur when they are large enough, so we look forward with confidence to greater sharing in the future.

Notes

1. The textbook by Paul Milgrom and John Roberts (1992) is a sophisticated introduction to analyses in which behavior is intentional. Peyton Young (1998) demonstrates the mimetic evolutionary mechanisms.

2. For example, Harold Cole, George Mailath, and Andrew Postlewaite (1992) develop a model in which the importance of social status can influence growth rates. Within their framework, Maristella Botticini (1999) examines Florentine dowries.

3. Though there is no bright line between the models referred to as "partial equilibrium" and "general equilibrium," general equilibrium models take more variables as being determined endogenously and include a fuller description of the economy.

4. Other motivations include the perceived success of a theoretical or empirical apparatus from another field.

References

Botticini, Maristella. 1999. "Social Norms and Intergenerational Transfers in a Premodern Economy: Florence, 1260–1435." Unpublished paper.

Coase, Ronald. 1937. "The Nature of the Firm." *Economica* 4: 386–405.

Cole, Harold L., George J. Mailath, and Andrew Postlewaite. 1992. "Social Norms, Savings Behavior, and Growth." *Journal of Political Economy* 100(6): 1092–1125.

Greif, Avner. 1994. "Cultural Beliefs and the Organization of Society—A Historical and Theoretical Reflection on Collectivist and Individualist Societies." *Journal of Political Economy* 102(5): 912–50.

———. 1999. "The Study of Organizations and Evolving Organizational Forms Through History: Reflections from the Late Medieval Family Firm." *Industrial and Corporate Change* 5(2): 473–501.

Hannan, Michael T., and John Freeman. 1989. *Organizational Ecology.* Cambridge, Mass.: Harvard University Press.

Merton, Robert K. 1936. "The Unanticipated Consequences of Purposive Social Action." *American Sociological Review* 1(6): 894–904.

Milgrom, Paul, and John Roberts. 1992. *Economics, Organization, and Management.* Englewood Cliffs, N.J.: Prentice-Hall.

Williamson, Oliver E. 1991. "Comparative Economic Organization: The Analysis of Discrete Structural Alternatives." *Administrative Science Quarterly* 36: 269–96.

Young, Peyton H. 1998. *Individual Strategy and Social Structure: An Evolutionary Theory of Institutions.* Princeton, N.J.: Princeton University Press.

Chapter 6

Black Ties Only?
Ethnic Business Networks,
Intermediaries, and African American
Retail Entrepreneurship

James E. Rauch

An ethnic business network can be a tool that allows entrepreneurs to avoid or overcome the effects of discrimination. The first objective of this chapter is to show, for the case of retail trade, how careful study of the interaction of networks and markets can improve understanding of the ways in which ethnic business networks benefit their members. The second objective is to demonstrate that this understanding can be used to generate new, workable ideas for policy where ethnic business networks are weak or absent. In particular, I argue that large, diversified commercial trade intermediaries already provide many of the same benefits as business networks to majority retailers, and that they can be induced to provide these benefits for minority retailers as well.

My fieldwork in Brooklyn, New York, supports, for retail businesses, the claims of earlier scholars that African American businesses have been ineffective in organizing "mutual self-help" compared to businesses in many immigrant groups of color that also suffer from discrimination. At the same time, the low rates of participation and success of African Americans in retail entrepreneurship have been important issues for the African American community. African American retail entrepreneurship thus seems a natural subject to which we can apply the new ideas for policy developed here.

I argue later in the chapter that an important way in which ethnic business networks help their retailer members is by facilitating their connections to a broad array of vendors who reliably provide merchandise that is well suited to their clienteles. The power of ethnic ties in retailing is illustrated here with the example of Korean wig merchants. I also show that existing large-scale intermediaries such as independent buying offices, contract wholesalers, and franchisers provide these benefits to majority retailers, but there are important shortcomings, I contend, in the ability of these intermediaries to serve African American retailers. I present a policy proposal that aims to overcome these shortcomings, focusing on apparel and accessories within retailing. I suggest subsidizing the affiliation of African American apparel and accessory retailers with a large independent buying office. Affiliation with a common buying office would yield the same sharing of information that occurs in an ethnic business network, increasing the efficiency with which African American retailers find vendors of the products most desired by their clienteles. African American market representatives employed by the independent buying office to serve its African American retailers could develop relationships with these vendors that would enable them to turn the most successful African American retail concepts into African American–owned franchises. I conclude with some thoughts on the likelihood that my policy proposal would succeed if implemented.

The Importance of African American Retail Entrepreneurship

The low rate of overall entrepreneurship among African Americans is well known. Robert Fairlie and Bruce Meyer (1996), using a sample from the 1990 U.S. Census of the Population of nonagricultural workers at least sixteen years old, compute self-employment rates of 10.8 percent for all males and 4.4 percent for African American males.[1] According to the U.S. Bureau of the Census, blacks accounted for just over 12 percent of the U.S. population in 1992, but as the 1992 Survey of Minority-Owned Business Enterprises (SMOBE) shows, they accounted for only 3.6 percent of small-business entrepreneurs.[2] The black share of retail trade small-business entrepreneurs is almost exactly the same (3.5 percent), despite the low capital-intensity of retail trade.[3] Black retail trade entrepreneurs are also less successful than U.S. retail trade entrepreneurs overall, with sales per firm of roughly $80,000 compared to $292,000, and share of firms with paid employees equal to 13.9 percent compared to 29.1 percent. Within this latter subset of firms, however, employees per firm is roughly equal (6.9 versus 7.3 employees), and the ratio of black firm size to overall U.S. firm size is higher (roughly $462,000 versus $921,000).

Are the low rates of African American participation and success in retail trade entrepreneurship of any consequence? Let us first take note of the quantitative importance of retail trade small business in the U.S. economy. In the United States in 1992, 44.7 million people worked in 17.3 million small businesses, of which 27.4 million were paid employees of the subset of 3.1 million small businesses that had paid employees (U.S. Department of Commerce 1996, 73, table 10). Retail trade accounted for 21.1 percent of small-business workers: 14.4 percent of entrepreneurs and 25.4 percent of paid employees. Among major industry groups, retail trade was second behind services in all of these statistics, the comparable figures being 38.1, 45.1, and 33.7 percent.

Overall, retailing accounts for 40 percent of Americans' first jobs (Moss 1995). Recent research has shown that black businesses are more likely than nonblack businesses to hire blacks, even controlling for ethnic composition of business location (Bates 1993, chapter 5; Holzer 1996). Increased African American participation and success in retail trade entrepreneurship may also facilitate successful African American entrepreneurship in other lines of business. Speaking of a maker of African American toys, Marlene Cimons (1988) observed: "Eason's toughest battle is getting distributors to place her products in stores. 'The distribution system is where many black businesses get stopped out,' she said, 'especially when you're distributing in an area that doesn't already have a layer of black businesses.'" Clearly, there is a synergy between the formation of African American retail trade businesses, the establishment of an African American presence in distribution networks, and successful African American entrepreneurship more generally.

Retail trade makes an essential contribution to community economic health. Not only does a strong retail sector prevent the blight of vacant commercial space, but it makes life more convenient for community shoppers. In 1994 Columbia University conducted a survey on behalf of the New York City Empowerment Zone of northern Manhattan between 110th and 175th Streets (excluding the area surrounding the university itself), a community that is 72 percent black and 16 percent Hispanic. Although this community is home to more than 200,000 residents, the survey found that more than 70 percent of them shopped elsewhere for clothes and shoes, electrical appliances, furniture, and gifts (New York City Empowerment Zone 1994, appendix H, table 4). Much of the absence of retail business from such communities surely reflects their unattractiveness for retailers, but a low supply of local retail entrepreneurs is a contributing factor.

Last but not least, the visibility of retail trade makes it a lightning rod for frustration over the low representation of African Americans among the ranks of entrepreneurs. There was a grim reminder of this frustration on December 8, 1995, when a gunman walked into a white-owned clothing store on 125th Street, the main commercial strip of Harlem, and set it afire, killing himself and seven store employees. The store had been the target of demonstrations because of its plan to expand and evict a subtenant, a black-owned record shop.[4]

The Benefits to Retailers of Network Ties

How can ethnic business networks be of help to small retailers? I begin this section by describing how, in theory, retailer ties to vendors and ties among retailers can both be important assets. I then review evidence in the literature that African American retailers lack effective ties among themselves, particularly in contrast with Asian immigrant groups. I conclude the section with a concrete example of how ties have helped Koreans dominate an area of retailing in which African Americans should have had an advantage.

Ties and Information

Network ties can be important sources of information for retailers searching for products that suit their clienteles. Suppose a retailer uses impersonal information sources such as the business-to-business Yellow Pages or the Internet to locate potential vendors (who could be manufacturers but for small retailers are more likely to be wholesalers). Because these sources do not convey the "feel" or quality of the products, many subsequent visits to vendors will turn out to be false leads, especially for what the *Economist* (2000, 12) calls "high-touch goods" (clothing and housewares, for example, as opposed to computer software). Such visits are time-consuming and expensive (if long-distance travel is involved) and may generate unproductive purchases. A retailer therefore has an advantage if he enters business with a stock of preexisting ties to vendors, connections he may have accumulated from his own previous businesses or from his experience as a buyer for other retailers. The information content of these ties includes, above all, thorough familiarity with the vendor's product lines, but also knowledge of factors such as the vendor's ability to meet rush orders or propensity to offer volume discounts.[5] These ties may also have a "trust" content, reflected, for example, in a greater willingness by the vendor to sell on credit. Not all of his ties will meet a retailer's needs, but many will, especially if the retailer's choice of specialty was influenced by his stock of ties.

Not only ties to vendors but also ties among retailers themselves can be helpful. Consider, for example, two hypothetical retailers whose entrepreneurs are "tied" in the sense that they are familiar with each other's product lines and business strategies. Retailer 1 specializes in women's shoes, and retailer 2 specializes in men's shoes. Suppose retailer 1 is searching for products to stock and visits an unfamiliar vendor who carries both men's and women's shoes. He does not see women's shoes that are appropriate for his clientele but notices men's shoes that would be perfect for retailer 2. If he transmits this information to retailer 2, and this kind of behavior is reciprocated, clearly both retailers will be better off. I observed this behavior from the sellers' side among New York Garment District wholesalers, who routinely referred to their competitors (that is, other wholesalers) potential customers whom they thought would be interested in their competitors' product lines.

Just as tied retailers can realize economies of scope in searching for new vendors, they can in effect pool their ties to the vendors with whom they are already conversant. A retailer may have preexisting ties to vendors who do not meet his needs but are useful to other retailers he knows, and he can refer these retailers to them.[6] For economies of scope in the search for or pooling of ties to vendors to be realized effectively, however, the tied retailers must be familiar with each other's businesses. If one retailer urges another to whom she is tied to take the time and incur the expense of visiting a vendor, she should be confident that the visit will be productive. Since retailers have no reason to do business with each other directly, mutual familiarity among them will not arise automatically. Social contacts are helpful, but more formal business associations are likely to provide the forum where business characteristics are experienced and needs are discussed most intensively.

These arguments concerning the benefits of ties between buyers and sellers and within groups of buyers or sellers are consistent with work showing that international information-sharing networks increase the volume of international trade.[7] Such evidence has been found for business groups operating across national borders (see, for example, Belderbos and Sleuwaegen 1998), immigrants (see Gould 1994), and long-settled ethnic minorities that maintain coethnic business societies, such as the overseas Chinese (Rauch and Trindade, in press).[8] David Gould (1994) and James Rauch and Vitor Trindade (in press) find that these groups have less effect on trade in more homogeneous products, for which prices can effectively convey the relevant information, than on trade in more differentiated products, for which matching of multifarious characteristics of buyers and sellers is more important.

Ties among retailers may, of course, be useful for purposes other than sharing information. Examples are joint advertising and cooperative volume buying of certain common inputs like modern transactions equipment (point-of-sale, credit-card terminal, and check-cashing protection systems). These additional benefits should be kept in mind later in the chapter when I consider the ability of commercial intermediaries to substitute for ties.

Ties and African American Retailers

We can expect potential African American retail entrepreneurs to be endowed with smaller and less useful stocks of ties to vendors than their white majority counterparts. The low rate of African American retail entrepreneurship in itself makes a potential African American retailer less likely to have accumulated ties from his own previous businesses or inherited family businesses. Moreover, discrimination may keep African Americans out of buying positions with larger retailers where valuable contacts with vendors can be made. Making deals is often a social affair, and because white vendors may have trouble "bonding" with African American buyers, some employers may practice this subtle form of discrimination.[9] By the same token, the trust content of any ties to vendors that African American retailers do have is likely to be lower.

What about ties *within* African American retailers? Sociological work has drawn an especially sharp contrast between the propensities of Asian immigrant groups and African Americans toward collective action to promote business. William Julius Wilson (1987, 33) states that "the discontinuation of large-scale immigration from China and Japan enabled those already here to solidify networks of ethnic contacts," while African American migration to the urban North continued in substantial numbers for several decades even after European immigration was drastically restricted. Ivan Light (1972, 124–25) writes:

> Among the Chinese and Japanese, kinship and locality ties carried over into the community's division of labor. As a result, *kenjin,* or "cousins," tended to pile up in the same occupations. Since the same sort of ties were so weak among urban Negroes, these particular loyalties could not structure that community's division of labor. Hence, the black business population which arose was composed of unrelated competitors.

Light argues that this difference deleteriously affected the ability of African American trade associations to recruit members and conduct mutual aid: "Because these associations were not immigrant brotherhoods, they lacked informal social sanctions so extensive as those of the Oriental trade guilds" (125). Light singles out for discussion the failure of the Colored Merchants Association, which "proved unable to recruit enough Negro grocers and to secure adequate cooperation from those who did join" (126). A different kind of evidence is provided by tabulations by Timothy Bates (1994) from samples of 893 Korean immigrant-owned and 3,803 black-owned small businesses formed between 1979 and 1987. These show that, of the 69.0 percent of Korean firms and 40.4 percent of black firms that used debt capital at start-up, 24.9 percent of the former but only 11.3 percent of the latter listed "friends" as a major debt source.[10]

Light's discussion suggests that not only is collective action helpful in overcoming discrimination, but discrimination may actually facilitate collective action by creating a small world in which business information is transmitted more effectively and trust is maintained more easily, in part because sanctions against those who do not cooperate have more bite. Mark Granovetter (1995b) has argued that immigrant groups may have an advantage in striking the right balance between "coupling" and "decoupling," where the latter is helpful for business by preventing a drain on reinvestible profits by community claims and permitting "antisocial" aggressive business practices. On the other hand, one must be careful not to make exaggerated claims for the benefits of ethnic business networks. Bates (1994, 243) notes that self-employment is often underemployment for immigrant groups whose poor English limits their employment options. Although successful entrepreneurs typically work long hours, the goal of policy presumably should not be to increase African American participation in lines of retailing that involve extremes of self-exploitation.[11]

I can now summarize the problem of African American retail trade entrepreneurship from the perspective of ties and information. On the one hand, compared to their white competitors, African American retailers lack ties to vendors that would help them find the varieties of differentiated products best suited to their clienteles. On the other hand, compared to their Asian immigrant competitors, African American retailers lack, or have been relatively ineffective in using, ties among themselves that would allow them to realize economies of scope in the search for differentiated products and to pool the ties to vendors they do have. Insofar as retailers can use ties among themselves to generate benefits in addition to those from sharing information, African American retailers may be still further disadvantaged relative to their Asian competitors.

An Example of Ties in Action: Korean Immigrants in Wig Retailing

In general, immigrant retailers would not be expected to be endowed with better ties to vendors than their African American counterparts.

An important exception, however, occurs when the retailers are selling products made in their native country. When these preexisting ties
to vendors are combined with the high density and use of ties that appears to prevail among Asian immigrant entrepreneurs in particular,
the likelihood of high participation and success in retailing is especially
great. Pyong-Gap Min (1993, 196) states: "By virtue of the advantages
associated with their language and ethnic background, many Korean
immigrants have established import businesses dealing in Korean
exports. Korean importers distribute Korean-made consumer goods
mainly to co-ethnic wholesalers, who in turn distribute them mainly
to co-ethnic retailers."

Ironically, one of these trade-based Asian retail concentrations is
in the supply of wigs and other hair care products to African American
beauty shops and women consumers. I learned of this when looking
into the supply of these African American beauty shops as a possibility for either cooperative buying by the beauty shops themselves,
or for African Americans to be retailers or wholesalers to an important part of their community demand. My informant was an African
American entrepreneur who owned a complex that housed a number of service businesses catering to an African American clientele, including a beauty shop and a fitness center. He produced a catalog
of hairstyles for African American women and was distributing it in
partnership with Korean wholesalers who served between 1,700 and
2,000 Korean-owned hair care supply stores nationwide.

The Korean dominance of retailing in this area can be traced back
to the near-monopoly on wig supply to the United States that Korea
had established by the early 1970s. The fascinating story of how Korea
came to dominate the world wig industry is told by Illsoo Kim (1981,
123–28). Here I concentrate on how that dominance was translated to
the retail level in the United States. Min (1984, 21) provides an explanation based on his personal interviews with 159 randomly selected
Korean business owners in Atlanta and his own experience as a wig
retailer:

> Korean immigrants have a number of advantages in establishing and
> operating wig and other retail businesses dealing in Korean-imported
> items. In starting up a business, they have advantages not only in
> terms of business information but also in terms of business capitaliza-

tion because they can buy merchandise on a credit basis from Korean wholesalers. In operating a business they receive preferential treatments in item selection, price, speed of delivery, and credit. Moreover, in the case of the wig business, a retailer almost needs to speak the Korean language because Koreans have a complete control over wig wholesales. My experience as a wig retailer suggests that Korean wig wholesalers are reluctant to respond to orders by non-ethnic retailers. This may be one of the major reasons why few blacks run wig stores, although blacks constitute more than 75 percent of customers for the wig business in this country. Eighteen of 20 retail owners in our sample were found to deal largely in wig and other Korean-imported items, and 16 of them reported that they received business information and training from other Korean businessmen to help start their business. Three of the wig store owners indicated that they bought wigs from Korean wholesalers on a credit basis to start their business.

Min describes not only the informational advantages enjoyed by Korean retailers owing to their ethnic ties to wholesalers and ties among themselves (in particular, the willingness of those with useful information to teach coethnics what they know), but also the active discrimination by Korean wholesalers in favor of Korean retailers and against other retailers. My informant asserted that the active discrimination has since abated, but the other benefits of the Korean ethnic business network remain.

Grassroots Business Organizations Among Black Retailers in Brooklyn

Strategy for Field Research

The case for policies to improve the ability of commercial intermediaries to substitute for ties within African American retailers is predicated on the inability of the latter to organize themselves. An organization that brings retailers together for the express purpose of discussing business is the form of tie most useful for building the mutual familiarity needed for economies of scope in search or pooling of ties to vendors to be realized effectively. The evidence for the lack or weakness of such organizations among African Americans is decades old. The purpose of the field research described in this section is to provide an up-to-date assessment of the prevalence and performance of grassroots business organizations among African Americans in order to check whether the old findings are still valid. A secondary purpose is to gain a richer (albeit anecdotal) sense of how grassroots business organizations serve their members, as well as some insight into how they form. By "grassroots" I mean organizations that are sustained by member contributions rather than a dependence on outside funding, though they may have received start-up funding from an outside source such as a city government. I limited my more intensive survey to organizations with significant participation by retailers.

My approach presumes that businesspeople who share strong informal ties and practice mutual self-help tend to form grassroots organizations that reinforce and amplify the benefits of these ties. If, on the contrary, strong informal networks do not give rise to grassroots business organizations, then by focusing on the latter I risk missing the former, which might be an important omission if purely informal business networks are substituting for many of the functions of grassroots business organizations. I cannot rule out this possibility. The idea that strong informal business networks do not lead to grassroots business organizations is inconsistent, however, with my own perceptions in the field, with the work of Light described earlier, and with the recent work of AnnaLee Saxenian (1999, 21), who writes of Chinese and Indian entrepreneurs in Silicon Valley:

> As their communities grew during the 1970s and 1980s, these immigrants responded to the sense of professional and social exclusion by organizing collectively as well. They often found one another socially first, coming together to celebrate holidays and family events with others who spoke the same language and shared similar culture and backgrounds. Over time, they turned the social networks to business purposes, creating professional associations to provide resources and support structures within their own communities.

I conducted my field research in New York City during the academic year 1995 to 1996. As a "control group," I selected black immigrants from the English-speaking Caribbean, whom I call "Caribbean Americans." Because they speak English, it is no more "necessary" for them to work together owing to language barriers than it is for African Americans. Among the five counties (boroughs) of New York City, the largest populations of both African Americans and Caribbean Americans are in Brooklyn, though the Caribbean Americans are more concentrated there. According to the 1992 SMOBE, the New York primary metropolitan statistical area (PMSA) contained the largest number of black-owned small businesses of any PMSA in the United States, though total receipts of black-owned small businesses were highest in the Los Angeles-Long Beach PMSA (U.S. Department of Commerce 1996, table 4). Within New York City, Brooklyn (Kings County) contained the most black-owned small businesses, though total receipts were highest in Manhattan (New York County) (table 5). It stands to reason that the New York metropolitan area, and Brooklyn in particular, is a good place to learn about black grassroots business organizations.

Although I did not attempt to gather evidence regarding the ties of African American retailers to vendors relative to white retailers, my research in New York City did at least provide anecdotal confirmation of the importance for African American retailers of the search problem described earlier. A saying in the business was: "You make money in buying, not selling." An African American retailer I interviewed, describing his search for products to carry in his store, said that a local retailer's "head spins" when confronted with the range of wholesalers. The importance of the search problem for the consumers these retailers wish to serve is indicated by the New York City Empowerment Zone Survey, which found that the top three reasons respondents gave for shopping outside their neighborhood were quality of goods and services (33 percent first mention), prices (28 percent first mention), and selection (26 percent first mention) (New York City Empowerment Zone 1994, appendix H, table 5). Note that two of these reasons, quality and selection, are inherently issues relating to differentiated products.

African American Organizations

I succeeded in identifying two predominantly African American grassroots business organizations in which retailers participated at significant rates.[12] One was the local "Black Pages," which describes itself as "The Networking Directory of Black-owned Businesses, Professionals, and Organizations." This publication was celebrating its tenth annual edition. It carries advertisements from black-owned (predominantly African American) businesses in New York City and Long Island. Most of the advertisers are service-sector businesses, but there is a significant retailer presence. It was clear from my conversation with the publisher that it was not the mission of her organization to directly stimulate deeper cooperation among black-owned businesses, though her publication could have stimulated such cooperation indirectly by helping black-owned businesses learn about each other's existence.

The other organization was based in a historic and relatively affluent African American Brooklyn neighborhood, and its main goal was to make this neighborhood "a highly desirable consumer/tourist destination" through joint advertising and other efforts. Other goals included provision of technical assistance and acquisition of commercial real estate for member businesses. In June 1996, the organization was nearly a year and a half old. The businesses most intensively targeted for membership were the estimated 150 black-owned businesses in the neighborhood, though all neighborhood businesses were welcome to join. The basic concept appeared sound to me and to the Brooklyn Economic Development Corporation, which was providing some start-up funding and technical assistance. In our interview, the founder told me that the most common line of business among those that had expressed interest in the organization was apparel and accessories retailing, followed by restaurants and hair salons.[13] Although more than half of the businesses were owned by African Americans, a large minority were owned by immigrants of African descent. Ten to 20 percent of the owners were Muslims. It appeared that what had brought these businesses together (at least the core group) was not, strictly speaking, coethnicity, and certainly not religious affinity, but rather Afrocentric ideology. Of the sixty to seventy black-owned businesses that had expressed interest in the organization by attending at least one meeting, only ten regularly attended meetings and paid dues. The organization was making a push to expand dues-paying membership by setting a less ambitious dues structure.

Caribbean American Organizations

In the Caribbean American community, there was one dominant grass-roots business organization to which all informants referred me. This organization was founded in 1985 with ten members, all Caribbean Americans, and by June 1996 had grown to more than twelve hundred members, many of which were African American–owned businesses and white-owned businesses.[14] About 15 percent of the members were retailers, and 5 to 6 percent were importers, exporters, and/or wholesalers, a category that tended to include the larger businesses. The organization had three categories of membership: newly started businesses, defined as less than one year old; small businesses, defined as having annual sales less than $3 million; and large businesses, defined as having annual sales of more than $3 million. Annual membership dues for the three categories in June 1996 were $150, $375, and $2,000, respectively. Among its many activities, the organization maintained a "comprehensive business resource center," sponsored "seminars on how to start, operate, and manage a business," coordinated "trade missions to the Caribbean along with trade fairs and expositions," and conducted monthly "Power Breakfast Business Networking meetings." The organization also had an international business committee that met quarterly to exchange information regarding import-export opportunities and especially investment opportunities in the Caribbean. A membership benefit of special interest was discounted advertising through member radio stations. The organization had also organized cooperative advertising by member businesses in member newspapers.

I attended a "Power Breakfast" meeting at which there were three speakers on the theme of small-business financing. One speaker was a vice president of a major bank, one was a vice president of a specialty financial services firm, and one was a representative of the New York City Department of Business Services. Two of the speakers were Caribbean Americans, and the other had done business in a Caribbean country and met the organization's president through that connection. The meeting was attended by sixty to seventy individuals, about 90 percent of whom were Caribbean Americans or African Americans, and many of whom were not (yet) members. At least one-quarter of those in attendance were women, many looking to start their own business. Most of the time at the meeting was taken up with exchange of business cards and self-introductions, interspersed with exhortations by the president to do business with each other and to use the financial resources being presented at the meeting.

I sat next to an African American woman who had recently been downsized by a major New York bank and was looking to strike out on her own. Her husband was Jamaican, and she was investigating opportunities to get involved in Caribbean trade. At an International Business Exposition attended by this organization, she had met a retailer and mail-order supplier of cosmetics for black women (an organization member) who was interested in breaking into the Caribbean market. She was attending the meeting to learn more about the organization and about starting a business exporting to the English-speaking Caribbean. A member sitting directly across from her said that he would be traveling to Jamaica soon and would be happy to make some contacts for her, and a trade finance specialist with the major bank represented by one of the speakers gave her his card and briefly described some of the services he could offer.

In our interview, I questioned the president (and founder) closely about how his organization had grown. He told me that the organization had been able to establish its networking meetings and small-business seminars six months after its founding, after which it grew rapidly to four hundred dues-paying members within four years. Most members have been unsolicited—they hear about the organization through friends, who themselves may or may not have been members. When I doubted the attraction for Caribbean American small-business people of the networking function of his organization when it still consisted of only the ten founding members, he responded that from the beginning the organization linked them to services such as technical assistance and finance provided by economic development agencies like the Brooklyn Economic Development Corporation. But why did they come to his organization for services they could obtain elsewhere? Why did they not go directly to the economic development agencies, for example? His answer was that his organization "speaks their language," by which he, of course, did not mean English! As his organization has grown, it has come to include more businesses owned by the children and grandchildren of Caribbean immigrants, many of whom identify themselves as African Americans, and it has become stricter about charging nonmembers higher fees for its services and for admission to meetings.

Summary

In New York City, there is no African American grassroots business organization, with or without significant retailer participation, that is even close in size or effectiveness to the Caribbean American organization just described. I conclude that my New York City field research supports the claims of sociologists that African Americans have been ineffective in using collective action to promote business compared to immigrant groups of color that may also suffer from discrimination.

Examining the reasons why African American businesses have difficulty organizing along ethnic lines compared to some immigrant groups of color is beyond the scope of this chapter. I do not believe that arguments based on the effectiveness of social sanctions are relevant for the grassroots business organizations I studied. Many or even most members of these organizations do not expose themselves to enough risk from the actions of other members (for example, by lending them money) to benefit from the threat of collective punishment of cheaters. Nor did I find any "peer pressure" in the Caribbean American community to join the Caribbean American organization described here, although I looked for it. Instead, I conjecture that certain immigrant groups are able to form successful grassroots business organizations because their shared backgrounds give them the belief that they can learn most effectively from each other rather than from society at large: they "speak a common language," in not only a literal but a metaphorical sense. This belief is most important before the organization reaches a "critical mass" above which its attraction for target businesses is irresistible.

Buying Groups for U.S. Retailers

Motivation

Explanations of economic problems based in part on inadequate networks can discourage the search for solutions to those problems, given that the efficacy of networks is seen as determined by deeply rooted cultural patterns and hence as difficult to change, except perhaps in the very long run. It is the argument of this chapter that in the case of retail entrepreneurship, institutions can be developed that substitute for business networks by providing many of the same benefits, and that commercial intermediaries are the most promising institutional raw material.

More specifically, we have identified at least two benefits provided to retailers by ties among them: economies of scope in the search for new vendors and connection to a large pool of vendors. Although I have argued that retailers from the white majority are on average better endowed with ties to vendors than minority retailers, we can expect many of them to be willing to pay for such services, especially given that they are in all probability no more tied to each other than are African American retailers. We should not be surprised if commercial suppliers emerge to cater to such a large demand. At the same time, we should not take this emergence for granted: I argue later in the chapter that there may be a "market failure" that leads to undersupply of the kind of large-scale, diversified intermediaries needed to mimic the benefits supplied by an ethnic business network.

Whether or not they are in optimal supply, it turns out that such commercial intermediaries, known in the retail trade field as "buying groups," do indeed exist. I discuss all the major forms, each of which supplies some of the same services provided by retailers' ties. I argue that each type has important shortcomings in its ability to meet the needs of African American retailers. Nevertheless, I conclude that modifying these existing institutions is a sounder (less experimental) way to make policy than developing institutions from scratch.

It is helpful to a discussion of these institutions to build on figure 6.1, the left-hand panel of which depicts an idealized organized exchange, and the right-hand panel of which depicts an unorganized market. Many homogeneous commodities like grains or metals are traded on organized exchanges, such as the Minneapolis Grain Exchange. One of the functions of these exchanges is to match buyers and sellers efficiently. In contrast, most goods handled by retailers are differentiated or brand-name products, for which organized exchanges do not exist and for which trade is more appropriately described by the right-hand panel of figure 6.1, in which buyers and sellers become individually connected as the end product of a search process and may be ignorant

Figure 6.1 Connecting Buyers to Sellers

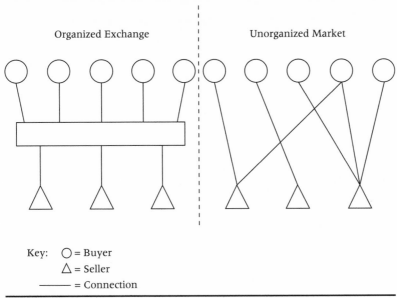

Key: ○ = Buyer
      △ = Seller
      ——— = Connection

Source: Author.

of the many buyers or sellers to which they are not connected. I think of the various buying groups as partly attempting to mimic the matching and aggregation services provided by organized exchanges, so that differentiated product markets will look less like the right-hand panel and more like the left-hand panel.

Independent Buying Offices

Despite their name, independent buying offices do not usually make purchases for their retail clients but rather act as their representatives in wholesale markets such as New York City.[15] The typical services of an independent buying office are described by Patrick Cash, John Wingate, and Joseph Friedlander (1995, 51–52):

> First, one-to-one assistance is given before, during, and after market visits of store buyers. This includes researching the markets to locate

buyers' specific needs, recommending preferred lines, making appoint-
ments for buyers' visits to showrooms, and accompanying buyers to
markets. After the buyer returns home, the services include following
up on the orders placed, placing reorders and special orders, and handling vendor problems. Second, market reports advise stores of market
trends, special offerings by vendors, and best sellers.

Besides these basic services, independent buying offices may prepare
displays and promotional materials, train salespeople, pool orders so
that small retailers can qualify for quantity discounts, and even develop private label merchandise in conjunction with manufacturers
(Diamond and Pintel 1996, 213–17).

It is significant that all descriptions of independent buying offices
stress their importance as loci for information exchange. Cash and
his colleagues (1995, 51), for example, state that "information exchange . . . is considered by some the single most important benefit of
a buying office affiliation." Jay Diamond and Gerald Pintel (1996, 210)
elaborate: "The other retail organizations being represented should be
similar to one's own. Clientele, merchandising policies, price ranges,
and image are just some areas of significance. If the other stores are
unlike your own operation, the information exchange will be mean-
ingless." On the other hand, both of these sources warn against membership of direct competitors in the same independent buying office,
precisely because information exchange is so important. Just as in the
earlier example of women's and men's shoe retailers, a certain amount
of separation of clientele (which could be purely spatial) is necessary
to sustain cooperation.

What does the retailer pay for these services? According to Irving
Burstiner (1998, 145):

> The independent buying office usually requires the retailer to sign an
> annual contract. Typically, the cost runs to about 0.5 percent of an-
> nual sales. When sales are quite low, the buying office may substitute
> a minimum fee of several hundred dollars for the customary percent-
> age arrangement. The fee is payable over the year in equal monthly
> installments.

The independent buying office model shown in figure 6.2 gives
a schematic representation of the function of independent buying

Figure 6.2 Types of Buying Groups

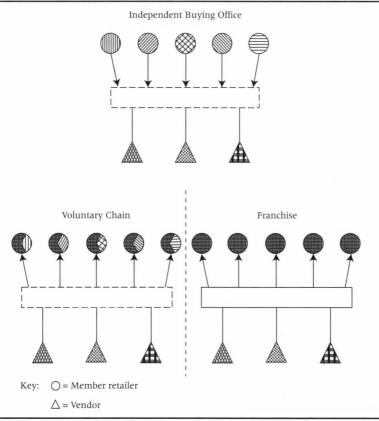

Independent Buying Office

Voluntary Chain

Franchise

Key: ○ = Member retailer

△ = Vendor

Source: Author.

offices that builds on the concepts and symbols introduced in figure 6.1. The buying office itself is represented by the central rectangle, inside of which member retailers (circles) are matched with appropriate vendors (triangles). The direction of the arrows indicates that the ultimate decision on product mix is being made by the retailers, albeit with the advice of the buying office. The rectangle is drawn with a broken rather than a solid line to indicate that there is hedging on both sides of the retailer-buying office relationship: the retailer can conduct his own search in addition to the search the buying office does for him, and the buying office does not normally have to actually buy the goods.

We can recognize that, by affiliating with a common independent buying office, retailers are benefiting from economies of scope in the search for vendors. In one respect, independent buying offices have an advantage over ethnic business networks in this area because they supply personnel who are specialized in search—in other words, they realize economies of scale in the search for vendors as well as economies of scope.

In considering their usefulness to African American retailers, we must note that most independent buying offices specialize in apparel and accessories (and to a lesser extent in home furnishings). African Americans have distinctive tastes in apparel and accessories; for example, they have created demand for Afrocentric garments and for what people in the clothing trade call "ethnic urban sportswear." Most African American apparel and accessory retailers serve the African American niche market. Independent buying offices serve retailers nationwide who are, of course, overwhelmingly catering to a white clientele. It may not pay for a given African American retailer to affiliate with an independent buying office if the office has little or no experience researching vendors appropriate for the African American niche market, though coordinated affiliation of many African American retailers with a given independent buying office could alleviate this problem. According to an informant, independent buying offices do not handle many African American retailers.

Does an African American niche market exist, and is it profitable? There are a number of commercial enterprises whose existence makes sense only if both questions can be answered yes. For example, Target Market News is a twelve-year-old business that "provides corporations with a full range of consumer marketing and media research services specifically designed for the unique characteristics of the African American consumer market" and runs an annual conference and trade show called the Marketing to African Americans Expo. African American retailers are not, of course, restricted to targeting the African American market. However, it would appear to be the most convenient way for large numbers of African Americans to succeed in small retail businesses given the extent to which African Americans are residentially segregated.[16]

Wholesaler-Sponsored Voluntary Chains

Two other major forms of interstore cooperation involve centralized buying by joint retailer-owned wholesale establishments or wholesaler-sponsored voluntary chains. "When it is neither possible nor economic to buy directly from the producer," Cash and his colleagues (1995, 59) point out, "advantages are gained by setting up a wholesale subsidiary cooperatively or by associating with a wholesale distributor. These approaches assume certain wholesaling functions (such as scouting, assembling, storing, and delivering in economic size lots)." The cooperative approach requires what may be substantial financial investments by retailers and assumes away the problem of lack of ties between retailers that we are trying to solve. For both these reasons, I concentrate my attention on the second approach of contracting with a common wholesaler.

Today, wholesaler sponsors of voluntary chains have a tendency, Cash and his colleagues (1995, 59–60) note, "not only to sell at low markups, but also to provide management services. These may include merchandising, accounting and record keeping, joint advertising, and supervision. The contract wholesaler usually insists that member stores follow suggestions about store fronts, signs, and merchandising policies." Financing is the most important omission from this list. Many wholesalers extend credit to their retail customers through delayed billing, but contract wholesalers even provide long-term financing for store modernization, erection of new buildings, or purchases of existing businesses (Burstiner 1998, 144). If the loan is not repaid, or if the retailer does not concentrate his purchases with the wholesaler, the latter can repossess inventory or the store itself.

In the voluntary chain model shown in figure 6.2, the wholesaler is represented by the central rectangle, inside of which the products purchased from vendors (triangles) are "packaged" for member retailers (circles). The "package" is represented by the pattern that is common across the circles. The direction of the arrows indicates that the ultimate decision on product mix is being made by the wholesaler, though feedback from the retailers inevitably influences the wholesaler's buying choices. The rectangle is drawn with a broken rather than a solid line to indicate that the member retailers do not have to buy all of their stock from the contract wholesaler.

To provide all these services and put together "packages," these intermediaries need to be much more diversified than the typical wholesalers whose proliferation made my retailer informant's "head spin." We can recognize that member retailers obtain from the contract wholesaler the benefit of connection to a network of vendors much larger than any pool of vendors to which an individual retailer is connected, as well as other benefits that an ethnic business network can provide, such as cooperative volume buying and joint advertising. However, members of an ethnic business network can use their pooled ties to vendors to design their *own* product packages. Clearly, something is lost in the voluntary chain model shown in figure 6.2 by comparison: the closeness to the market and flexibility in adapting to consumer preferences that independent retailers provide, and the possibility of identifying new, winning ideas for product packages that can be franchised. Contrasting independent buying offices and voluntary chains, one can argue that the former are better suited to increasing the success of existing retailers, while the latter are better suited to increasing participation in retail entrepreneurship by facilitating start-ups, given the ready-made product package and much higher service level such chains provide. Both the strengths and weaknesses of voluntary chains are heightened by franchising, the last form of buying group I examine.

Franchising

Franchising is not usually thought of as a form of buying group for the franchisees, but in fact, it is a short step from voluntary chains to franchising (compare the voluntary chain and franchise models in figure 6.2). The main difference is that much greater effort is made by the franchiser than by a voluntary chain to make the franchisees identical: the franchisee must buy all (not just most) of his stock from the franchiser and receives substantial training in the ways of the franchise. The franchisee then identifies his store completely with the franchise and expects large benefits from the use of the franchise name.

Franchising has several drawbacks as a means of increasing African American participation and success in retail entrepreneurship. Applying for a franchise is not unlike applying for a bank loan, and it follows that African Americans may run into the same problems with franchises that have been documented for banks: redlining of African American communities and discrimination against African American applicants.[17] (By extension, the same problems may arise for African American membership in voluntary chains.) The charge for the use of the franchise name and other benefits of the franchise also raises capital requirements considerably. (It can cost in excess of $1 million to open a McDonald's store.) The mix of merchandise offered by some franchises and the image they seek to create may be a poor fit for African American communities.

These drawbacks suggest that, in general, franchising will be most successful in stimulating African American retail entrepreneurship if the franchisers are themselves African American, especially if they have roots in African American communities that help them to identify niches that are not well served by existing franchises. A natural source of African American franchisers is African American wholesalers, who have already accumulated the requisite ties to vendors (manufacturers). Unfortunately, as table 6.1 shows, at least in small business the representation of black entrepreneurs in wholesale trade is the lowest for any major industry group except mining.[18] Nevertheless, it seems that much could be learned from the African American–owned retail franchises that do exist, despite this hindrance.

I was able to find only one African American–owned franchise that met my definition of retail (which excludes restaurants) and was tailored to the African American community (at least to some extent).[19] This was an athletic footwear franchise targeted, according to the entrepreneur with whom I spoke, at the "inner-city African American and Hispanic market." It was founded in 1993, had seven stores in the mid-Atlantic area as of June 1996, with three more scheduled to open within two months, and was planning a major expansion to nationwide operation with the backing of several banks and venture capitalists. This entrepreneur works in partnership with a friend whose mom-and-pop business provided a rough template for his franchise. He had met the sales representatives of the various manufacturers through his

Table 6.1 Small Businesses Owned by Blacks, by Major Industry Group, 1992

Industry	Percentage of All U.S. Small Businesses
All industries	3.6
Agricultural services, forestry, and fishing	2.3
Mining	0.3
Construction	2.4
Manufacturing	2.0
Transportation and public utilities	7.0
Wholesale trade	1.4
Retail trade	3.5
Finance, insurance, and real estate	2.1
Services	4.3

Source: Author's computations based on U.S. Department of Commerce (1996, 9, table 1; 74, table 10).

participation in promotional events for a National Basketball Association team. He also received some help in identifying vendors from the Association of Black Sporting Goods Professionals.

The franchise works in partnership with local governments to raise the capital to open the stores from a variety of public and quasi-public sources such as community development corporations. Often the stores have been opened in urban enterprise or empowerment zones. The franchisee must bring $250,000 to the table, of which 20 to 25 percent is his equity, making the equity investment required comparable to what is needed to buy an upper-middle-class dwelling.

The entrepreneur claimed that his franchise has an advantage over competitors such as Footlocker because he and his partner "know the market better." The idea of their franchise is to move the product "from an athletic statement to more of a fashion statement."

I conclude that this one case confirms the importance of preexisting ties to manufacturers for African Americans who wish to start retail franchises, so that lack of these ties presents a significant obstacle. It also demonstrates, however, that the potential obstacle of bank discrimination against African American franchisees can be overcome through judicious use of government programs, at least for cheaper franchises.[20]

A Modest Proposal

The Possibility of Market Failure

At the core of my policy proposal are subsidies intended to modify the behavior of at least one large independent buying office to better serve African American retailers. It is then natural for an economist to ask: If the benefits of this proposal exceed its costs, why does the market not provide this service on its own? In this section, I briefly describe a theory of why the services provided by large independent buying offices might be undersupplied in general, and why the problem might be especially severe for the African American niche market.

The first step of the argument is to conceive of the service provided by an independent buying office as "match-making" between retailers and vendors. Diamond and Pintel (1997, 94) write:

> The key to successful merchandising is making desirable merchandise available to customers. The bringing together of vendors and retailers whose merchandise needs and offerings blend is a function of the resident buyer. . . . The resident buying office provides the supplier with potential users and also gives the retailer new resources. The "marriage" of the two can make the retailer's business more successful.

The second step of the argument notes that successful match-making requires "deep knowledge" of the capabilities and preferences of the seller, buyer, or both. Of export trading companies, Yung Whee Rhee and Christine Soulier (1989, 25) write:

> As highlighted in our Hong Kong survey, the most important resource that ETCs [export trading companies] have is their deep knowledge about external markets/buyers and local production capabilities/producers. Without such information, ETCs can hardly be effective in matching potential overseas buyers to local producers. . . . The effectiveness of Japanese, Korean, and Hong Kong GTCs [general trading companies] has been based on the depth of their product-market knowledge and of the supplier-buyer network.

In the third step in the argument, we observe that the need for deep knowledge makes the quality of service provided by the independent buying office to the retailer unverifiable and hence inherently noncontractible. In the absence of an enforceable contract based on payment for surplus created, the intermediary must rely on his bargaining power, but this is limited because the specificity of each match leaves the intermediary with poor alternative transactions if bargaining breaks down. The end result is that independent buying offices and similar intermediaries lack adequate incentives to make socially profitable investments in the acquisition of deep knowledge of buyers or sellers.[21]

At least two factors tend to mitigate this problem. First, potential intermediaries may accumulate deep knowledge as a by-product of other remunerative activities (employment as store buyers, for example), and then decide to cash in on their knowledge by starting independent buying offices. Although these offices can be expected to be small and specialized, they can form the nuclei for large, diversified offices. Second, the cost of investments needed for a small office to diversify its knowledge base is reduced by the concentration of vendors into clusters, such as the New York Garment District. There are in fact perhaps nine large independent buying offices in the United States (Diamond and Pintel 1997, 80). As argued earlier, the first mitigating factor probably operates less effectively for African Americans. At the same time, entrepreneurs who are not African American are less likely to start out with deep knowledge of many African American retailers, and as we have seen, there are few grassroots organizations for the latter that could reduce the cost of investments in such knowledge.

Focus on Apparel and Accessories

There are at least seven reasons why efforts to increase African American participation and success in retail trade by building ties to vendors and across retailers are most likely to yield results if aimed at the apparel and accessory sector of retailing. (Apparel and accessory stores include men's and boys' clothing stores, women's clothing stores, women's accessory and specialty stores, children's and infants' wear stores, family clothing stores, shoe stores, and miscellaneous apparel and accessory stores.)

1. *Although I noted earlier that African Americans form a niche market within apparel and accessories on which independent buying offices serving*

retailers nationwide may fail to focus, it is an important niche nevertheless. Tyler Biggs and his colleagues (1994, 13–14) state, citing a marketing study, that "56 percent of African Americans enjoy shopping for clothes and like viewing a store's new merchandise compared to 29 percent for whites." According to the 1993 Consumer Expenditure Survey (U.S. Department of Labor 1995), blacks spend 7.9 percent of their income on apparel and services compared to 5.3 percent for whites, yielding an estimate (216, table 58) of roughly $17 billion for black expenditures on apparel and services in 1993.

2. *Given the first reason, it is not surprising that African American retailers have been more successful in apparel and accessories than in other sectors, providing a base for economies of scope and scale for any retail trade buying group that might handle a large fraction of them.* Among categories of a comparable level of aggregation, the black share of small-business entrepreneurs is highest for apparel and accessory stores (5.6 percent, based on computations from U.S. Department of Commerce 1996, 9, table 1; 73, table 10).

3. *Despite this relative success, a need is felt for apparel and accessory stores in the African American community.* In the New York City Empowerment Zone Survey, clothing stores led the list of stores that residents would like to see added to the neighborhood, narrowly topping supermarkets (New York City Empowerment Zone 1994, appendix H, table 14).

4. *Apparel and accessories constitute a quantitatively important sector of retailing.* According to the 1993 Consumer Expenditure Survey, apparel and services is by far the largest category of nonfood expenditures on nonfood retail items (U.S. Department of Labor 1995).

5. *At least in New York City, African Americans have established a significant presence in clothing design and manufacturing (albeit in a very upscale segment of the market), as evidenced by the Black Fashion Collective.* Hence, the prospects for synergy with other African American entrepreneurial ventures are relatively good in the apparel and accessories sector.

6. *Casual observation suggests that African Americans are fashion leaders, especially in the youth market.* It follows that the potential for successful African American apparel and accessory retailers to branch out of the African American community is relatively high.

7. *It would be difficult for any immigrant group to "lock up" distribution of clothing the way Koreans did with wig distribution,* given that more than twenty different countries are significant clothing exporters to the United States (Gereffi 1999) (partly a consequence of export quotas imposed under the Multi-Fiber Arrangement).

The Roles of Independent Buying Offices and Franchising

Figure 6.3 gives a schematic illustration of my proposal. I noted earlier that the area of apparel and accessories is well covered by independent buying offices, but that these may lack experience catering to an African American clientele. The obvious way to build expertise in serving the African American niche market is practice. By paying most of their affiliation fees with a selected independent buying office (or a few, if the response to this incentive is overwhelming), it should be possible to induce coordinated affiliation of many African American retailers. After a period during which the independent buying office acquires deep knowledge of African American retailers, this affiliation will realize economies of scope and scale in search for vendors for these retailers, so the incentive should be phased out.[22] A start-up period of five years should prove adequate for the independent buying office chosen to develop sufficient expertise for the affiliated African American retailers to find it worthwhile to pay the full costs of their affiliation.[23]

If it works, this part of the proposal will increase the success of existing African American apparel and accessory retailers. But we have seen that the nature of the independent buying office is not conducive to establishing new retail businesses, and the pull of the example of success is a slow and relatively weak process compared to voluntary chains or franchising.

The need for the second element of the plan depicted in figure 6.3 follows: in return for what amounts to a subsidy for their business, the independent buying office chosen should be strongly encouraged or even required to employ African American market representatives

Figure 6.3 Stimulation of New Franchises by Chosen Independent
Buying Office

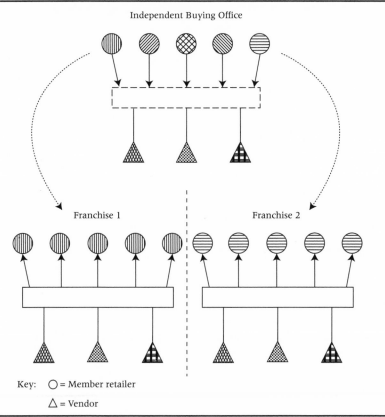

Independent Buying Office

Franchise 1

Franchise 2

Key: ○ = Member retailer

△ = Vendor

Source: Author.

for its African American clientele.[24] These African American market
representatives can then develop relationships with vendors that
will enable them, in the long run, to turn the most successful African
American retail concepts into African American–owned franchises.[25]
It is important to be clear that this part of the proposal is highly speculative: the fact that it is possible for the African American market representatives to start franchises once they have established relationships
with a broad array of vendors does not mean they will actually do so.

The direct cost of the proposal is modest.[26] According to the 1992 SMOBE, there were 6,391 black-owned apparel and accessory stores in the United States (excluding large businesses), of which 796 had paid employees (U.S. Department of Commerce 1996, 9, table 1). Average annual receipts for the latter group of stores were roughly $158,000, yielding an affiliation fee of roughly $800 using the 0.5 percent of sales formula quoted earlier. We can round this affiliation fee up to $1,000 and apply it to the *total* number of black-owned apparel and accessory stores existing in 1992, yielding an estimate of roughly $6.4 million (in 1992 dollars) annually.

This expenditure would recur for perhaps five years. Actual expenditure should fall well below this estimate because the average affiliation fee is overestimated, less than the full affiliation fee is being subsidized, and not all existing retailers will participate, while it is unlikely that there will be a substantial number of start-ups within the subsidy period. On the other hand, most independent buying offices are headquartered in New York City, and it may be necessary to pay travel expenses for retailers outside of the New York metropolitan area who are accustomed to visiting smaller local wholesale markets. If necessary, additional cost reduction can be achieved by limiting coverage of the proposal to one or more regions of the country. I believe that the cost of this proposal could be brought within the range of feasible financing by African American, corporate, and foundation philanthropy, thus avoiding the need for formal legislation.

Conclusion

The ability to produce new ideas for policy is perhaps the acid test of a novel approach in social science. In this chapter, I have tried to show that integrating network and market views of economic behavior passes that test. Nevertheless, there remain grounds for skepticism regarding whether my proposal would work if put into practice.[27] Perhaps the weakest part of the proposal is that it is based on a textbook knowledge of independent buying offices. Despite my best efforts, I simply could not discover a scholarly literature devoted to this subject, or to large-scale, diversified domestic trade intermediaries more generally. A combination of field and statistical work investigating the clienteles, detailed operations, and growth paths of the larger independent buying offices would have been very helpful.

Nevertheless, government efforts to stimulate the formation of the large-scale, diversified *foreign* trade intermediaries known as "general trading companies" provide some cause for optimism. International trade intermediation is an area in which investments in deep knowledge are likely to be especially expensive, and hence the incentive problems described earlier are likely to be especially severe. The well-documented dearth of general trading companies is therefore not surprising. Fields (1995), Rauch (1996b), Peng (1998), and references in these works describe successes in creating viable commercial intermediaries of this type in Japan, Korea, and Turkey, as well as failures in Taiwan and the United States.[28] If government intervention can successfully establish new large-scale intermediaries that link domestic manufacturers to foreign distributors and retailers, successful intervention to reshape existing large-scale intermediaries to improve the links between domestic and foreign vendors and an underserved group of domestic retailers should be within reach.

Epilogue

The fieldwork for this chapter was completed in June 1996. In May 2000, I followed up on the major case studies. I feel it is more informative to report here the changes that occurred than to update the descriptions in the main text, which were written four years earlier. As of May 2000:

- The founder of the African American grassroots business organization described in this chapter had gone out of business. By 1998 the organization had become inactive. At that time, a new executive director reinstated monthly meetings and rejuvenated the organization in general. More than twenty businesses now regularly attend monthly meetings, and the organization is currently in the midst of an attempt to expand membership and increase annual dues from $20 to $100.

- The Caribbean American grassroots business organization described here had expanded to more than thirteen hundred members.

According to my source in the Brooklyn Economic Development Corporation, it had added new member services and was continuing to draw large and enthusiastic crowds at all its events.

- The African American–owned athletic footwear franchise had expanded to fourteen stores in 1998, but only five stores remained open by May 2000. The entrepreneur with whom I spoke felt that the chief problem was a shift in inner-city youth demand away from athletic footwear as the key fashion accessory. Promised financial backing from several prominent African American sports figures had fallen through, and the franchise was searching for new venture capitalists as it repositioned itself in the market.

This chapter is a revision of "Trade and Networks: An Application to Minority Retail Entrepreneurship," written while I was a visiting scholar at the Russell Sage Foundation. Previous versions were presented at the Russell Sage Foundation, the University of California at San Diego, Brown University, and the Santa Fe Institute. I especially wish to thank J. Philip Thompson for his invaluable help. I would also like to thank the many unnamed individuals who generously permitted me to interview them for this research. Alessandra Casella and Marta Tienda made many useful suggestions for revision, and David Riker supplied the title pun. Financial support was provided by NSF grant SBR-9709237. I am solely responsible for any errors.

Notes

1. Fairlie and Meyer (1996, 759) define African American as "those people whose race is black and ancestry is African American. These individuals are a separate group from Black Africans because the latter group's members are more specific about their exact origin and are almost entirely first generation immigrants." In the remainder of this study, "black" refers to the racial identification category used by the U.S. Bureau of the Census, and "African American" refers to the native-born subset of blacks.

2. Author's computations based on U.S. Department of Commerce (1996, 9, table 1; 74, table 10). Here I am using the term "small business" to describe the firms covered by the SMOBE. These are individual propri-

etorships or self-employed persons, partnerships, and subchapter S corporations, where "a subchapter S corporation is a special IRS designation for legally incorporated businesses with 35 or fewer shareholders who, because of tax advantages, elected to be taxed as individual shareholders rather than as corporations" (U.S. Department of Commerce 1996, V). The three categories accounted for 45.0, 14.7, and 40.3 percent of all small-business workers, respectively, with proprietorships dominating the ranks of entrepreneurs (84.6 percent) and subchapter S corporations having the most paid employees (60.0 percent) (U.S. Department of Commerce 1996, 74, table 12).

3. In this study, I define "retail trade" as resale to final consumers of goods purchased from producers or intermediaries such as wholesalers, with further processing limited to repackaging. This differs slightly from the SMOBE definition, which includes eating and drinking places that involve a substantial element of food preparation service. If eating and drinking places are omitted, the black share of retail trade small-business entrepreneurs falls to 3.4 percent.

4. For students of African American retail entrepreneurship, this story is laden with irony. The owner of the building that housed both the clothing and record stores was the United House of Prayer for All People, an African American church founded in 1926 that preached economic self-reliance and started to build its present wealth in the 1930s by selling a line of products that included coffee, eggs, shoe polish, and toiletries (Frantz and Pulley 1995). The owner of the clothing store claimed that he needed more rent from his subtenant to make his own lease payments to the church. At one point, the church asked the owner of the record store to call off the demonstrations in return for space in another church-owned building on 125th Street, but the two sides were unable to come to agreement on the terms of a lease.

5. A tie brings familiarity with not only the vendor's product lines currently in stock but also with her "depth"—her ability to keep up with changing fashions and seasons. One wholesaler summed up the information content of ties for me with the phrase "know what you're all about."

6. I conjecture that the information content of ties to vendors is easier than the trust content for one retailer to pass on to another through referral.

7. Because trade is recorded when it crosses national borders, it is much more feasible to estimate statistically the influence of networks on international than on domestic trade. Rauch (in press) provides an extensive survey of the literature on business and social networks in international trade.

8. Business groups are "sets of firms that are integrated neither completely nor barely at all" (Granovetter 1995a, 96–97), and the lineages of their members can often be traced back to a founding family or small number of allied families. Typical mechanisms serving to integrate the firms include mutual stockholdings and frequent meetings of top executives. Business groups are common throughout Asia, continental Europe, and Latin America but are rare to nonexistent in Great Britain and the United States.

9. An especially vivid example of the sociability of deal-making is provided by sales practices in the auto industry. A saleswoman for a parts supplier to the Big Three automakers is suing her (former) employer because of its practice of making deals over lunch in topless bars. Robyn Meredith (1997) reports, "Many salesmen love these strip clubs because they speed up the male bonding that can lead to lucrative contracts."

10. Such friends presumably include the broader community and not just other small-business people.

11. Grocery stores are the leading example. The need for daily purchases of fresh food and the expectation of U.S. consumers that grocery stores will be open at their convenience make running a grocery store significantly more taxing than other forms of small-business entrepreneurship. Rauch (1996a, 34–36) expands on this point in the context of Dominican bodegas and Korean greengrocers.

12. I am fairly certain that these organizations are the only two in either the Manhattan or Brooklyn boroughs of New York City. I did not investigate the Bronx or Queens boroughs as thoroughly, partly because no trails ever led there. (There are very few African Americans in Staten Island.) I am deliberately excluding street vendor cooperatives, partly because I did not get the sense that they were sources of upward mobility to retail storefronts and partly because they appeared to be dominated by immigrants. I came across several grassroots African American business organizations with no retailer participation, most notably the Black Fashion Collective of upscale clothing designers and manufacturers.

13. In response to my question concerning cooperation in buying, the founder asserted that there was a clear opportunity to engage in joint, bulk buying of black and white T-shirts and ash sweatshirts, on which several of the apparel retailers printed different things, but that group cooperation had not yet reached this stage.

14. An informant estimated that 80 percent of the member businesses were Caribbean American, with the balance mostly nonwhite, of which a majority were African American. The same informant felt that the

networking benefits of this organization for African American businesses were weakened by the "tension" between the African American and Caribbean American communities. This tension was not evident in the meeting described below. Even if this organization were ultimately to prove capable of substituting for the ability of African American businesses to organize themselves, the broader implications of this would be limited by the lack of sizable Caribbean American populations in most African American communities.

15. Independent buying offices are a subset of "resident buying offices," so-called because they are resident in the major wholesale markets.

16. Using data from the 1990 U.S. Census, Douglas Massey and Mary Fischer (1999, table 1) show that affluent blacks are more residentially segregated than the poorest Hispanics or Asians.

17. Evidence is presented by Faith Ando (1988) that established black businesses are more likely to have their loan applications rejected, controlling for other factors that influence credit risk, and Timothy Bates (1993, chapter 5) presents evidence for the redlining of minority areas by commercial banks. I am not aware of any systematic studies of whether either redlining of African American communities or discrimination against African American applicants is a problem in franchising. Anecdotal evidence suggests that neither is a problem in the fast-food industry, but some of my informants claimed that both were problems in other sectors.

18. African Americans may be significantly underrepresented in wholesaling because of problems in forming ties to manufacturers related to the sociability of deal-making, as mentioned earlier.

19. I am aware of an African American–owned airport bookstore franchise, which grew out of a minority set-aside at an Atlanta airport and now covers more than forty airports. I did not discover any African American–owned voluntary chains. Given my search procedure, I feel fairly confident that if the franchise I describe is not the only one in the snowbelt of the United States that meets my qualifications, it is one of an extremely small number.

20. The various minority lending programs typically do not make loans of more than $500,000. Other conversations with African American small-business people and officials of community development corporations tended to confirm that these programs are quite effective for African American entrepreneurs *with credible business plans in hand*. Of course, applicants with poor business plans tend to be turned down for loans. These applicants can confuse researchers by stating that their businesses are doing poorly because of lack of capital.

21. As we saw earlier, independent buying offices are paid fees whose per-
    centage rate or dollar amount is not based on quality of service but set
    by custom. The point here is that, if the expectation of these fees does
    not provide adequate incentive to make socially profitable investments
    in deep knowledge, the independent buying office may have little lever-
    age to raise its return through side payments or other means.

22. If one wants the stores to be serious about using the services of the cho-
    sen independent buying office, one should not subsidize the entire cost
    of affiliation. There is a trade-off: the greater the subsidy, the greater
    the incentive for African American apparel and accessory retailers to
    join, and the bargaining power with the chosen independent buying
    office is greater as well.

23. An adequate length for the start-up period of five years is an educated
    guess based on the experience of Turkey in stimulating the creation of
    large-scale, diversified international trade intermediaries, the most re-
    cent success for this kind of government intervention. (I know of no
    similar intervention on behalf of domestic trade intermediaries.) As part
    of an export drive that Turkey began in 1980, special tax rebates were
    offered to trading companies exporting more than a specified amount,
    and starting in 1985 trading companies exceeding both minimum cap-
    ital and export volume requirements qualified for additional incentives.
    The percentage of Turkish exports handled by large trading companies
    grew from 7 percent in 1980 to more than 50 percent by the end of 1988
    (Krueger and Aktan 1992). Most of these remained viable after the sub-
    sidies were phased out. This experience concerns foreign rather than do-
    mestic trade, so a shorter start-up period is justified.

24. It was asserted by one of my informants that when African Americans
    become successful, they often cut their ties to African American commu-
    nities, an argument also made by Wilson (1987). It is thus worth point-
    ing out that these market representatives, however successful, cannot
    cut their ties to the African American community because their success
    is dependent on the success of retailers selling to that community.

25. This may be an unattractive possibility from the point of view of the in-
    dependent buying office. However, it is understood to be part of any
    business that employees may split off and take some clients with them.
    Aside from the possibility of discrimination, the fact that the indepen-
    dent buying office is unlikely to be able to capture this benefit to their
    African American market representatives implies that its own interests
    cannot be relied upon to lead it to choose African Americans over whites
    for these positions.

26. I do not attempt to assign a number to the social benefits of my proposal. Even with the best data, we lack a theoretical framework sufficiently well developed to measure the social "output" of large independent buying offices or similar large-scale, diversified commercial intermediaries.

27. Even in the best case, the proposal could only supplement rather than supplant other policies, such as elimination of bank discrimination aimed at increasing African American participation and success in retail trade (and other) entrepreneurship.

28. The 1982 U.S. Export Trading Company Act eased antitrust constraints for registered export trading companies and allowed banks to participate indirectly in exporting, but no subsidies accompanied these regulatory changes. Similarly, Fields (1995, 214) attributes the failure of Taiwan's Large Trading Company program to "the feeble nature of incentives," though it may also have been the case that the overseas Chinese network made general trading companies redundant for Taiwan.

References

Ando, Faith. 1988. *An Analysis of Access to Bank Credit*. Los Angeles: UCLA Center for Afro-American Studies.

Bates, Timothy. 1993. *Banking on Black Enterprise*. Washington: Joint Center for Political and Economic Studies.

———. 1994. "An Analysis of Korean-Immigrant–Owned Small-Business Start-ups with Comparisons to African-American– and Nonminority-Owned Firms." *Urban Affairs Quarterly* 30(December): 227–48.

Belderbos, René, and Leo Sleuwaegen. 1998. "Tariff Jumping DFI and Export Substitution: Japanese Electronics Firms in Europe." *International Journal of Industrial Organization* 16: 601–38.

Biggs, Tyler, Gail R. Moody, Jan-Hendrik van Leeuwen, and E. Diane White. 1994. "Africa Can Compete!: Export Opportunities and Challenges for Garments and Home Products in the U.S. Market." Discussion paper 242. Washington, D.C.: World Bank.

Burstiner, Irving. 1998. *How to Start and Run Your Own Retail Business*. Secaucus, N.J.: Carol Publishing Group.

Cash, R. Patrick, John W. Wingate, and Joseph S. Friedlander. 1995. *Management of Retail Buying*. 3rd ed. New York: Wiley.

Cimons, Marlene. 1988. "Creation of Black Firms Gets Harder." *Los Angeles Times*, July 2.

Diamond, Jay, and Gerald Pintel. 1996. *Retailing*. 6th ed. Upper Saddle River, N.J.: Prentice-Hall.

————. 1997. *Retail Buying.* 5th ed. Upper Saddle River, N.J.: Prentice-Hall.

The Economist. 2000. "Survey: E-Commerce." Vol. 354 (February 26).

Fairlie, Robert W., and Bruce D. Meyer. 1996. "Ethnic and Racial Self-employment Differences and Possible Explanations." *Journal of Human Resources* 31(Fall): 757–93.

Fields, Karl J. 1995. *Enterprise and the State in Korea and Taiwan.* Ithaca, N.Y.: Cornell University Press.

Frantz, Douglas, and Brett Pulley. 1995. "Harlem Church Is Outpost of Empire." *New York Times,* December 17.

Gereffi, Gary. 1999. "International Trade and Industrial Upgrading in the Apparel Commodity Chain." *Journal of International Economics* 48(June): 37–70.

Gould, David M. 1994. "Immigrant Links to the Home Country: Empirical Implications for U.S. Bilateral Trade Flows." *Review of Economics and Statistics* 76(May): 302–16.

Granovetter, Mark. 1995a. "Coase Revisited: Business Groups in the Modern Economy." *Industrial and Corporate Change* 4(1): 93–129.

————. 1995b. "The Economic Sociology of Firms and Entrepreneurs." In *The Economic Sociology of Immigration,* edited by Alejandro Portes. New York: Russell Sage Foundation.

Holzer, Harry J. 1996. "Employer Hiring Decisions and Antidiscrimination Policy." In *Demand-Side Strategies for Low-Wage Labor Markets,* edited by Richard Freeman and Peter Gottschalk. New York: Russell Sage Foundation.

Kim, Illsoo. 1981. *New Urban Immigrants: The Korean Community in New York.* Princeton, N.J.: Princeton University Press.

Krueger, Anne O., and Okan H. Aktan. 1992. *Swimming Against the Tide: Turkish Trade Reform in the 1980s.* San Francisco: Institute for Contemporary Studies.

Light, Ivan. 1972. *Ethnic Enterprise in America.* Berkeley: University of California Press.

Massey, Douglas S., and Mary J. Fischer. 1999. "Does Rising Income Bring Integration?: New Results for Blacks, Hispanics, and Asians in 1990." *Social Science Research* 28: 316–29.

Meredith, Robyn. 1997. "Male Bastion for Dealmaking Under Attack." *New York Times,* September 20.

Min, Pyong-Gap. 1984. "A Structural Analysis of Korean Business in the United States." *Ethnic Groups* 6(June): 1–25.

————. 1993. "Korean Immigrants in Los Angeles." In *Immigration and Entrepreneurship,* edited by Ivan Light and Parminder Bhachu. New Brunswick, N.J.: Transaction.

Moss, Mitchell L. 1995. "Harlem's Economic Paradox." *New York Times,* December 13.

New York City Empowerment Zone. 1994. *Appendices.* Unpublished paper. Columbia University, New York.

Peng, Mike W. 1998. *Behind the Success and Failure of U.S. Export Intermediaries.* Westport, Conn.: Quorum Books.

Rauch, James E. 1996a. "Trade and Networks: An Application to Minority Retail Entrepreneurship." Working Paper 100. New York: Russell Sage Foundation (June).

———. 1996b. "Trade and Search: Social Capital, Sogo Shosha, and Spillovers." Working paper 5618. Cambridge, Mass.: National Bureau of Economic Research (June).

———. In press. "Business and Social Networks in International Trade." *Journal of Economic Literature.*

Rauch, James E., and Vitor Trindade. In press. "Ethnic Chinese Networks in International Trade." *Review of Economics and Statistics.*

Rhee, Yung Whee, and Christine Soulier. 1989. "Small Trading Companies and a Successful Export Response: Lessons from Hong Kong." Industry Series paper 16. Washington, D.C.: Industry and Energy Department (December).

Saxenian, AnnaLee. 1999. *Silicon Valley's New Immigrant Entrepreneurs.* San Francisco: Public Policy Institute of California.

U.S. Department of Commerce. 1996. *1992 Survey of Minority-Owned Business Enterprises: Black.* Washington: U.S. Government Printing Office.

U.S. Department of Labor. 1995. *Consumer Expenditure Survey, 1993.* Washington: U.S. Government Printing Office.

Wilson, William J. 1987. *The Truly Disadvantaged,* Chicago: University of Chicago Press.

Discussion

Ethnic Ties and Entrepreneurship: Comment on "Black Ties Only? Ethnic Business Networks, Intermediaries, and African American Retail Entrepreneurship"

Marta Tienda and Rebeca Raijman

The high rate of business ownership among recent immigrants, particularly Asians, has directed attention to the strategies that enable new arrivals to establish a foothold in the U.S. economy through small-business ownership. Ethnic networks link producers, distributors, and consumers vertically and horizontally to enhance the social "embeddedness" of economic transactions (Granovetter 1985; Portes 1996). Rauch acknowledges that ethnic networks not only permit entrepreneurs to transcend market discrimination but also contribute to the economic vitality of communities. He poses a vexing question: If recent immigrants can succeed in small businesses, why are African Americans seemingly less able to do so? This is not a new question, yet few studies provide any insights into an answer.

Focusing on the retail sector, Rauch acknowledges that ethnic networks are a powerful resource to enhance economic transactions by linking buyers and sellers. He builds on this idea to expose a weakness in the community of African American retailers and proposes a policy solution. Despite the "natural markets" provided by residentially segregated neighborhoods, Rauch perceives the absence of intermediaries linking buyers and sellers as a crucial reason for the relatively limited presence and success of African Americans in retail and other small businesses. His fieldwork suggests that African American business owners have thinner business networks; that their networks are less conducive to information-sharing and thereby to linking buyers and sellers; and that there are relatively few formal business associations that cater to African American concerns to provide the market linkage. Accordingly, he proposes the establishment of commercial intermediaries to carry out the economic functions currently performed by ethnic networks in immigrant communities.

Rauch acknowledges that social contacts among retail business owners are beneficial for economic transactions because they enhance information about both merchandise and potential suppliers. Moreover, he maintains that business functions are discussed more intensively and productively in the context of formal organizations. To develop his case about commercial intermediaries as functional alternatives for ethnic networks, Rauch documents the glaring absence of predominantly African American grassroots business organizations that cater to co-ethnic retailers, in sharp contrast to thriving Caribbean American business organizations. He provides richly textured evidence about the exchange of information at the "Power Breakfast" meetings, illustrating how this formal organization fosters exchanges conducive to the establishment and growth of small retail businesses. Presumably, commercial intermediaries can provide one of the crucial benefits of informal ethnic ties or ethnic grassroots business organizations, namely, information. In the market niche that Rauch studies—the retail sector—such information seems vital for a tighter linkage of buyers and sellers.

His proposal that commercial intermediaries are a functional substitute for informal ties has merit inasmuch as it responds to an identified problem (limited horizontal and vertical linkages among buyers and sellers) and offers a compelling and plausible solution, namely, formalizing ties between buyers and sellers to enhance the flow of information. However, the anecdotal evidence he provides does not indicate what share of current African American business owners actually participate in such formal business organizations, or would participate if the financial barriers to organizational membership were significantly reduced or eliminated. Systematic evidence that retailers who are members of business organizations also are more successful would render his proposition more convincing, assuming it is operationally viable. Evidence that new or prospective entrepreneurs routinely seek information about business start-ups from such organizations would be even more compelling.

Rauch's discussion leaves the impression that formal business organizations are an alternative to informal business networks and that commercial intermediaries can furnish the information often transmitted informally along ethnic lines. In fairness, he acknowledges that such organizations at best can *supplement* the functions performed by informal business ties, serving instead to bolster information flows among existing businesses and possibly—although this is less clear from his proposals—encourage new business start-ups. For this to occur, prospective business owners would have to know about the commercial intermediary organizations, and they would have to be willing to utilize their services. Both requirements are reasonable enough, yet in the absence of evidence establishing a real demand for these services— both the need for information about goods and consumers and the ability to pay for the intermediary services—the viability of his policy recommendation remains unclear. Formal business networks may be necessary, albeit insufficient, conditions to promote and enhance small-business development. Much depends on whether business owners use the commercial intermediaries, and what it would take to institutionalize this practice among small-business owners.

In what follows we pursue these questions by drawing on a unique study that sought to understand the mechanisms through which ethnicity influences entrepreneurship, with a special focus on the roles that households, families, and ethnic communities play in stimulating or undermining business activities. Our study includes interviews with both entrepreneurs and household heads residing in a community known as Little Village, which is one of the largest Mexican communities in the Midwest.[1] In addition to standard demographic and socioeconomic characteristics, the survey instrument solicited information about inputs for business start-up, including: sources of capital; sources and use of credit; economic difficulties and financial barriers; and clients, suppliers, social networks, and participation in formal business organizations. The uniqueness of the instrument resides in its emphasis on how ethnicity structures economic transactions both formally and informally.

In this exercise, we illustrate the degree and nature of own-group ties in vertical and horizontal market transactions, and we present information about membership and participation in formal business organizations. Mexican immigrants are an informative comparison to African Americans because they too have low rates of business ownership and are highly residentially segregated. According to the 1990 U.S. Census, Mexican self-employment rates ranged from 3 to 4 percent, for males and females, respectively (Raijman 1996). Mexican immigrants also have relatively low incomes and financial assets, and like African Americans, they experience difficulties qualifying for credit. A notable difference, however, is that Mexican immigrant retailers are embedded in thick ethnic networks that connect them to clients and customers, credit sources, suppliers and distributors, and information about economic opportunities—the roles Rauch proposes commercial intermediaries could perform for African American business owners. Given this policy recommendation, it is worthwhile to ponder whether, when confronted with the option of consulting a formal business organization, drawing on informal ethnic resources, or both, Mexican immigrants actually use the former and why.

Following a description of the community studied and the business survey conducted in Little Village, we present descriptive information about the prevalence of economic ties among own-group members and show that formal business organizations play a relatively minor role in both business start-ups and expansions of existing businesses. We find that, for Mexicans, economic transactions are highly structured along ethnic lines and take place in multiple formal and informal settings. Therefore, we conclude that commercial intermediaries may not adequately perform the roles of ethnically circumscribed social ties in fostering successful minority businesses, even in a supplementary role. Whether dense ethnic ties are essential to promote the establishment of formal business organizations is debatable. However, the Caribbean American case that Rauch documents involves both strong informal ties and strong grassroots organizations; the African American case has neither; the Mexican community has strong informal ties but apparently weak grassroots organizations. This variance provides a weak foundation from which to draw inferences about the viability of Rauch's proposition.

The Little Village Study

Little Village is one of two Mexican immigrant neighborhoods on the southwest side of Chicago. Previously a Czech immigrant neighborhood, this community is surrounded by small to moderate-size nondurable-goods factories that employ immigrant workers at low wages. The vibrant shopping district on Twenty-sixth Street is populated by small businesses that serve the steady stream of new immigrants: this neighborhood has become a magnet for recent immigrants of Mexican origin who seek employment in the low-wage jobs available within and surrounding the neighborhood.[2] Between 1970 and 1990, when most of Chicago's low-income communities lost population, Little Village witnessed an increase from 63,000 to 81,000. Residential succession has been equally rapid, as the Hispanic share (virtually all Mexican) of the community rose from 33 to 82 percent during this period. More than two out of five Little Village residents were foreign-born in 1990, and nearly one in four families had incomes below the official poverty level in 1990. The official unemployment rate was about 15 percent. Thus, despite its dynamic business community, the community is far from affluent.

Little Village is an interesting case study for our purposes because Chicago, like many northern industrial centers, has experienced massive job losses since the mid-1970s, even as immigration has continued to increase. As low-wage job opportunities declined in Chicago, the lure of business ownership as a gateway to the formal labor market has grown stronger. The residential concentration of Mexican immigrants is conducive to the development of a strong retail trade sector that caters to ethnic concerns. Thus, Little Village offers a strong retail section through which we can evaluate Rauch's claims for this ethnic market niche.

The survey of businesses in Little Village is based on a stratified random sample of establishments that were in operation in the spring of 1994. Our canvass of the neighborhood yielded approximately one thousand business establishments, which were stratified according to primary type of industry, product, or service.[3] Relatively uncommon businesses, such as bridal shops, bakeries, ironworks products, and factories, were sampled at a rate of 100 percent. Abundant enterprises like restaurants, bars, auto repair shops, and hair salons were sampled at a rate of 35 percent. All remaining establishments were sampled at a rate of 50 percent. Weights inverse to the sampling ratio were applied to represent the Little Village business community. With a target sample size of 200 enterprises, we surveyed 286 establishments and successfully interviewed 200 business owners, yielding a response rate of 71 percent.[4] This is a highly successful response rate, considering that we insisted on interviewing the owners of the establishments and declined interviews with managers or other employees. Bilingual interviewers conducted all interviews.

Although predominantly a Mexican *residential* neighborhood, Little Village is a multi-ethnic business community where, not surprisingly, Mexican-owned businesses dominate. Three in four of Little Village business owners are of Hispanic origin, the majority of them Mexican and foreign-born.[5] Koreans represent 13 percent of Little Village business owners, and the remaining share consists of Middle Eastern, other South Asian (Indian and Pakistani), and non-Hispanic whites. Korean business owners concentrate in clothing and other general retail concerns, including electronics, jewelry, and beauty supply outlets. Not surprisingly, Mexicans dominate the restaurant business and other concerns that cater to an ethnic clientele, such as hair salons and barbershops. Approximately 40 percent of non-Hispanic entrepreneurs and U.S.-born Hispanic business owners engage in the sale of furniture, music, jewelry, photo processing services, and laundry services.

To examine our case about the importance of ethnic ties in both formal and informal business transactions, we first consider the ethnic foundations of economic transactions by examining the extent to which Little Village entrepreneurs acquire services and products from suppliers who are of the same ethnicity. This helps portray the extent of vertical integration among distributors, suppliers, and vendors. Subsequently, we examine the participation of Little Village entrepreneurs in formal business organizations to evaluate the salience of formal organizations in structuring economic transactions in an ethnic economy. Finally, we provide more in-depth information about the breadth of ethnic networks in Little Village and their importance not only for business start-ups—a dimension not addressed by Rauch's proposal about commercial intermediaries—but also for the routine conduct of business. Taken together, these considerations suggest that even if commercial intermediaries strengthen links among African American business owners, they are unlikely to substitute for ethnic networks in both promoting business start-ups and encouraging expansions.

Ethnic Foundations of Economic Transactions

In this section, we document the extent to which vertical integration of small businesses is ethnically circumscribed. Vertical integration has been singled out as an important mechanism promoting economic growth within residentially circumscribed communities (Wilson and Martin 1982). Based on a study of Miami's Cuban enclave, Alejandro Portes and his numerous collaborators have argued that the ability of certain ethnic economies to reproduce themselves stems from their higher capacity to structure economic transactions along ethnic lines (see Wilson and Martin 1982; Portes and Bach 1985; Portes 1987). That is, by increasing the circulation of income flows within the ethnic economy, vertical integration increases the demand for goods and services that creates a continuous source of business opportunities for aspiring entrepreneurs (Wilson and Martin 1982). That Mexican immigrants have relatively low aggregate rates of business ownership does not necessarily imply thinner social networks or ethnic ties less conducive to sharing information or linking buyers and sellers than Cubans, Koreans, or the Caribbean Americans Rauch describes. To address whether this is so, we first consider whether groups differ in their propensity to engage in business transactions along ethnic lines.

Table 6.2 shows the propensity of Little Village business owners to transact services (horizontal integration) or products (vertical integration) with members of their own ethnic group. Nearly 90 percent of Korean, 73 percent of Mexican, 66 percent of Middle Eastern, and 57 percent of non-Hispanic white business owners in Little Village use

Table 6.2 Homo-Ethnicity of Economic Transactions for Little Village Entrepreneurs (Percentage)

	Mexican	Korean	Middle Eastern and Asian	Non-Hispanic White
Business service providers				
Use service suppliers of own ethnicity	72.7	89.0	66.7	57.1
Use accountant	86.6	85.2	58.3	94.4
Use accountant of own ethnicity	72.8	100.0	42.9	83.0
Use attorney	27.0	30.8	18.2	66.7
Use attorney of own ethnicity	25.5	0.0	33.3	84.6
Use insurance services	45.4	46.2	54.5	83.3
Use insurance agent of own ethnicity	39.3	75.0	20.0	75.0
Product suppliers				
Have at least one coethnic product supplier	50.0	81.0	25.8	72.0
Use product suppliers of same ethnicity	35.4	60.0	20.6	66.7
Product suppliers also provide credit	44.9	82.6	79.4	61.0
N	187	27	12	18

Source: Little Village Business Survey.

the services of coethnic professionals. With the exception of Middle Eastern and South Asian business owners, all groups tend to hire accountants from the same ethnic group. This difference probably reflects the scarcity of Middle Eastern and South Asian accountants more than the expressed preferences of these groups. By contrast, the majority of firms that use legal services contract with American (white) lawyers. Several Mexicans told us that they have two attorneys—a coethnic lawyer for routine business matters and an American (white, often Jewish) lawyer for more complicated matters. Three in four white and Korean business owners utilizing insurance services contract these from coethnic suppliers, compared to only 40 percent of Mexican and 20 percent of Middle Eastern and Asian business owners.

Ethnic differences in propensity to procure product supplies from members of their own ethnic group are somewhat lower, but still quite high.[6] Half of Mexican merchants in Little Village have at least one coethnic supplier compared to 81 percent of Koreans, 72 percent of non-Hispanic white businesspeople, and only 26 percent of Middle Eastern and South Asian merchants. Another indicator of the extent of vertical integration is the proportion of all economic transactions conducted with a supplier of the same ethnic group. Group differences are rather striking. Just over one-third of all business transactions of Mexican business owners are conducted with coethnic suppliers, and for clothing retailers and restaurant owners, Mexicans rely on coethnic suppliers more extensively—54 and 40 percent, respectively. These figures compare with 60 percent of Koreans, two-thirds of non-Hispanic whites, and only 21 percent of Middle Easterners and South Asians who own and operate businesses in Little Village.

There are several explanations for the observed differences in reliance on own-group service and product suppliers. One is that business owners prefer members of their own group because they find it easier to establish trust and to communicate with them. Another is that own-group members provide more favorable credit terms to business owners, thereby reducing financial stress when cash flows are tight. As shown in the third line of the lower panel of table 6.2, the shares of product suppliers who provide their clients with credit are not trivial. Third, some groups may be underrepresented in concerns that lend themselves to ethnically circumscribed vertical integration, particularly for demographically small populations, like Middle Easterners and South Asians in Chicago.

To explore the reasons associated with the selection of service and product suppliers, business owners who reported using at least two suppliers of their own ethnicity were asked whether they generally prefer to work with members of their own ethnic group, and if so, why. Cultural reasons are the modal response for choosing a coethnic service supplier. Among the most common responses to this question are: "It is easy to work with them," "Language problems [that limit transactions beyond the ethnic network]," and, "You understand each other better." Trust is the second most frequent reason for selecting a coethnic professional supplier. Not surprisingly, Koreans—among the most successful immigrant entrepreneurs—are more likely than others to report common culture as a motivation for hiring a coethnic service supplier. Virtually all respondents identify coethnics as "less corrupt" and "more efficient." Seeking the best prices for the highest-quality goods and services, non-Hispanic white business owners claim to consider job performance over racial affinity in selecting their suppliers and producers.

In addition to cultural reasons (language, common understandings, and trust), the selection of product suppliers also is governed by the availability of distributors offering a particular product line. Herein lies the power of ethnically grounded vertical integration for promoting ethnic entrepreneurship. Unlike the Cubans in Miami, where vertical and horizontal linkages are bolstered by residential segregation, those for the Korean community are generally residentially dispersed but ethnically contained (except for businesses located in the Korean residential neighborhood). Korean business owners report that when coethnic suppliers specializing in the products they retail in Little Village are available, they prefer own-group suppliers, but when they trade in goods that cater to a Mexican clientele, they generally have to find non-Korean distributors. Koreans also report that coethnic suppliers offer them good prices and better credit conditions than other groups. Non-Hispanic white business owners are equally likely to report choosing coethnic suppliers because "they provide the [necessary] merchandise" these owners need and also because these suppliers approach them and are "well known in the market." Only 11 percent of Mexican business owners see their reliance on coethnic suppliers as coincidental rather than a deliberate choice.

Although ethnic entrepreneurs may prefer a coethnic supplier of products, when none exists in the specific industry or coethnics do not provide the best market terms, they are forced to trade with other ethnic groups, as Little Village Mexican business owners do. Because of the relatively low rate of Mexican business ownership outside of Little Village, many business owners report having no choice in the selection of product suppliers. Mexican, Middle Eastern, and South Asian business owners who do not rely on coethnic suppliers are more likely than non-Hispanic white business owners to report that they do not use coethnic suppliers for this reason.

In summary, Korean business owners in Little Village report higher preferences for coethnic suppliers, are less constrained by availability to purchase their supplies outside of their ethnic network, and also prefer to do trade with coethnics for economic reasons (better terms and credit availability). Mexicans report lower preferences for coethnic suppliers and are also less likely than Koreans to report economic reasons for choosing them as coethnic suppliers. But when Mexican business owners go outside the ethnic network to procure supplies and services, they do so because members of their own group who can supply the goods and services are unavailable. This situation is probably analogous to that encountered by African Americans engaged in retail trade. The question, then, is whether vertically integrated African American businesses would provide better credit terms, and whether the nature and frequency of economic transactions would be mutually beneficial for buyers and sellers. Rauch provides more theoretical than empirical evidence on this question.

At issue for assessing the viability of commercial intermediaries as an alternative to ethnic networks is the value of coethnicity in structuring preferences and economic transactions. Assuming optimal price and credit terms, when given a choice, Korean immigrants, and to a lesser extent Mexican immigrants, *prefer* coethnic product suppliers and service providers. It is unclear whether economic transactions by commercial intermediaries would be more efficient if structured along ethnic lines, but our evidence suggests an affirmative answer.

Would business owners actually patronize commercial intermediary organizations if organized along ethnic lines? In response to this empirical question, table 6.3 reports the organizational participation and use of institutional services by Little Village entrepreneurs. We recognize that business associations are not the same as commercial intermediaries dedicated to the functions outlined by Rauch. However, his illustration using the Caribbean American organization to contrast with the absence of grassroots organizations in the African American community prompted us to consider this possibility.

Because the tabulations reported in table 6.3 are based on a representative sample of business owners, they provide a different perspec-

Table 6.3 Organizational Participation and Use of Institutional Services by Little Village Entrepreneurs, by Ethnicity (Percentage)

	Mexican	Korean	Middle Eastern and Asian	Non-Hispanic White
Belong to business association	28.9	33.3	8.3	49.4
Same ethnic group, association 1	84.6	33.3	0.0	50.0
Same ethnic group, association 2	67.0	66.7	0.0	100.0
Know about programs for business owners	16.0	7.4	8.3	27.8
Use these services	14.3	33.3	0.0	16.7
N	187.0	27.0	12.0	18.0

Source: Little Village Business Survey.

tive than that afforded by studying a particular organization. More important, they address a question relevant to Rauch's proposal, namely, business owners' willingness to participate in formal organizations that putatively offer the benefits provided by ethnic networks. These tabulations show that only between 29 and 33 percent of Little Village Mexican and Korean business owners belong to a business association, compared to almost half of white and less than 10 percent of Middle Eastern and South Asian business owners. However, of those who participate in formal business associations, most Mexican business owners, but only one-third of Korean business owners, are involved in coethnic organizations.

Just as important is the information (rows 4 and 5) indicating a lack of knowledge about programs for new business owners. Less than 20 percent of Mexican business owners in Little Village know about programs that serve new business owners, and less than 10 percent of Korean and Middle Eastern and South Asian business owners are familiar with such organizations. This compares with approximately one in four non-Hispanic whites. Somewhat surprisingly, of those who are aware of such programs, less than 20 percent of Mexicans and non-

Hispanic whites take advantage of the services provided. One-third of Korean business owners use such services, conditional on familiarity. Combined, these tabulations indicate that only a tiny fraction of Little Village entrepreneurs actually benefit from formal programs for business owners. Partly this reflects imperfect information, but largely this results for other reasons. Before assuming that the commercial intermediary solution would apply to small business owners, an understanding of who does and does not participate in formal business organizations seems crucial. Unfortunately, our survey can provide little insight into this issue.

However, one possible reason is that Little Village business owners prefer to draw on informal ethnic ties rather than participate in formal organizations whose overall mission may be too broad to provide concrete benefits. Respondents were asked how they obtain information about business start-ups and whether there is a group of business owners with whom they confer regularly. Tables 6.4 and 6.5 report whom current business owners consulted when they considered starting their business and whom they regularly consult about routine business matters. These tabulations illustrate the importance of social ties in busi-

Table 6.4 Social Networks in Business Start-Ups, by Ethnicity (Percentage)

	Mexican	Korean	Middle Eastern and Asian	Non-Hispanic White
Social networks used during start-up				
Family	71.1	37.8	52.9	51.1
Friends	20.0	32.2	41.2	22.4
Business associate	8.9	30.0	5.9	26.5
Same ethnicity	93.6	90.0	85.3	89.4
Places of interaction[a]				
Home	67.7	32.2	61.8	30.6
Phone	2.6	28.9	—	6.1
Business workplace	25.0	47.8	47.1	36.7
Other	6.4	10.0	—	18.4
N	187	27	12	18

Source: Little Village Business Survey.
[a] Percentages exceed 100 because respondents gave multiple answers.

ness activity because the vast majority of *all* groups relied heavily on coethnics. Although groups differ in their relative reliance on friends, family, and business associates, 85 to 94 percent of their advisers are coethnics. Discussions about business start-ups were not restricted to formal settings, although Koreans and Middle Easterners and South Asians are more likely than Mexicans and non-Hispanic whites to confer at a place of work or business. That business discussions occur in a myriad of settings, including churches, restaurants, and homes, partly explains the salience of ethnicity in business ties.

Strong ethnic ties persist beyond the business start-up phase. As table 6.5 reveals, between 40 and 56 percent of Little Village business owners confer regularly with other business owners, with whom they discuss a myriad of topics ranging from technical advice and merchan-

Table 6.5 Social Networks in Doing Business, by Ethnicity (Percentage)

	Mexican	Korean	Middle Eastern and Asian	Non-Hispanic White
Discuss matter with other business owners	43.9	44.4	41.7	55.6
Same ethnicity	96.1	100.0	73.3	62.5
Topics discussed				
Everything	63.2	44.2	26.7	53.1
Technical advice	9.0	3.8	—	12.5
Customers	4.5	3.8	—	15.6
Merchandise	15.8	40.0	36.5	40.0
Financing	7.4	3.8	13.3	—
Expansion	25.5	28.8	86.7	40.6
Places of interaction[a]				
Home	26.1	23.1	13.3	18.8
Phone	17.1	26.9	13.3	25.0
Business	46.8	36.5	86.7	34.4
Restaurants	9.0	23.1	—	15.6
Professional settings	6.5	—	—	—
Other	3.2	—	—	18.8
N	187	27	12	18

Source: Little Village Survey.
[a]Percentages exceed 100 because respondents gave multiple answers.

dising to financing and business expansion. These interactions also take place in many settings, but only Mexicans report professional settings as a venue for these discussions. Especially striking is the finding that virtually all Mexican and Korean and nearly three-fourths of Middle Eastern and South Asian entrepreneurs discuss business matters with coethnics. This suggests that Rauch's proposal about commercial intermediaries might be even more successful if it capitalized on ethnic ties that strengthen forward and backward linkages among producers, distributors, and retailers. That is, designating commercial intermediary institutions to foster vertical and horizontal linkages among African American businesses may meet with limited success if they do not consider the value of "black ties" in structuring the organizations.

Conclusions

That formal business organizations play a relatively minor role in either business start-ups or the expansion of existing businesses does not mean that they cannot provide some of the functions currently offered by informal ethnic ties. However, based on our survey and fieldwork, we remain skeptical that, at least for small business enterprises, formally organized commercial intermediaries would serve African American business owners in the same way, or to the same extent, as the informal ties embedded in ethnic networks. Moreover, for retail trade, a consumer base to patronize retail shops may be as critical for business success as good information about reliable suppliers and distributors. On this score, we note that 74 percent of Mexican business owners in Little Village report that the success of their business depends on the income levels of the community in which they operate, compared to only 56 percent of Korean business owners and 28 percent of non-Hispanic whites. For African Americans, this issue is also germane for understanding the viability of small retail businesses that cater to an African American consumer base. Thus, even if the commercial intermediaries are dedicated to the retail industry, the constraints of the consumer base also need further exploration in the context of residential segregation that for African Americans appears less conducive to business success than is common among immigrant minorities.

The results reported in tables 6.3, 6.4, and 6.5 also temper optimism about the ability of commercial intermediaries to provide the benefits currently offered by ethnic networks. For such a proposal to be successful, the implementation strategy must be accompanied by a strong information campaign to inform business owners about the benefits and services provided. This challenge is more complicated for serving prospective business owners—individuals like those who attended the "Power Breakfasts" of the Caribbean American grassroots organization. For prospective entrepreneurs, perhaps the informal ethnic ties have no functional substitutes. In fact, there is some evidence that ethnic economies operate as a training sector for future entrepreneurs because employment in a coethnic firm increases the likelihood of acquiring skills relevant to owning a business (Raijman and Tienda 2000). This is particularly so in the retail sector. However, until such training opportunities expand, creating a broad base for would-be entrepreneurs to acquire know-how for establishing and operating a business, the role of ethnic economies in perpetuating further business start-ups is likely to be small. Nevertheless, it is not clear that this training function can be negotiated by intermediaries either.

Our evidence about the salience of ethnic ties in business transactions suggests that Rauch's proposal to establish commercial intermediaries to provide African Americans with the benefits currently enjoyed by businesses embedded in thick ethnic networks might be enhanced not only by considering how to strengthen the ties among existing retailers but also by encouraging the growth of new businesses in product and service lines that lend themselves to vertical integration, particularly if this interpretation can capitalize on ethnic ties. The success of Korean business owners is a strong testimonial to the value of this strategy. This consideration is especially important for segregated communities like African American ones because it means that the economic effects of ethnically encapsulated markets can be harnessed within minority communities (Wilson and Martin 1982).

This research was supported by core grants from the MacArthur Foundation and the Rockefeller Foundation to the Center for the Study of Urban Inequality at the University of Chicago (Marta Tienda, Richard Taub, and Robert Townsend, principal investigators). We acknowledge institutional support from the Office of Population Research at Princeton University and the University of Haifa.

Notes

1. Understanding Mexicans' underrepresentation in entrepreneurial activity cannot be gleaned from existing data sources. Analyses of self-employment based on the U.S. Census of Population or the Survey of Minority-Owned and -Operated Businesses lack crucial information about financial arrangements, needed business supports, and the like. Nor can they address questions about information sources, suppliers and creditors, or plans for expansion.
2. A *Wall Street Journal* article (May 7, 1997) described Twenty-sixth Street, the main drag in Little Village, as "a vibrant thoroughfare of furniture and clothing stores, travel agencies, photography studios, flower shops and cafés—all advertising their wares in Spanish. Shoppers of all races come from as far away as Wisconsin and Michigan. The area is surpassed in Chicago's business volume only by the 'Magnificent Mile,' the upscale corridor along North Michigan Avenue, whose stores include Marshall Field's, Neiman Marcus and Bloomingdale's."
3. We excluded professional services such as legal and health services because the formal licensing and educational requirements for self-employment in medicine and law are quite different from those needed for nonprofessional business firms.
4. We drew a sample of 340 establishments, of which 36 were closed by the date of the interview; 10 were franchises or not-for-profit operations, 5 were secondary businesses of an individual included in the primary sample, and 3 were owned by Cantonese-speaking Chinese, whom we did not interview.
5. Because the vast majority of Hispanic respondents were of Mexican origin, for simplicity we refer to them as Mexicans.
6. Respondents were asked to provide information regarding the three most important product suppliers. The reported figures are averages from the three responses.

References

Granovetter, Mark. 1985. "Economic Action and Social Structure: The Problem of Embeddedness." *American Journal of Sociology* 91: 481–510.

Portes, Alejandro. 1987. "The Social Origins of the Cuban Enclave in Miami." *Sociological Perspectives* 30: 340–72.

———. 1996. *The Economic Sociology of Immigration*. New York: Russell Sage Foundation.

Portes, Alejandro, and Robert Bach. 1985. *Latin Journey: Cuban and Mexican Immigrants in the United States*. Berkeley: University of California Press.

Raijman, Rebeca. 1996. "Pathways to Self-employment and Entrepreneurship in an Immigrant Community in Chicago." Ph.D. diss., University of Chicago.

Raijman, Rebeca, and Marta Tienda. 2000. "Training Functions of Ethnic Economies." *Sociological Perspectives* 43: 439–56.

Wilson, Kenneth D., and W. Allen Martin. 1982. "Ethnic Enclaves: A Comparison of the Cuban and Black Economies in Miami." *American Journal of Sociology* 88: 135–60.

Chapter 7

Concluding Remarks: Questions for Policy

Alessandra Casella

The unifying theme of the contributions to this volume is the relationship between networks and markets, as seen from the perspective of two neighboring but different disciplines in social science. The novel aspect of the volume is in part the close interdisciplinary collaboration, but more fundamentally the emphasis on studying markets and networks *together*, not as alternative institutional structures, each of which supplants and excludes the other, but as different organizations for the exchange of information, assets, and goods that coexist in our societies and affect and shape each other. In fact, it can be said that the formal pairing of sociologists and economists matches the substantive focus on the interdependency of markets and networks.

In the chapter by Robert Feenstra and Gary Hamilton, for example, the observation that business groups in Taiwan and Korea have different structures is interpreted in terms of different patterns of integration across industries. Feenstra and Hamilton show that both of the observed structures can be chosen rationally to maximize economic opportunities within the constraints imposed by market discipline. Thus, the shape that the network takes is conditioned by the rules of the market, but multiple outcomes are equally possible, and the specific network structure that emerges determines the final economic results. Networks and markets inform each other, and both belong to the more general problem of finding the most profitable channels for allocating resources.

Markets and networks also interact at an equal level in James Rauch's chapter on the scarcity of African American retail businesses in New York City. The absence of African American grassroots organizations is seen as a major business handicap that prevents African Americans from establishing profitable market niches. To overcome the problem, Rauch suggests subsidizing African Americans' use of independent buying offices, a formal market substitute for the informal and personal interaction of business associations. Rauch is an economist, and to an economist the motivation for subsidizing an activity comes down to the need to overcome a coordination problem that prevents its optimal provision. The chapter states that successful entry into a market—the decentralized, anonymous, mostly efficient institution at the heart of economic theory—demands coordination, or in other words, membership into a network. If the network does not form spontaneously, it should be subsidized. Although this view, in the best tradition of Granovetter's "embeddedness" hypothesis, is hardly surprising to sociologists, it is unusual among mainstream economists.[1] But notice also that the policy suggestion is to encourage reliance on a formal, for-profit organization, the buying offices. This is the market equivalent of the personal ties that are found missing: if a successful market presence requires reliance on a network, it is also true, in this reading, that the market itself can sell services that approximate the transmission of information provided by the network. It is not surprising then that Marta Tienda and Rebeca Raijman look at this prescription with some skepticism. The implied general question is very important for policy, and I return to it below. If membership in a network provides tangible advantages, is there room for a network entrepreneur, or for a policymaker, to organize and sell "network services" for profit? To what extent can formal institutions substitute for missing personal ties?

If markets and networks interact "horizontally" in these two chapters, their relationship is instead "vertical" in the work of John Padgett and Alan Kirman. According to Padgett, the pattern of business transactions in Renaissance Florence, in particular the lines along which Florentine banks were organized, reflected the personal networks that in each period individuals had come to see as dominant—in fact, as essential to their sense of identity. Thus, personal networks were the fundamental prior that conditioned the formal institutions and the form of market exchanges. More controversially, personal networks were the foundation of individual identity: the individual existed only as a member of a group, while external political events affected the choice of which interpersonal relation would be privileged. As remarked in chapter 1, this view is problematic for our existing theories of the market, because it questions the methodological focus of economics on the individual—not necessarily a self-interested individual living in isolation from his fellow men, but certainly an individual with well-defined, if possibly evolving, preferences. Without embracing this more extreme reading, the conclusion that the networks provide the soil on which market relations grow is also reached in Kirman's study of the fish market in Marseille. Here the network is the personal and repeated bilateral relation between a specified seller and a regular customer, whereas the market is the aggregation of all these individual transactions, and in particular the resulting well-behaved price-quantity relationships for each type of fish. Following the logic of the argument, Kirman poses a rather paradoxical question: If the complex and heterogeneous bilateral relations give rise to the much simpler market outcomes predicted by traditional economic theory—if, in Becker's (1962) startling words, "households may be irrational, and yet markets quite rational"—does it matter what the correct characterization of the microstructure of transactions really is? The answer, however, must remain yes, because both the evaluation of a given market outcome and the response to a policy intervention are bound to depend on the nature of individual interactions.

In fact, the chapter by Ronald Burt and its discussion by Joel Sobel make this point very clearly. When describing the role of gossip in transmitting information, both authors conclude that communication from close associates is more likely to confirm one's prior. But in Burt's analysis, these communications are essentially uninformative, and managers' reliance on them is counterproductive. In Sobel's view, on the other hand, information received from closely connected third parties can be highly informative, exactly because there exists an infrequent but precise scenario in which the manager's own view will be contradicted. Thus, managers relying on information from close ties will do worse (according to Burt) or better (at times, according to Sobel) than managers with weaker ties. There is a single crucial difference between the two alternative interpretations: whether the informant is following the rules of "etiquette," the desire not to counter the opinion of a friend, or whether he is pursuing an objective of his own, possibly in line with the goals of the person requesting his opinion, but leading him to manipulate the information he is transmitting. In other words, is the informant following the conventions of good behavior within a network or is he acting like a rational economic agent? As in Kirman's chapter, what is empirically observed—close associates confirm managers' prior information—does not allow us to distinguish between the two alternative views. But as Sobel remarks, the optimal design of the work environment would differ in the two cases. Sobel's discussion of Burt's chapter is particularly apt because Burt's theory of structural holes provides very fertile ground for economic analysis; in fact, in the eyes of an economist, Burt's theory demands such analysis. The language itself—"monopoly power," "entrepreneur," "competitive advantage"—suggests that the path toward a network equilibrium evolves through the rigor and opportunities of economic competition. The market, intended here as the purposeful pursuit of individual profit (and power), becomes the underpinning of equilibrium network formation.

An integrated view of markets and networks is important for the intellectual richness it provides to our analyses of economic transactions. But it is more important still because of its burgeoning influence on economic policy. Consider the position of the World Bank—given its size, political role, and ideological identity, we can say quite safely that ideas spearheaded by the World Bank have entered the policy consensus, and statements drawn from its publications, in the specific realm of development policy, can be read as examples of views that have gained influence more widely. The last three issues of the World Bank's *World Development Report* (World Bank 1997, 1999, 2000) devote a great deal of attention to the existence of personal networks in developing economies and to the role that these networks play in alleviating the institutional weaknesses that prevent or retard the establishment of a market economy.

The change in emphasis is remarkable. Throughout the 1980s, the bank's main message was that markets needed to be opened and liberalized, and it was delivered with the confidence that market discipline would be sufficient to bring opportunity, development, and prosperity. It is telling, for example, that the central argument of the 1983 *World Development Report* was summarized in a table that presented a series of (negative) correlations between a country-by-country index of price distortions and various indicators of economic growth (World Bank 1983, 61, table 6.1). However, the experiences of the 1990s—the difficulties of transforming planned economies into market systems, East Asian growth, and its financial crisis—have led the World Bank to reevaluate the importance of institutions in supporting and complementing markets. And it is not only formal institutions that have come in for reevaluation, but also the preexisting ties among groups that often are the original and only source of cooperative behavior.

Thus, in the 1999 to 2000 *World Development Report* (2000, 18, 171), we read: "It is hard to overemphasize the importance of networks of trust and association for sustainable development." The bank's policies should "facilitate the formation of new networks where the old ones are disintegrating" because, as shown in the example of a study of rural-urban links in Tanzania, "ties of ethnicity, religion and kinship are a source of social capital and support flexible production arrangements." The World Bank has organized a large research project on social capital, and an increasing number of its research papers are devoted to the topic (see www.worldbank.org/poverty/scapital and, for examples, the surveys by Grootaert [1998] and Woolcock [1999]). Following the same logic, nongovernmental organizations (NGOs) figure more prominently in the bank's development strategy: a recurrent theme is the desirability of forming alliances with NGOs because of their important connections to local groups. Indeed, most of the case studies described in the latest *World Development Reports* amount to the successful mobilization of local groups by NGOs, which start reforms that are then institutionalized by the local government. The examples, to choose only a few, range from the role of religious NGOs in Bolivian schools (World Bank 1997, 90) to campaigns for legal reforms favoring the poor in Peru (World Bank 1997, 101), to successful efforts to eradicate river blindness across several African countries (World Bank 1999, 60), to the provision of health services through the training of local women in a poor region of Brazil (World Bank 1999, 122). All of these cases present innovative solutions to a problem of public good provision—or, more generally, to a market failure.

But it is not the case that the World Bank has simply lost its confidence in markets as vehicles of development. Its position is more interesting: successful markets require successful institutions, and as emphasized, for example, by the work of Robert Putnam (Putnam, Leonardi, and Nanetti 1993), successful institutions require successful networks. Thus, the interaction between markets and networks that is the focus of this book has entered the realm of policy discussions, and the policy puzzles analyzed by the book's contributors assume new urgency.

There are three broad questions we must ask. First of all, is the confidence in networks as a stepping-stone to efficient markets justified? Or, on the contrary, do successful networks hamper the establishment of impersonal exchanges? Avner Greif (1994) has argued that it was the lack of cohesion among medieval Genoese traders that forced them to develop accounting rules and a formal legal system. These institutions in turn allowed them to incorporate non-Genoese employees into their firms and set the bases for an open and profitable market economy. The Maghribi traders, on the other hand, paid for the short-term advantage of a reliable network of personal connections with the inability to grow beyond that network—and the eventual loss of their position in medieval world trade. From this perspective, one of the World Bank's case studies is particularly interesting. Myrada is an NGO operating in rural southern India with the goal of making credit more readily available to the poor. It does not, however, provide micro credit itself—as does, for example, the Grameen Bank in Bangladesh—but instead organizes groups of borrowers and trains them to establish and maintain links with the regular banks. Its goal, formalized in a detailed time table, is to leave the groups on their own within three to five years from their formation. The purpose of the NGO is explicitly to ease the entry of poor borrowers into the formal credit market, without relying on its continuous presence. If encouraging the establishment of personal networks becomes a routine tool of development policy, then it seems that an integral part of the policy should indeed be a plan ensuring a smooth transition from network to wider market—or more generally, an evaluation, however tentative, of the effect of the network on the development of the market and on individuals' opportunities to break loose from the network.

Following this logic, a second question seems natural and important: What about those individuals who are excluded from the network? And a related point: presumably not all networks are equally valuable. Which ones should be supported, and which ones should not? The question is difficult because what makes the network valuable is the same strength of personal ties that induces it—in fact, at times requires it—to keep outsiders out. Ethnic groups, for example, are exclusionary by definition. The implication is that a policy intervention affecting the group has distributional implications, entering the difficult grounds of political evaluations. Should policy then select networks that favor the downtrodden? Or should policy limit itself to those instances when coordinating the few can yield benefits to all? Or should it require that the targeted network be open to all those who want to participate?[2] But notice that if the network is open to all, then it has lost some of the features that sociologists in particular have emphasized: the sense of shared norms and the common language that make it impossible to engineer a network where none has formed spontaneously. It follows that networks that are "generalizable" can indeed be created artificially, or at least approximated by suitable institutions.

If institutions that replicate networks can be designed, then we are faced once again with an issue that was raised earlier. If networks are valuable and can be constructed, a "network entrepreneur" could organize a group and provide "network services" while retaining part of the surplus and making a profit.[3] Can markets then produce and supply networks? This is our third question, and we have returned to Rauch's independent buying offices and their role in stimulating retail trade. Two comments may be appropriate before pursuing the idea further. First, as stated earlier, marketable networks are a natural object of study if we conclude that policy should favor the exchange of information within nondiscriminatory groups, and thus exactly because they will not function as channels of shared history, trust, and close personal connections. But how much added value would they still provide? Second, the functioning of markets is predicated on well-defined property rights, on predictable enforcement of contracts, and on acceptable quality of information. If, as in many of the World Bank case studies, the networks are organized as embryonic institutions to supply these missing underpinnings, then the networks themselves cannot be provided by the nonexistent or malfunctioning market. Market provision of "network services" is more relevant for developed market economies.

The following two examples are suggestive of the type of services that can be marketed. Consider first the functions of the middleman, the role naturally defined as "entrepreneurial" by Burt in bridging the structural holes between unconnected networks. A prospective exporter to an unfamiliar foreign market can buy the services of McInsey, Arthur D. Little, BCG, or in fact any of the large international consulting firms and obtain not only a traditional market study but names, phone numbers, and direct introductions to potential contacts and partners in the foreign country. Increasingly, the exporter can also choose to address directly consultants familiar with his country of origin but located in the target market.[4] Thus, he can purchase, at a price, the connections that coethnic groups scattered among many countries have always been able to extend freely to their members.

As remarked by Burt, the entrepreneur exploiting his privileged position can earn, for a time, a monopoly rent. A classic case where the lure of monopoly rents leads to the market provision of a public good is the creation of standards. (Here the community sharing the established standard is a network, in its more literal sense.)[5] Standards can be developed by individual firms: technological races and disputes following the exploitation of the winner's monopoly position are part of our daily experience. And standards can also be provided by groups, again presumably held together by the expectation of market profits. In most Western countries, regulations concerning safety, health, and the environment are issued by governments; however, technical standards, including at times the specific measures that satisfy the objectives of the government regulations, are often left to private industry organizations and publicized as voluntary standards (UNIDO 1991). Expenditures for the development of standards and certification procedures are substantial and mostly sustained by private firms.[6] Predictably, here too concerns about antitrust violations have been voiced (U.S. Department of Commerce 1977; Federal Trade Commission 1983). Although the World Bank extols the role of NGOs in organizing private networks for enforcing milk quality in rural India (World Bank 1999, 73), in mature market economies, private certification is led by market forces and at times comes uncomfortably close to suspicions of collusion.

These two examples demand to be studied in more detail, but for now they help establish two points. First, market-provided network services are common, and it would be good to devote more systematic thought to distinguishing between those services that can be sold through the market and those that cannot. Second, ex ante there is no presumption that such market provision will in general be efficient or inefficient. The statement that the market can at times overcome the coordination problems of networks should not carry a value judgment per se—as always, the precise details of the different cases will determine the outcome.

The three policy questions outlined here are all too broad to hold hope of an answer. They are meant as suggestions for lines of inquiry that future research will have to make more precise and richer. But after much work on markets and networks, it is important to stimulate debate on the policy lessons that have been learned and to design new projects targeted at least in part at increasing our understanding of policy choices. If this book plays any role in encouraging such a debate and such projects, it will have been a success indeed.

Notes

1. An important distinction that I am skipping here is between markets for homogeneous goods and markets for differentiated products. It is in the case of these latter markets that Rauch makes his recommendation.

2. Portes and Landolt (1996), in describing some of the undesirable features of close personal networks, discuss the network's ability to limit participation, and thus the obstacles it can pose to the achievement of the common good, the pressure toward conformity and against innovation among network members, and the downward leveling influence of inner-city social ties.

3. The private organization of groups devoted to the provision of a public good is the subject of the theory of clubs in economics. For a synthetic exposition, see, for example, Starrett (1988).

4. For example, a U.S. producer interested in entering the Italian market could contact the Boston office of GEA, a well-established Italian consulting firm whose American office has exactly this purpose.

5. A standard is a public good because it is jointly consumed by all individuals using it; in fact, it derives its value from being shared by a community. But property rights over a standard can in general be defined, and therefore the return from establishing it can be appropriated. In economics terminology, a standard is excludable, but not rival.

6. In the United States in 1977, it was estimated that they amounted to $1 billion annually (U.S. Department of Commerce 1977).

References

Becker, Gary. 1962. "Irrational Behavior and Economic Theory." *Journal of Political Economy 27*: 69–89.

Federal Trade Commission. 1983. *Standards and Certification: Final Staff Report* (April).

Greif, Avner. 1994. "Cultural Beliefs and the Organization of Society: A Historical and Theoretical Reflection on Collectivist and Individualist Societies." *Journal of Political Economy* 102: 912–50.

Grootaert, Christiaan. 1998. "Social Capital: The Missing Link." Social Capital Initiative working paper 3. Washington: World Bank.

Portes, Alejandro, and Patricia Landolt. 1996. "The Downside of Social Capital." *American Prospect 26*(May–June): 18–21.

Putnam, Robert, with Robert Leonardi and Raffaella Nanetti. 1993. *Making Democracy Work: Civic Traditions in Modern Italy*. Princeton, N.J.: Princeton University Press.

Starrett, David A. 1988. *Foundations of Public Economics*. Cambridge: Cambridge University Press.

United Nations Industrial Development Organization. 1991. *International Product Standards: Trends and Issues*. Vienna: UNIDO.

U.S. Department of Commerce. 1977. *Voluntary Standards: Problems, Issues, and Alternatives for Federal Action* (July).

Woolcock, Michael. 1999. "Managing Risk, Shocks, and Opportunity in Developing Economies: The Role of Social Capital." Unpublished paper. Washington: World Bank.

World Bank. 1983. *World Development Report 1983*. New York: Oxford University Press.

———. 1997. *World Development Report 1997: The State in a Changing World*. New York: Oxford University Press.

———. 1999. *World Development Report 1998–1999: Knowledge for Development*. New York: Oxford University Press.

———. 2000. *World Development Report 1999–2000: Entering the Twenty-first Century*. New York: Oxford University Press.

INDEX

Boldface numbers refer to figures and tables.